D1083653

Blasian Invasion

RACE, RHETORIC, AND MEDIA SERIES
Davis W. Houck, General Editor

Blasian Invasion ★

Racial Mixing in the
Celebrity Industrial Complex

MYRA S. WASHINGTON

University Press of Mississippi / Jackson

www.upress.state.ms.us

The University Press of Mississippi is a member of
the Association of American University Presses.

First printing 2017

∞

Library of Congress Cataloging-in-Publication Data available

ISBN 978-1-4968-1422-7 (hardcover)
ISBN 978-1-4968-1423-4 (epub single)
ISBN 978-1-4968-1424-1 (epub institutional)
ISBN 978-1-4968-1425-8 (pdf single)
ISBN 978-1-4968-1426-5 (pdf institutional)

British Library Cataloging-in-Publication Data available

For Clarence

Contents

Acknowledgments

At the risk of being that person with the overlong and overwrought acknowledgments section, here is my overlong and overwrought acknowledgments section.

Kent Ono is perhaps the most generous, kind, and helpful person ever. He has patiently answered questions—usually emailed in all caps—ranging from the most important to the mundane. Thank you also to the wonderful and brilliant Lisa Nakamura, Norman Denzin, and Angharad Valdivia for offering incisive critiques of this book. An additional thanks to Anghy, who like Kent, answered panicked, all-caps text messages at all hours about this project and life in general.

I know that I am particularly lucky to be able to call upon an amazing cadre of ICR (and ICR-adjacent) folks—thank you, Robert Mejia, Vincent Pham, Jungmin Kwon, Rachel Dubrofsky, and Peter Campbell for your excellent insights and support and for being on conference panel after conference panel with me. Peter and Robert especially have been clutch in thinking through this book and offering encouragement at all the right times. The University of Illinois introduced me to so many wonderful colleagues and lifelong friends who humble me with their generosity and genius, but thank you especially to Michelle Rivera, Jillian Baez, Molly Niesen, Safiya Noble, Andre Brock, Geneene Thompson, Katie Walkiewicz, Emily Skidmore, Yaejoon Kwon, and Bryce Henson, who read and/or discussed versions of this work. Outside of Chambana Amanda Murphyao, Isra Ali, Joo Young Lee, Wendy Thompson Taiwo, Emily Haas, and Mitzi Uehera Carter have offered feedback and modeled exceptional scholarship.

I am indebted to so many amazing scholars who have offered career and life advice, polished my writing, connected me to key works (and academics), encouraged me, and pushed my theoretical boundaries through their own phenomenal work. Thank you, John Sloop, LeiLani Nishime, Roopali Mukherjee, Shilpa Davé, Gregory Carter, Chuck Morris, Tina Harris, Tom Nakayama, Laura Kina, Rudy Guevarra Jr., Mary Beltrán, Ralina Joseph, Camilla Fojas, Madhavi Mallapragada, Jennifer Ho, Barry Brummett, Daniel McNeil, Minelle Mahtani, WeiMing Dariotis, Catherine Squires, Mimi Nguyen, Fiona Ngo, Julie Dowling, Isabel Molina-Guzman, and Junaid Rana.

Thank you to Vijay Shah, who is the most patient, insightful, and hilarious editor. His excitement for this book paired with his keen observations have been invaluable to me. I am glad that we get to make up words that will obviously take the world by storm. Thank you also to Lisa McMurtray, who patiently answered all of my very basic questions and probably fixed a million things I have no idea about.

There are not enough thanks in the world for my friends who have offered me support, reassurances, and, most importantly, super-fun times while I alternated between procrastinating and freaking out over this book. Thank you to Josh McElroy, Celeste Lee, Sharmaine Davis, Ken Harris, and Rachel McNary, who have been my friends for so long they know where all the bodies are buried. Also thanks and so much love go to Heather Choi, Amber and Andrew Kemp-Gerstel, Ankita Rakhe, Jeremy and Alexandra Payne, Bryan Parr and Antonio Gomez, Brooks Alford and Dave Bragg, and Tim Miller, who all have managed to both cheer me on and cheer me up when I needed it. In Albuquerque, I am grateful for friends like Rory and Kim Jensen, Elise Oviedo, Elyse Sewell Thompson, and MG McCullough, who made sure to include me in non-university-related fun. I am also grateful for finding amazing friends and brilliant colleagues at the University of New Mexico like Kirsten Buick, Szu-Han Ho, Kency Cornejo, Ray Hernandez-Duran, Ana Alonso Minutti, Tiffany

Florvil, Kimberly Huyser, Tyson Marsh, Olla Ali, Faith Mikalonis, Nancy Lopez, Mary Jane Collier, Jaelyn deMaria, Tony Tiongson, Carolyn Dang, Patrick Kelley, Victor Chacon, Shinsuke Eguchi, and Erin Watley, who have all sustained me intellectually and socially. An extra dose of thanks goes to Kirsten Buick, who read iterations of this work and helpfully pointed out weaknesses to be strengthened and introduced me to parts of Albuquerque I would not have sought out on my own.

My grandmother Priscilla, Aunt Gloria, and Uncle Bob continue to be fountains of unending love, support, and encouragement, but I am most thankful for Clarence. My father died as I was doing the revisions for this book, and so he never got to see this final version, but he has always been my biggest supporter and ally. He spent my entire life helping me work through what I thought about being Blasian and the ideas I explore in this book. He, more than anyone, encouraged me to write and made sure I followed a path that would get me here. He was simply the best.

Blasian Invasion

CHAPTER ONE

Theorizing Blasians

In March 2015 the Miss Japan beauty pageant created a slew of headlines and think pieces after crowning its newest queen. There were criticisms that the newest Miss Japan was not Japanese "enough."[1] That is because, though Ariana Miyamoto is Japanese through citizenship, parentage, and various cultural practices, she is also Black.[2] Not only is Miyamoto Japan's first obviously multiracial winner, she is also its first Black one.[3] Many of the news stories focused on the backlash surrounding the crowning of Miyamoto, centering on Miyamoto's "non-Japanese" look and the resistance by many in Japan to even acknowledge that she is Japanese. The tenor of the comments proliferating online made claims that she had "too much black blood to be Japanese,"[4] or that she did not "even look Japanese,"[5] or that the pageant should have crowned a "pure-blooded Japanese"[6] woman instead. During CNN's story on her historic win, the reporter asked a group of high school students on the street their thoughts on the decision to crown Miyamoto as Miss Japan. One student replied, "Half is not 100% Japanese. If someone is chosen as Miss Japan, both her parents should be Japanese."[7] The responses to Miyamoto highlighted the tensions between the perceptual and the performative aspects of racial identities that all of the subjects in this book navigate.

Miyamoto's response to the critiques around her mixed-race identity attempts to meet both constitutive notions of race: the performative, *doing*, and the essentialist, *being*. When asked why she got involved in the pageant, Miyamoto discussed how the death of a mixed-race friend motivated her attempt to "change Japan."[8] Later Miyamoto told reporters about the racism she faced through childhood but asserted, "I'm Japanese through and through, but in Japan if you look 'foreign' you are often not accepted as Japanese. But I am Japanese—100 percent."[9] Miyamoto also stresses her Japanese cultural competencies, such as holding a fifth-level expertise in Japanese calligraphy, and donning a kimono for her coming-of-age ceremony. Still, despite her assertion that she is Japanese, nearly every news piece in the weeks following her crowning made sure to mention how Miyamoto spoke either "fluent" or "perfect" Japanese. Which is, of course, only noteworthy if one assumes she is not Japanese and thus might not be able to speak the language.

Not all stories focused on how other Japanese people thought of Miyamoto; there were news stories that focused on how her win might shift (perhaps necessarily) the image of Japan as something other than a country so hostile to outsiders that it thrives on its continued isolation and homogeneity. Miss Japan has won the Miss Universe title only twice, in 1959 and 2007, and both times the competition was held in Japan. Miyamoto represented Japan in the 2016 Miss Universe pageant in Las Vegas, which featured nearly 100 women who are all symbols of national pride for their respective countries. That Miyamoto was the first visibly multiracial representative for Japan is notable because it "expands and contests the idea of whose ideal beauty represents a country."[10] Additionally, as Sarah Banet-Weiser notes, national pageant winners' bodies are inscribed with narratives "that articulate dominant expectations about who and what [Japanese] women are and should be at the same time as it narrates who and what the nation itself should be through promises of citizenship, fantasies of agency, and tolerant pluralism. Therefore the beauty pageant provides us with a site to witness the gendered construction of national identity."[11] The crowning of Miyamoto, then, becomes a strategic attempt by the organizers of Miss Japan to "remain competitive in the Miss Universe arena"[12] by garnering both national and international attention, and appealing to a transnational judging body with their obviously transnational contestant. Though pageant participants and organizers would probably not see these competitions as political arenas, they are, especially in the sense that the "presentation and reinvention of femininity that takes place on the beauty pageant stage produces political subjects."[13] Miyamoto becomes, then, the perfect trope for Japan, as through her the nation comes to embody both modernity and tradition.

This opening vignette about Miyamoto suggests her identity in media is racialized in very particular ways, specifically how narratives about her identity focused on themes of nationalism, beauty, and authenticity. Miyamoto is framed as Black according to a hegemonic understanding of race and racial mixing in the United States, Japanese for the purposes of shifting the national identity of Japan, and Blasian (mixed-race Black and Asian) according to the ways she describes herself and the celebratory rhetoric in various news articles. This book attempts to explain how Blasian, a concept and a term likely still unknown to some today, went from being undefined to taking an identifiable place in popular media culture. Today it is not just an identity that Black and Asian/American[14] mixed-race people can claim but also a popular identity with meaning within media and a relevance that works in productive ways. This book explores the transformation and branding of Blasian from being an illegible and unmentioned category to a legible classification that is then applied to other Blasian figures in media. By "legibility" I mean the "ease with which [one] can be recognized."[15] I use branding as a tool to map out the process of conferring meaning, legibility, to Blasians. Importantly, I also use Blasians as an example of what Leslie Bow has described as transracialism because they "enable the formation of alternative concepts of community, of alliances that contest those sedimented by nationality and belief in biological inevitability."[16] This book ultimately reveals that even though Americans have mixed in every way possible, racial mixing is talked about in certain ways (which seems to almost always involve Whiteness) and not others. Importantly, Blasians contest the hegemony of race constructed around the lives of not just Blacks and Asian/Americans, but all members of US society, as we are all embroiled in the illogical (and contradictory) discourses framing our identities. After all, as Stuart Hall notes, "the future belongs to the impure."[17]

The Politics of Naming

I contend in this book that, like Ariana Miyamoto, Blasian celebrities are the focus of contested racialized media discourses, and through media

coverage of these celebrities the need for alternative narratives for understanding racial identity and multiracial identity arises. Blasian, which first
appeared in print in 2001 when high school swimmer and Korean adop-
tee Zak Heaton used the term to describe his racial mixture,[18] broke into
mainstream consciousness at the height of the Tiger Woods scandal in
2009. I use the term Blasian to refer to the celebrities and stars in this
book because they self-identify with these socially constructed racial/
ethnic categories of Black and Asian/American. This is also why stars I
would categorize as Blasian, like Bruno Mars, do not appear in this book.
Of course, Blasian joins a number of other labels used to describe multiracial individuals, labels like *hapa, mulatto/a, métis, half-breed, creole,*
biracial, hybrid, and *colored,* among others. I chose Blasian over those
terms because the historical meanings and the commonsense understandings of those labels are directly dependent on Whiteness. For example, *hapa (haole)* carries with it a history of violent White colonization of
indigenous Hawaiians.[19] Though it has been appropriated since then by
mixed-race Asian/Americans to refer to themselves, implied in its use is
Asian/American and White racial intermixing. The terms *mulatto/a, col-*
ored, half-breed, métis, and *biracial,* common terms in early literature on
mixed race, carry similar connotations, but instead of White and Asian/
American mixtures, those terms refer to White racial mixing and speak
to the history of colonizer violence against indigenous people and slaves.
While it is sometimes used in other ways, *biracial* has primarily come to
stand in for those who identify themselves or are identified as Black and
White, excluding those of other racial mixtures. There are also biological
implications of sterility and superiority tied in with labels like *mulatto,*
half-breed, and *hybrid. Mulatto* and *half-breed* have historically circulated
the idea that mixing "breeds" will result in a new breed that will be sterile
and subsequently unstable because of that sterility.[20] *Hybrid's* mooring in
biology carries with it the idea that (racial) mixing produces a biologically
superior end result,[21] one that is stronger, more attractive, and all-around
better than the individual components.[22] *Hybrid* and *half-breed* are also
problematic considering how often people of color are already compared
to animals and objects. Using the term Blasian allows me to talk about a
particular subjectivity while acknowledging the work of Blackness but
not making it the default racial position, as hypodescent does when terms
like *mulatto* or *biracial* are used. There are other terms, reflective of the
multicultural 1990s, terms like Amerasian, Eurasian, and Austronesian.
Amerasian has been used to refer to mixed-race Asians, especially those

who came about as a result of US military interventions in Asian countries. I use Blasian partially because it is a term that has acquired and continues to gain public attention and acceptance. Mainly, I use Blasian because it recognizes racial mixing that occurs outside of Whiteness even though Whiteness obviously works to racialize Blasians. Research on mixed-race people highlights the need for racially mixed people to label themselves as a response to being labeled by others. Self-identification is especially important for Blasians, as people of color who are often labeled according to how they are phenoperceived,[23] because their self-identification strategies point to the fluidity and multiplicity of racialized identity.

Used interchangeably with the label Blasian is the term *mixed race*. *Mixed race*, like some of the other aforementioned labels, can be criticized for giving the impression that multiracial people are "mixed up" or confused and/or unstable because of racial mixing. It has also been criticized as a label for people because it privileges the idea that race must be essentially pure, so *mixed race* has connotations of racial impurity. However, given that race is socially constructed and does not derive from biology, within this book the terms *mixed race, racially mixed*, and *multiracial* are used interchangeably, as they all signify the dynamic nature of racial classification. Additionally, I still find it to be a useful term because mixed-race people use it to describe themselves. *Mixed race* does not carry with it the racially exclusive connotations that labels and descriptors like *biracial, hapa, mestizo/a, colored*, Eurasian, or *mulatto/a* all do. Also, *mixed race* is a label that allows people who categorize themselves as such to divulge their particular mixtures or not, conferring on multiracial folks a small amount of agency in determining how they identify. *Mixed race* as a descriptor also enables multiracials who use the label to become part of a larger mixed-race community. So, while all multiracial people do not use *mixed race* to describe themselves, many do and it is one of the most recognizable terms both inside academia and outside in the multiracial community and in the spaces where those two worlds overlap.

As with the term *mixed race*, there are some who might find the term Blasian to be problematic, because it stems from superficial color/racial designations, but despite the problematic branding aspects of using the term and the less-than-satisfactory identity-producing dimension of it, I use the term here to signal the need for language that breaks out of old and outdated racial schema. Blasian also allows me, despite criticism to the contrary, to acknowledge that the terms Black and Asian refer to a diverse population of people; yet, despite that diversity, the racial structure of US culture classifies each group according to some socially constructed conventions centered mostly on perceived phenotypical markers or what Spivak terms "chromatism."[24] Additionally, the constructed nature of race and how individuals interpret its meanings are crucial to how we understand race in this country. I do not put quotations around the term *race*, despite the fact that it is socially constructed and without any real biological moorings, as it has very real power which is deployed unevenly and oppressively and has a very real impact on the lives of people everywhere.[25]

As people are increasingly embracing terms like *mixed race*,[26] *multiracial*,[27] and Blasian, analyses of racial mixing and identity formation are crucial and make projects such as this one all the more essential. When multiracial political organizations like Project Reclassify All Children Equally (Project RACE) and the Association for MultiEthnic Americans (AMEA) grew in popularity during the 1990s, they employed the same strategies used by ethnic immigrants (e.g., Irish, Italians, Jews) at the turn of the twentieth century to Whiten themselves. These organizations used Blackness as their foil, focusing their ire on hypodescent, which they felt unfairly constrained the identities of mixed-race people by rendering them Black. For example, Maria P. P. Root's "Bill of Rights for Racially Mixed People"[28] rhetorically positioned Blacks as trapping biracial people into Blackness through enforcement of the one-drop rule.[29] For these organizations, mixed-race people were almost exclusively Black and White, and all other combinations of racial mixtures were mostly ignored.[30] Thus, the movement used racial mixing as a means for escape from Black identity, offering up mixed-race people as exemplars of progress and change.

The groups that made up this early wave of the multiracial movement claimed not to be Whitening themselves, but to be working toward the end of race as a classification category by calling for multiraciality to be recognized as its own category.[31] Yet, despite criticisms the movement was anti-Black, those leading these groups appropriated the language of the civil rights movement and its ideologies to argue that the refusal to let mixed-race people identify as they choose, in concert with the use of the one-drop rule to recruit (unwillingly, according to the movement) members to the Black community were violations of the rights of multiracial people. Activists within this first wave of the mixed-race movement and early scholars researching multiracial people argued the one-drop rule was racist because its enforcement maintained racial categories. In order for hypodescent to be applicable, the biologically based nature of race had to exist: Whiteness had to be considered biologically pure, and transitively Blackness had to be biologically impure. Interestingly, those same activists and many early multiracial scholars insisted on framing the discussion of mixed race in terms of a multiracial baby boom/rapid growth in numbers, which, despite their intentions, reinforced those very biological differences they wished to avoid with the application of hypo-descent. Meaning, in order to have and count multiracial bodies, "biologi-cally" identifiable monoracial people need to exist (Black, White, Asian, Indigenous, etc.), so that when they mix they can be tracked and counted.

Nevertheless, through legal and political maneuvering based on per-ceived civil rights violations, the multiracial movement's mobilization to allow those filling out the US census to check more than one box was successful. This policy approach won out over creating a *multiracial* cat-egory, which some members of the movement claimed would have at least challenged the existing categories. The movement declared chang-ing the census would allow mixed-race people to be counted fairly and finally represented accurately in numbers. In addition to Root's "Bill of Rights for Racially Mixed People," Nathan Douglas's "Declaration of Racial Independence"[32] also focused on the "rights" of multiracial people to self-identify. The multiracial movement's rallying point in having the need and ability to self-identity was validated partially at the state, federal, and cultural levels. The success has varied from state to state, and other than in the census, has yet to be implemented full-scale within the federal government, but the movement has had some success in making it more culturally appropriate to self-identify.

Mixed-Race Studies and Its Discontents

Despite talk of rights and fair representations, many of the criticisms against the multiracial movement focused on its anti-Black orientation and the erasure of other groups of color. Jared Sexton points out that the way "multiracialism operates [is] by way of a historic double standard— endorsed when it does not involve blackness in significant ways, abjured whenever it does."[33] That key organizations within the multiracial move-ment found support from neoconservatives like Newt Gingrich and Ward Connerly certainly seems to buttress the claims of anti-Blackness. The tensions between critics and supporters of the multiracial movement pre-2000 census centered on how state and federal agencies would disburse resources to communities of color should *multiracial* become a census category. Racial groups previously represented on the census believed the change in the census would see first their numbers, then subsequently their resources, diminish. In addition to those very possible political and economical implications of the changes proposed by the multiracial movement, supporters made the discursive claims that biracial identity should stop being viewed as a subset of Blackness. Critics pointed out that *multiracial* would simply become another category added to the racialized hierarchy in the United States, further separating Blacks from Whites and Blackness from Whiteness.

Like many but not all multiracial people, Blasians attempt to trouble the notion of hypodescent in the way they accept being racialized as people of color, who are oftentimes but not always also Black. Blasian is an intentional identity, meaning this is not an identity that is thrust upon people, but rather one that is chosen deliberately. While other researchers have discussed whether or not biracial people really challenge the one-drop rule,[34] Blasians—without the benefit of Whiteness—are an unavoidable test of the one-drop rule. Blasians shift discussions of multiracialness from being a threat to Whiteness, or being anti-Black, and/or functioning as a racial salve, to strategically using Blackness and Asianness (sometimes in combination, other times singly) to assert a particular subject position that has its own benefits and advantages. Structural anti-Blackness and anti-Asianness work in both concert and contention with each other to highlight the ordering power of White supremacy as it forces groups against each other. It is important to note how the protection of Whiteness, which can be enacted for White racially mixed people, does not extend to Blasians or similarly non-White racially mixed people. While research has addressed the whitening of multiracial people by virtue of their mixed-race status,[35] and the whitening of Asian/Americans,[36] I argue that the Mobius strip of their coexisting Black and Asian/American identities in large part keeps them from benefiting from those Whitening strategies and entitlements in the same ways.

I focus on Blasians to demonstrate how their mixed-race status has been used to frame them in specific ways, especially as they all represent a segment of the multiracial population often ignored by both academe and the multiracial movement. The mixed-race movement has been dominated by White + other biracial members, while minority + minority mixed-race people are only now moving into positions of leadership and gravitating toward the center of the movement. Blasians have been left out as a meaningful category of people in academic research by all but a few scholars, despite an extensive history of Black and Asian/American interactions within the United States and abroad.[37]

Four key narratives emerged from the first wave of research on multiracial people. The first narrative is that of the tragic mulatta/o, which depicted multiracial individuals as survivors of the unfortunate act of miscegenation.[38] The second narrative is a proscriptive, boundary-setting discourse that resigned the mixed-race person's experiences to fit within one racial discourse, usually based on perceived phenotypical features.[39] The third narrative is full of celebratory rhetoric focused on how hybrid vigor is responsible for mixed-race people as attractive, exotic, smart, different, unique, ideal mating partners, best of (both) all worlds, and so on.[40] The fourth theme focused on the colorblind and/or postracial narratives that declared racial mixing responsible for the lack of color (race) now, and the rendering of racial categories obsolete in the future.[41] These trajectories of multiracial discourse rely on two overarching frames: mixed race as uniquely new phenomenon, and mixed race as resistant to dominant paradigms of race and racism. Both have been necessary for multiracial activists and the mixed-race movement and have served as the foundation for much of the research in mixed-race studies. As a response to these narratives, the critical turn in mixed-race scholarship has begun to question and critique the assumptions and conclusions of earlier works.[42] For instance, analyzing the social conditions and boundaries trumpeted by early participants in the multiracial movement and mixed-race studies has exposed an uncritical embrace of Whiteness[43] and the call for the erosion of solidarity within communities of color. Others have introduced previously ignored and elided racial mixtures and subjectivities, emphasizing the intersecting nature of these identities and calling for analyses that address those transecting categories.[44]

This critical turn in mixed-race studies critiques much of the early wave of mixed-race organizing and research as endorsing "the delusional, inverted worldview in which the oppressive power of racism is generated from the ground up, propagated by blacks, its prototypical targets, rather than by whites, its prototypical agents."[45] Furthermore, the establishing of Critical Mixed Race Studies (CMRS) as a field arose in part to look "back critically and [assess] the merit of arguments made over the past two decades."[46] CMRS examines both how "multiracials become subjects of historical, social, and cultural processes" and the "institutionalization of social, cultural, and political structures based on dominant conceptions of 'race.'"[47] CMRS pushes for acknowledging what constitutes mixed race changes depending on location, history, class, gender, ethnicity, sexuality, and other important factors.

Other critical mixed-race studies scholars point out how early organizing and scholarship fall "prey to binary traps of categorization, where a majority 'mixed race' group (with some white heritage) exists and other minority 'mixes' [found] themselves silenced or ignored."[48] The rise of CMRS corresponds with a rise in analyses of multiraciality addressing the multiplicities of mixtures and experiences.[49] Critical mixed-race scholars continue to further differentiate themselves from prior mixed-race research and the multiracial movement by accounting for the sexual politics around miscegenation, as well as racial mixing globally.[50] While earlier research and efforts rarely made the existence of racial differences and the subsequent hierarchies the focus of analysis, CMRS focuses attention on the very specific ways racialized hierarchies are used to frame race, multiracial people, and interracial relationships.

Blasians as Transracial

Borrowing heavily from transgender theory and theorists, I am using the term *transracial* to operationalize how representations of Blasians function within our current racial landscape. When individuals begin the process of transitioning, it is expected that they pick a gender, because picking neither, both, other genders, or moving constantly back and forth are not held up as viable options as they do not make the individual legible. Still there are people whose presence calls for an expansion of this regime of gender. For example, Fausto-Sterling writes about intersex individuals and how their presence, their "unruly bodies" disrupt our need to classify them into identifiable categories.[51] It is the same desire for legibility that motivates mixed-race individuals to select a category, and their bodies become "sites where culture's investments in category distinction become visible."[52] Transgender theorists are "concerned with anything that disrupts, denaturalizes, rearticulates and makes visible the normative linkages we generally assume to exist between the biological specificity of the sexually differentiated human body, the social roles and statutes that a particular form of body is expected to occupy, the subjectively experienced relationship between a gendered sense of self and social expectations of gender-role performance, and the cultural mechanisms that work to sustain or thwart specific configurations of gendered personhood."[53]

I am not equating being transgender with being transracial, but rather attempting to link the discourses around gender to those of race, since they do similar work and have similar expectations and share similar discriminatory forces and practices. Also, I recognize that transracial has long been used to describe adoptions and adoptees who do not share the same racial identity as their parents, and I do not intend my use of it here to delegitimize or weaken its usage in that context. However, as with the gender dissonance that we are forced to address by the presence of transgender, intersex, gender-fluid bodies, *transracial* is useful for addressing the racial dissonance of mixed-race bodies. Leslie Bow notes how "the transracial individual does not so much constitute a third race . . . as much as she provides a similar site of cultural disruption that may likewise signal the limitations of existing social organization and our investment in similarly naturalized racial categories."[54] The interstitial nature of mixed-race bodies and the racial dissonance wrought by Blasians mount a challenge to our devotion to and participation in a system that values categories and categorizing. Blasian subjects are "site[s] of both cultural anxiety and potential disruption, site[s] where status hierarchies are made visible and potentially reconciled to cultural norms."[55] Transgender theory asks that we denaturalize and disrupt normative gender categories, and I use transracial theory to denaturalize and disrupt normative racial categories.

Importantly, *transracial* lets us think about Blasians as not just moving back and forth between racial categories, but as transecting race. As Henry Yu points out, simply crossing boundaries does not in and of itself challenge those boundaries; in fact, the crossing "highlight[s] stability of the categories."[56] Accordingly, an intersectional analysis of sociocultural identities is useful since it is concerned with the conception of "categories not as distinct but as always permeated by other categories, fluid and changing, always in the process of creating and being created by dynamics of power."[57] Still, Crenshaw notes in *Mapping the Margins* that her use of intersectionality necessarily "engage[s] dominant assumptions that race and gender are essentially separate categories."[58] Thus, "intersectionality can imply that social identities arise from social relations meeting at a single point, with a resolution at that site."[59] Parker and Song's use of transection is perhaps a more useful characterization, as it "refers not simply to the spatial dimensions of the intersection of social relations, but also to the temporal dimension of how distinct historical trajectories may be asynchronous, incommensurable and thus confound additive combinations through their interactive dissonance."[60] Meaning the bodies of mixed-race people have the ability to disrupt the continuity of biological lineages through potential rejection or the failure to embody essentialist markers of race. The failure to visibly locate mixed-race people according to ancestry or inherited familial characteristics interrupts the presumptive continuity of race. So, then, in cutting across categories, transracialness is about the "potential mutual transformation" of those categories.[61]

We find ourselves in a postmodern moment where culture has become flattened and emptied of meaning, only to be commodified and then sanitized and offered back to us as an indicator of authenticity. Blasians should be afforded the same access to symbolic identities as Whiteness affords, but they are not, because as people of color they are constrained by narrowly defined extant categories of racialization. Through a transracial paradigm Blasians access symbolic identities, moving betwixt, between, and through Blackness and Asianness (or neither/both) as they so choose. As Blasians are positioned and represented in ways that may push the limits of Blackness and/or Asianness, they convey the need for renovating and altering what can be included in these categories and what the categories themselves have come to signify. Thus, they transracially highlight how culture, and its progenitor authenticity, fall apart when asked to sort Blasians into understandable categories.

Transgender advocates and their allies call for the dismantling of gender as a category that organizes us biologically but also, more importantly, socially. This project examines the power and material consequences of racialization while simultaneously calling for a similar move to be made around race. While there is acknowledgment that race, like gender, is a socially constructed category with no meaning outside of the social and cultural boundaries it is placed within, the pernicious and persistent presence of racism forces us to hedge between recognizing the power of racism while decrying the continued reliance on an invalid concept such as race. In other words, erasing race from our vocabularies will not move us past the racialized inequalities that continue to structure and constrain our relationships with each other. As such, in this book I do not advocate for thinking about mixed-race people generally and Blasians specifically as "transcending" race. Instead I hope to utilize Blasians and transraciality as a way to answer Paul Gilroy's call that we move toward "the idea [that] 'race' is no longer secure as a way of understanding the world."[62]

While all racialized identities are performed against a White expanse, I would argue that the fluidity of Blasians is not quite the same as someone like Rachel Dolezal[63] claiming she is Black. The difference in a transracial identity for Blasians is that there are powerful lines and boundaries that must be constantly negotiated from positions of subjugation. Whiteness, however, works in such a way that people can position themselves authoritatively, while Blasians and people of color generally can and will have their identity denied or purposely misrecognized or subjected to disciplining. Dolezal could, after all, at any moment "change her appearance, style, and self-presentation; she could change her networks of social relations and activities; she could 'feel' black and identify, no doubt sincerely, with black culture and history; and she could exploit contemporary versions of the one-drop rule to pass as black."[64] An integral component of my transracial theory is remembering that it is ultimately about how people position themselves and move within this spectrum of power and is not so much about identity. For instance, in literature there has been recent focus on transracial narratives, which are similar to passing narratives, except these transracial narratives "depict a character's full assumption of a given racial identity, regardless of whether or not that identity represents the character's 'real' racial classification."[65] The emphasis on a "real" racial identity is an unnecessary distraction. It is in the social positioning of the identity that transracialness becomes disruptive and complicates the reliance on a racialized hierarchy. This also allows us to get out of the identity trap and into politics of race and positioning, and it is this space that allows for discussions on how Blasians are constructed by and negotiate social forces. Crucially, the paradigmatic potential of a transracial and transectional analytical frame is in its ability to "highlight the transformation of categories and social relations when they do not merely intersect, but transect one another in antithetical combinations where the component parts may not be aligned in the same plane."[66]

Branding Blasians

I use the language of brands to frame the emergence of Blasians, because legibility is essential to branding. The theory developed here explains how mixed-race subjects, specifically Blasians, come to gain cultural and social legibility. While commodities like laptop computers can be easily emptied of their actual meaning (a machine designed to do specific tasks) and replaced with a number of messages, meanings, and values,[67] people, especially of color, are not as effortlessly divorced from hegemonic meanings or history, but commodity processes try nevertheless. If Blasians had no meaning, experiencing a kind of invisibility or cultural illegibility initially, then branding becomes a way to recognize the processes that give them social meaning. In essence, I show how Blasian becomes a brand, a label, an identity with currency (albeit different levels of currency) beyond just the mixed-race celebrities discussed in this book.

Branding means coming up with a memorable label or identity around which particular meanings, references, and connections cohere, often for the purposes of selling something. However, the concept of a brand is no longer centered on its material markers (trademarks, logos, packaging, etc.), nor is it limited to being merely about economic transactions (purchasing products), now branding scholars are analyzing how brands establish and create social relationships.[68] Banet-Weiser has deemed brand culture as the "deliberate association of products and trademark names with things like ideas, concepts, feelings and relationships."[69] Branding scholarship now addresses in detail politicians/political parties, organizations, celebrities, institutions, trends, movements, religious groups, nations, and even public policy.[70] The focus on the symbolic function of brands is a crucial turn in the branding literature, as it enables tying brands more explicitly to identity construction, meaning making, and self-branding strategies. Banet-Weiser links the normalization of branding to late capitalism's focus on the individual. This suggests a crucial neoliberal shift, a willingness and acceptance of self-objectification, and evidence that neoliberalism is not just an economic policy approach or style, but a personal one. Since it is becoming more and more appropriate to talk about branding for things other than material products, its application here to racial identities is a timely intervention. Traditional branding is used to differentiate products or identify a good or service; personal branding is slightly different, because there may be no tangible service or functional benefit, though people have become (and always have been within capitalism) commodities. I use branding because the representations of the stars in my case studies operate more like products than not: like goods for sale, they can be "discontinued, modified, withdrawn from the market, relaunched and repositioned or replaced by improved products."[71]

My use of brand and branding differs from earlier research in a few significant ways. First, even as scholars address the symbolic function of brands, they still refer back to a physical or tangible product. Blasian is not a product that can be bought: there is not a BLSN stock of which shares can be purchased, and there is no single Blasian lifestyle or culture being sold that consumers can buy or be a part of. In other words, buying a Tiger Woods–branded golf club or a DVD of Kimora Lee Simmons's reality show does not make one Blasian. Second, branding research refers to how the meaning making of brands has created boundaries around identities. I am positing that identity is the brand, not part of the brand, or the brand community, or part of the symbolic function of brand that consumers coalescence around—it is the brand itself. Again it is the neoliberal shift toward the individual and subjectivities as consumable commodities that makes this possible. Last, because identity is the intangible product that is being branded here, it allows me to bring in transecting sociocultural markers such as race, gender, nation, sexuality, class, et al. as I talk about the way Blasian has emerged as a legible and popular brand. Additionally, the focus on the fluidity of identity supports the use of stars, whose celebrity allows them access to privileges not as readily available to non-celebrities,[72] in tracing out the process of branding an identity, since as Gray notes, "branding is a process that creates textuality."[73] It is not so important what these stars do, but rather what meanings are drawn from their representations.

This, then, is a media theory, but it is also a racial theory, for it not only theorizes the means by which media discourse functions to produce celebrities through their identities but also illustrates how racial identities gain social and cultural legibility, and thus, how racial identities become public and, through their publicness, politicized. Stuart Hall's well-known concept of negotiated meanings adopted by spectators of dominant televisual texts, wherein dominant texts do not have just one reading for viewers who negotiate meanings with those dominant texts, is useful here as well. I use negotiation similarly to suggest that media do not simply control the identities of the Blasian celebrities. Rather, Blasian celebrities participate in self-branding processes, along with their public relations intermediaries and other stakeholders, sometimes effectively contesting and challenging media constructions of their identities. Goffman referred to this process as impression management and noted it was a crucial part of the presentation of self.[74] Thus, this "negotiation" is in part a result of their social and cultural power, but power that facilitates their ability to participate in self-construction processes that interface, integrally, with mediatized discursive regimes.

Blasians as a racial group have benefited from personal branding strategies by participating in these discursive processes that address their specific cultural identities. They might play a Black character in a film, and an
Asian/American while endorsing a product, and assert their mixed-race
identity during interviews. Being able to negotiate their various identities does not necessarily point to some sort of unhappiness or insecu-
rity but is instead an example of how effective branding strategies can be
for multiracial people. What has happened with Blasians is what Klein
predicted would happen with corporations: their identities would no
longer be found in corporate products, but rather in "their attributes."[75]
Due to policing of racialized bodies through enforcement of practices
like the one-drop rule, multiracial celebrities have historically been pres-
sured to pass as monoracial entertainers[76] and distance themselves from
their mixed-race identity.[77] The Blasian celebrities featured in my project
have done neither. Instead of simply creating different ways to advertise
themselves to different markets,[78] Blasians as a brand "sell diversity itself,
to all markets at once. The formula maintained the one-size-fits-all cost
benefits."[79] Indeed, some might argue, prior to the media frenzy around
his storied sexual infidelity, Tiger Woods was literally the brand for multiracial America. So Blasians, a group marginalized within mixed-race
studies and the multiracial movement, have become a commodifiable,
increasingly visible, racialized brand.

Entertaining Blasians

I examine popular cultural discourses, tracing the way particular Blasian
figures, unknown initially, transform celebrity status into legibility in the
arena called the "celebrity industrial complex."[80] Gamson describes and
critiques this process of celebrity production "as a commercial industry
much like other commodity-production systems: those working within
it speak primarily in the language of commerce and machinery . . . marketing plays a key role in matching products to distributors and consumers, depending especially on strategies of product transformation
and the building of consumer loyalty."[81] In her book *The Importance of
Being Famous*, Orth would years later more simply refer to this as the
relationship among celebrity, media, corporations, and the entertainment
industry, all of which are involved in creating, producing, and promoting
a celebrity or an aspect of celebrity. She dubs it the "monster that creates
the reality we think we see, and the people who thrive or perish there."[82]

The distinctions Gamson and Orth make between entertainers as workers (the thing they do) and as celebrities (products that can be consumed) is key to understanding the usefulness of the celebrity industrial complex. The commodification and consumption of Blasian celebrities must be contextualized against the Whiteness default that powers the celebrity industrial complex.

Using the celebrity industrial complex coupled with the neoliberal push to commodify identities and subjectivities, I analyze the mechanisms at work, together with semiotics, to read the celebrities themselves as texts. Dyer reminds us that stars function to demonstrate that how "anything in society is made, how making is organized and understood, is inseparable from how we think people are, how they function, what their relation to making is."[83] I am interested in the way their racial identity as Blasians, initially confused by media that either read them monoracially or simply did not interact with the specificity of their identities, came to be a part of their social meaning as celebrities. The advantage of my branding theory is the explicit treatment of celebrities as commodities whose personae act as material markers for Blasians, while also acknowledging there are intangible assets/aspects built around their transracial identities that are understood (or not) by a diverse audience.

Celebrities were the focus for this project because they are an accessible entrée into the conversation around how cultures are organized and commodified through representations of key figures, mediatized discourses, and competing ideologies. Though celebrity/star studies has been derided as a discipline that is not serious or worthy of exploration, its coupling here with cultural and media studies emphasizes the importance of cultural and politically economical logics undergirding the production, distribution, and maintenance of culture. Despite moments when stars are "just like us!" the circular exchange that happens between the production of celebrity and its influence on our everyday lives reflects the circular exchange between the racialization of bodies and then the meanings conferred onto those bodies. Blasian celebrities were key because they offered opportunities for examining how media discourses were used to frame their images in recognizable ways, extending to Blasianness a currency within the celebrity industrial complex. Furthermore, these Blasian celebrities provide on their bodies an articulation between disparate areas like transnational movements, global popularity, national specificity, neoliberalism, citizenship, consumer capitalism, and identitarian ideologies.

Hollywood has begun to utilize multiracial stars and their ambiguity[84] more generally as box-office attractions both for their broad audience appeal and to reflect the diversity of the audience, which is beneficial economically for celebrities and the entertainment industry.[85] As US stars of color have become economically viable internationally, television and film have begun to trend toward using ethnically ambiguous mixed-race stars in their globally oriented projects. Beltrán notes how this "new ethnically ambiguous protagonist embodies contemporary concerns regarding ethnicity and race relations with respect to the nation's burgeoning cultural creolization and multiethnic population."[86] Multiethnic ensembles have become profitable, partly because they appeal to an array of experiences and cultures and to younger audience members who are already familiar with both multicultural and multiracial narratives. What has been ignored in the discussion around the utility of a multiracial cast is whether that utility is present for all combinations of multiracial stars. This book draws attention to the unevenness of that utility; all mixed-race stars are not treated the same, and it shows in the way these celebrities are read. While the branding of Blasians has an effect on other mixed-race groups and makes them more legible, this is a one-way path. The current framing of multiraciality does not make Blasians more legible; thus, a focus of this book is to examine how Blasians are branded and how they may participate in that branding themselves. If we think about mixed-race people as consumers, and not just merely objects of the gaze, as so much previous research on mixed race has situated them,[87] then it is necessary to point out that the political economy of mixed-race stars traditionally allows for identification in large part because of the ethnic ambiguity of those stars and now because of an increasingly ethnically ambiguous audience.

Within the last decade a shift has occurred in the discourses about multiracial identity. Part of the shift is due in part to the changes made in collecting data for the 2000 Census, which was the first time respondents were able to choose more than one racial category *and* have them all be counted.[88] Whereas racially mixed people denying parts of their racial makeup were/are met with cries of selling out, self-hatred, and/or whitewashing,[89] it is becoming more and more acceptable to play up (and down) all, none, one, or some portion of their particular mixtures. This characteristic of mixed-race identities highlights the political economic motivations that undergird the commodification of multiracialness and has made ethnic ambiguity trendy and extremely popular, particularly within the realm of popular culture. Using the popularity of various

Blasian celebrities and rhetorics that accompany their representations, I show that multiraciality challenges the essentialization of mixed-race people, and I offer a counter to the limiting binaries that frame the current discourse on race and racial mixing as a way to break further away from racial biologism. The branded Blasian is at the most fundamental level a cipher,[90] meaning Blasians have been imbued with meaning and act as a commodity. The process involved in the meaning making of Blasians, their "branding," is crucial to this project because it relies very much on the power circulated throughout the celebrity industrial complex. US culture and the uneven distribution of power has created a hierarchical racial order, which when paired with the emergence of the celebrity industrial complex[91] as a realm for both profit- and sense-making, makes popular culture an especially rich area for studying the circulation of ideologies.

Celebrity reinvention/presentation is not new in the realm of entertainment: however, the public nature of their presentation is. Whereas celebrities or, perhaps more accurately, their managers, agents, studios, labels, public relations representatives, or other sundry handlers once managed their images away from public scrutiny, the development of the celebrity industrial complex has brought about significant changes. Much of that shift in control can be attributed to the Internet, through which social media, innumerable blogs, entertainment and gossip websites, and even mainstream media outlets allow celebrities unprecedented access to their own images and to fans, and most importantly, vice versa. It is important to note that the popularity of digital media has not allowed these celebrities to create new personae, or a chance to start from scratch with their identities. In fact, a number of scholars[92] have pointed out that being online does not remove bodies from the constraints of materiality. For these celebrities, their digital representations are intimately linked to their embodied experiences. The Blasian celebrities I use as case studies are tethered to and traverse Blasianness, Blackness, and Asianness; they cannot claim a White identity online, because it is not available to them offline. For example, Kimora Lee Simmons's tweets and responses from fans are intimately tied to her particular performance of racialized gender. Additionally, popular culture now, in the age of the Internet, is as much about reception as production. Orth highlights why this turn within the celebrity industrial complex has become valuable to media and entertainment industries and celebrities, because "familiar faces . . . not only attract large audiences; they provoke sympathy, trust, and identification."[93]

It is notable that the emergence of Blasians within popular culture takes place at the precise time that colorblind politics have successfully saturated popular discourses. The narratives of a color-neutral and/or newly emergent postracial society rely on bodies of multiracial celebrities who are used as "emblem[s] of racial harmony, the Great Multiracial Hope."[94] The rhetoric of a color-neutral,[95] or postracial,[96] society allows for discussions of race to be ignored under the guise of celebrating diversity. Importantly, part of the Blasian brand confronts this narrative head-on, because, whether they are rhetorically positioned as Black, Asian/American, or both, they defy color-neutral framings. Additionally, using these celebrities as examples of how Blasians are represented provides examples of the discursive boundaries between racialized identities and what multiraciality[97] has come to signify within contemporary culture.

It is impossible to discuss the popularity of Blasians without contextualizing the interracial relationships that have produced them; thus, chapter 2 of this book provides some historical contextualization of the connections Blacks and Asian/Americans have made domestically and internationally. I discuss the policies and politics that have brought them together, particularly since the groups have "a common and often overlapping diasporic experience, and shared traditions of resistance and struggle have developed for liberation and equality."[98] Chapter 2 culminates by contextualizing the emergence of early Blasian stars and the subsequent explosion of Blasian video models featured prominently in music videos because of their valuable amalgamation.[99] These Blasians simultaneously challenge and reify the hierarchy of beauty by offering exoticism, which is packaged and traded for featured spots in videos. This strategy has made them very popular, while also augmenting the emergence of Blasian legibility. This chapter traces out how popular media have created, defined, and represented Blasians, and explores some of the ways Blasians themselves are destabilizing those media discourses.

Chapter 3 uses the global success of Kimora Lee Simmons as a case study to show how her particular branding strategy and utilization of camp works in tandem with transraciality to subvert hegemonic notions of both Blackness and Asianness. I argue that the presence of alternate readings of Simmons, like the one taken in this chapter, emphasizes the resistive potential of her class, race, and sexual politics—making her a camp object. Using camp as a lens in which to read the ways Simmons is represented allows for examining the ways the performance of her identity, through ghetto "fabulosity" and orientalist tropes, is definitely resistant to and potentially subverts dominant ideologies of race, mixed race, gender, class, and sexuality. Simmons's start in the fashion industry as model turned designer, her championing of a Kimora Barbie™, the naming of her children, the storylines on her reality television show, model castings, and her Twitter interactions, are all moments where dominant narratives meet resistance. The image of Simmons projected to the world self-consciously renders the artificial indistinguishable from the real, contributing to a representation that destabilizes what it means to be *both* Black and Asian/American. Her embodied performance of transraciality indicates a refusal to settle for what is visible and allows for the contestations of hegemonic notions of identity. As myriad representations of Simmons work to challenge reliance on racial authenticity, they also open up a space to question racial categorizations and hierarchies.

The next chapter deconstructs the rhetoric around Tiger Woods since his extramarital affairs became public, by tracing the contradictory and conflicting narratives that frame post-cheating-scandal Woods. Though there were very few narrative themes that addressed race explicitly, they were deployed in very specific ways that revealed a number of unspoken tensions about the state of race, mixed race, sexuality, and respectability in the United States. In other words, in order to shame, praise, emasculate, and mock Woods, the reaction and coverage had to engage not just his Blackness but his Asianness as well, purposefully leaving out any claim to Whiteness he might have gained with his declaration of multiraciality and his success in golf. This chapter ends with an examination of Woods's response to those mediated narratives via his apologia, which was deployed to save his brand specifically and the Blasian brand generally.

Chapter 5 continues the questioning of racial categorizations and hierarchies via media personalities Hines Ward and Dwayne "The Rock" Johnson. While government classifications had historically grouped Asian/Americans and Pacific Islanders (including Native Hawaiians and other indigenous groups) together until the 2000 census, when they were split into their own categories,[100] I am including these groups under the same pan-ethnic umbrella as a coalitional move. My inclusion of Pacific Islanders is a fraught move that has been and continues to be contested,[101] particularly given the rise in critiques[102] of Asian/American settler colonialism. I do this for the same reason AAPI/API/APA/APIA[103] organizations and initiatives continue to classify them together, as a political strategy. I focus on the positioning of Black Samoan, Dwayne "The Rock" Johnson as he transitioned from professional wrestler to A-list star, and former National Football League player Hines Ward, as they both embody and complicate a number of discourses ranging from racialized sexuality to Asian/American athleticism and model minority myths to national identities. Their racial identities often confound popular media who read them monoracially, or refuse to interact with the multiplicities of their identity despite the numerous opportunities to do so. Furthermore, Ward's role as part of the impetus for the redefinition of Korean nationalism ensures the Blasian branding process grapples with transnational movements of body and capital. I point out in this chapter that when multiple subjectivities are considered and acknowledged, it forces a reframing in definitions and narratives about everything from race to nationalism and citizenship to masculinity.

The lack of consistency between media on the coverage and representation of these celebrities illuminates how quickly some are able to keep up with dynamic changes in racialization, while many others maintain familiar notions of race. The lack of consistency also acknowledges that these celebrities and Blasians are not inscribed with a singular, "right" meaning, despite the presence of hegemonic narratives that try to convince us this is true. The conclusion also delves into the interventions this book makes by analyzing whether multiracial subjectivities are possible and whether those subjectivities can escape the uncritical embrace of Whiteness, narratives of self-loathing, or blindly celebratory logics of previous research on racial mixing. Blasians challenge extant identity models by recognizing the ways identities and subjectivities evolve and shift. Furthermore, if prevalent notions of racial authenticity, or realness, can be overcome, then the opportunities for building coalitions across the pluralities of subjectivities and identities grow exponentially. Lastly, I conclude by exploring the idea that emphasizing disruptions of the hegemonic racial order of society might ultimately force "race" into a moment like the Salem witch trials—a moment in which there were institutional and social supports for an idea that was ultimately rendered illogical and meaningless. I end by wondering if Barack Obama should be considered Blasian, thereby making him our first Black *and* Asian/American president.

Acknowledging that Blasians belong to more than one community, recognizing multiple histories and experiences, and trying to shift the rhetoric beyond the dominant discourses of pathology, celebration, binaries, and essentialisms, I am not concerned with defining or categorizing mixed race, but rather with recognizing the multiplicities of Blasians and the process by which Blasians come to have meaning, and with using that to illustrate a shift in narratives about identity. Using Blasians and the narratives that accompany their visible moves interrogates how culture both provides and still needs spaces in which mixed-race identities can be articulated. I use these celebrity case studies to highlight how Blasian subjectivities challenge and destabilize current racial discourse, creating spaces for themselves when there were none and spoiling the narratives that frame multiracial people. Furthermore, by analyzing where and why discourses framing celebrity and race diverge from dominant discourses of mixed race when it comes to Blasians, I highlight how the representations, reactions, and discourses around these stars are evidence of the fluidity of identities as they highlight the limitations of reductive and essentialist binary racial paradigms.

Finally, I am not concerned with adding more categories or with tracking the growing number of people who identify as mixed race, but rather in exploiting the interstitial nature of mixed race to disrupt racial hierarchies and rethink the primacy of perceived identity categories as the foundation for kinship and solidarity. As I point out throughout this book, Blasians trouble the usefulness of race as a means of categorizing, since their illegibility highlights how our current racial schema, which is predicated on the superficial and ocular, breaks down when having to account for race outside of phenoperception. Identifying a popular and, importantly, visible collection of Blasian subjects understandably points to celebrities, which allows me to ask the question "How did they become the fulcrum for Blasian legibility?" In this book, I explore how media processes, institutions, and discourses have "branded" mixed-race Black and Asian/American celebrities and hence made them legible and marketable to broad popular audiences. The way these Blasian celebrities challenge race is what constitutes their own brand. I am not replacing a biological understanding of race with an equally illogical and slippery cultural identity. I want to stress here that this project is challenging the primacy of both biology and culture as scripts for structuring by race (and by extension other identity markers). When we think of the ways in which Blasian celebrities both embrace and eschew their racial identities—as monoracially Black or Asian/American but also as multiracially Blasian—the tensions between the ambiguities, inflexibilities, and illegibilities coupled with the increased visibility, which in turn leads to legibility and successful commodification, not only highlights the inherently contradictory idea of race itself but also offers possible alternatives to racialization.

CHAPTER 2

Birth of a Blasian

In the last decade, global news media have been documenting the nascent sexual revolution in China,[1] with a focus on the increasing number of interracial relationships. A number of these stories have focused on the two-way movement of migrants—Chinese men working in various African countries and marrying local women,[2] and men from myriad African countries working in China and marrying local women.[3] Perhaps most surprising about this coverage is the focus on African and Chinese pairings and the astonishment conveyed about the existence and growing popularity of these intimate transnational connections. There exists a context for the transnational movements of Blacks and Asian/Americans that helps frame both their historical connections and the contemporary associations with each other. The context provides a space and chronology to understand the creation and emergence of Blasians as it draws on the ways Blacks and Asian/Americans have been imagined. Situating the images of both Black and Asian/American people socio-historically emphasizes how representations of these groups have been and continue to be both biologically and culturally

determined. The discourses framing these encounters underscore why
tensions and anxieties exist around Black and Asian/American connections, namely, the products of these interracial relationships—Blasians.
Furthermore, these Afro-Asian connections and contextualizations
are necessary to demonstrate how Blasian entertainment figures have
become visible and how their bodies act as racial scripts used to demar-
cate, sometimes poorly, racial divisions and hierarchies. Through explo-
rations of brief moments of illegibility, tensions, and solidarity as Blacks
and Asian/Americans intermingle and reproduce, I ultimately end on
how the connections Blacks and Asian/Americans have made with each
other also offer potential areas for rethinking culture, race, and societal
structure.

Mapping Out Afro-Asian Associations

African and Asian countries were trading with each other long before
Vasco de Gama led European expeditions that forced relationships with
countries outside of Europe. There were, for example, Chinese trade
expeditions to the African continent, which led to creating trade routes
between a number of Asian and African countries, leading to the uncov-
ering of xenophobia and ethnocentrism, which Prashad notes predates
the early modern world, as responses to "anxiety and cultural difference."[4]
In *Everybody Was Kung Fu Fighting*, Prashad offers an extensive explication of the ways African and Asian countries were not only familiar
with each other but also exhibited some of the earliest examples of what
he terms polyculturalism, via a long tradition of cultural exchanges and
encounters. One example of polyculturalism is the presence of Arabic
and Gujarati inflections and vocabulary in Swahili, which is a Bantu language spoken by a sizable portion of East African inhabitants. Prashad
also alludes to the intimate mixing of African and Asian (proto-Blasian)
peoples by noting the presence of Bajuni—Chinese/Swahili Africans—in
what is now Kenya, and the intermarriages of native inhabitants of Mad-
agascar and Indonesian slaves.[5] Furthermore, though the Indian Ocean
slave trade did not reach the numbers of the Atlantic slave trade,[6] the need
for slave labor magnified under the "flag of colonial powers."[7] Okihiro
notes the global system of labor triangulated the relationship between
Africans, Asians, and Europeans, which resulted in African slaves in Asian
countries, Asian slaves in African countries, and both African and Asian
slaves in European settlements and colonies.[8]

While Africans and Asians were already familiar with each other, it was not until the arrival of Chinese laborers that they encountered each other in the Americas. Thinking about these early associations forces us to recognize the intimacies that have led to "affective ties—loyalties, sympathies, desires, attachments, and affiliations—between and among racialized subjects."[9] The laborers in the United States and the Caribbean islands were overwhelmingly male, as they were not allowed to bring their families.[10] Chinese laborers, and later Filipino, South Asian, and Japanese workers, were also prohibited from living near Whites, and antimiscegenation laws prohibited them from forming relationships with White women. The exclusion by/from White society and lack of access to women drove these laborers into Black (and Indigenous) communities. While Asian laborers were forging relationships with the Black communities around them, they were simultaneously being used to highlight the potential of industrious, non-slave labor, then later to "depress the wages of the newly freed" slaves.[11] Blacks and Asian/Americans continued to be pitted against each other with each new labor development, such as the introduction of machines or the need for more specialized skills. The divide-and-rule strategy worked to maintain the social and political-economic control of Blacks and Asian/Americans, to the obvious benefit of White laborers and managers. Despite the efforts to drive a wedge between them, there were many moments of solidarity between the two groups, such as Frederick Douglass's speech calling for the inclusion of Asians in US society, which he claimed would benefit Blacks, because the number of similarities between the two groups far exceeded the differences;[12] and the lone dissenting vote against the Chinese Exclusion Act from Black Mississippi senator Blanche Bruce.

Other moments of solidarity occurred during wartime. For example, during the Philippine-American War (1898–1902) Black soldiers defected to fight alongside Filipino soldiers against the United States. After the war, a number of the soldiers stayed in the Philippines and married and started families.[13] During the Korean War, Widener notes, some North Korean broadcasts were aimed at the Black regiment of soldiers, feeding on the growing disenchantment of its members with the war. In prison camps run by either Chinese or North Korean forces, the captors would often use racial conditions back in the United States to encourage the Black soldiers "to go back to your country and help start a revolution," using mutual hatred of Whites to build up opposition.[14] Widener also notes that a few captured Black soldiers, when given the choice to go back to the United States or stay in North Korea, chose to stay in North Korea. Perhaps the best-known wartime moment of solidarity came via Muhammad Ali, né Cassius Clay, who famously declared his objection to fighting in Viet Nam by noting, "I ain't got no quarrel with those Viet Cong, anyway. They never called me nigger."[15] His declaration summed up nearly five decades' worth of social movements calling for the cooperation of Blacks and Asian/Americans, African countries and Asian countries, to collectively oppose Euro-American imperialism as a show of anticolonial solidarity. The cooperation included the Bandung Conference (1955) in Indonesia, and the joining of Black and Yellow Power (and Brown and Red Power) movements in the United States. In fact, the coalition building of racialized groups during the civil rights era led to what Chon-Smith sees as an "Afro-Asian vision of interracial coalition building that disavowed the essentialist and flattening gaze of racial magnetism, and their innovations in political organizing, social consciousness raising, and cultural fusion still have a lasting legacy today."[16]

While antimiscegenation laws did not explicitly prohibit relationships between Blacks and Asian/Americans, fighting wars in various Asian countries allowed for the gradual demise of anti-Asian miscegenation policies. The 1945 War Brides Act allowed White[17] soldiers to gain entry into the United States for the Asian women they married while fighting wars abroad, and the children from those marriages. The War Brides Act and its amendments eventually led to the reversal of the immigration policies that limited the number of Asian immigrants allowed entry into the United States, which allowed Black soldiers to also bring their war families into the country. However, the uneven application of the War Brides Act after World War II, coupled with xenophobic governmental bureaucracy, kept some military fathers from bringing their families back to the United States. Furthermore, there were other soldiers who either did not know or refused to acknowledge they had fathered children during their time in myriad Asian countries, or they abandoned their children upon returning to the States. This led to the emergence of both the military-dad narrative and the popularization of the term Amerasian. Coined by novelist Pearl Buck in 1930, Amerasian was used to refer to the mixed-race children of Asian women and American soldiers specifically,[18] and the passage of policies like the American Homecoming Act (1988), which was also referred to as the Amerasian Homecoming Act, cemented the label for these children. Movies such as Gail Dolgin's *Daughter from Danang*

(2002) and plays like Velina Hasu Houston's *Calligraphy* (2010) focus on these mixed-race children of military occupation couplings.

There are a number of factors that have played a part in eliding the historical connections between Asians and Africans, but the most important factors as noted by Fred Ho and Bill Mullen, are "race, racism, and capitalism [which] have conspired, according to Horne,[19] to both produce and manipulate the black world's understanding of Asia and the Asian world's understanding of the black 'West.'"[20] I would also argue that race, racism, and capitalism have also allowed for the continuous triangulation[21] of Blacks and Asian/Americans against each other, always for the benefit of Whiteness. Here, I think especially of the violence and tension between Black and Korean communities in New York City and Los Angeles, particularly in the late 1980s and '90s. Claire Jean Kim, in her book *Bitter Fruit*, deconstructs the maintenance of racial triangulation vis-à-vis White supremacy and how the end result of continuous racial triangulation is volatility between Blacks and Asian/Americans. Additionally, part of the reason why Blasians have not figured as prominently in either research or popular culture is because of the application of hypodescent, which renders any product of Asian/American and Black interracial relationships, de facto Black.[22] So just as White sexual violence against Black female slaves resulted in the deployment of the one-drop rule against the biracial children, the same has happened with early Blasians in the United States. Additionally, those Asian/Americans wanting to gain honorary White status had to eschew connections with Blacks; distancing themselves was a necessary move in order to move up the racialized hierarchy.[23]

For both Blacks and Asian/Americans "segregation in sex, marriage, and family [has been] a hallmark of intense racialization and entrenched inequality."[24] To study representations within popular culture, it is necessary to look at interracial relationships, particularly because it provides both a foundation and a frame for understanding the issues around sexuality and race while simultaneously highlighting popular culture's conflicted stance on Blasians. As the rates of intermarriage are rising, the growth is attributable mostly to interracial marriage between people of color and Whites, not between people of color with each other.[25] The percentage of interracial relationships between Blacks and Asian/Americans is so minimal that in the most recent Pew report on intermarriage, the pairing was not included.[26] Estimates for the percentage of interracial relationships between Blacks and Asian/Americans, however, put it at slightly under 1 percent of all interracial relationships. Based on data from the 2010 census, for every 1,000 interracial marriages, 14 are between Asian/American women and Black men, and only 2 are between Asian/American men and Black women.[27] The overwhelming prevalence of Black men Asian/American women pairings is due in part to US military intervention in Asian countries, which creates notable dynamics around gender and citizenship for these relationships. Undoubtedly the paucity of interracial relationships between Asian/American men and Black women is also attributable in part to the discourses of racialized sexuality used to frame these men and women. Whereas Asian/American men have been framed as feminized, asexual, and/or emasculated, Black women have been framed as hypersexual, sometimes masculine, overbearing, and emasculating. Both groups are framed as largely undesirable,[28] leading to a trend in the late 2000s encouraging more Asian/American men and Black women to date each other.[29] Fryer reminds us, however, not to assume the lack of Black and Asian/American intermarriage is caused by "negative preferences," especially when it can also be chalked up to relatively small population sizes when compared to the rest of the US population.[30] Still, as all relationships always involve the distribution and movement of power, interracial relationships become particularly complicated with narratives of race, sexuality, and desirability.

Just as historical examination and contextualization of Black and Asian/American encounters are sparse, despite evidence of their frequent exchanges and associations, analyses of popular mass-mediated images have also been sparse,[31] emphasizing the need for examining the politics of desire within Black and Asian/American interracial relationships. Interracial relationships on television and in films have been heralded as the progressive evolution of racial representations and race relations. However, underneath the veneer of racial advancement are hegemonic notions of racialized sexuality. While the narrative of the United States as a bastion of postracial ideology has become increasingly popular through its dissemination to countless media outlets,[32] the uneasiness of society over interracial unions comes out in popular culture. As couples, Blacks and Asian/Americans on primetime dramas are always relegated to one of two story arcs—either having sex without love or being in love without the sex. Interestingly, both storylines fall short of the heteronormative ideal for romantic couples on television—marriage *and* a baby.[33] Whereas the reliance on stereotypical tropes by these programs shows the United States is nowhere close to being a postracial utopia, it also reveals society's anxiety over the products of interracial, specifically Black and Asian/ American, unions—Blasian babies. Though my branding theory traces out the processes utilized to make Blasians legible, this portion is partially about illegibility as the desire for Blasian babies, the desire for each other, the desire for a postracial future, are all averted. Those babies represent a compelling challenge to the racial classification schema of the United States by virtue of the both/and nature of their racial mixture.

Blasian Invasion: The Emergence of Blasians

Charlie Mingus, an American composer and jazz musician, opens the documentary film *Triumph of the Underdog* by discussing his racial identity: "I'm Charles Mingus. Half-black man, yellow man, half-yellow, not even yellow, not even white enough to pass for nothing but black, and not too light to be called white. I claim that I am a Negro." Using archival footage of Mingus, interviews of family, friends, and musicians, and his original music, the film offers a compelling exploration of his life and career. As the son of a biracial man and a Blasian woman, biographers mention Mingus's multiraciality through his own words, his identity process, his reasoning regarding his identity, and his ultimate choice and designation for racial recognition. Though Mingus claimed a "Negro" identity for himself, it is clear his White, Black, and Asian ancestry made him Cablinasian[34] long before Tiger Woods coined the label; yet he rejected identification with multiraciality and, instead, identified with Blackness.

Mingus has been described as being race-conscious before the civil rights era logic about race permeated society.[35] His opening statement is perhaps the most compelling piece of audio from Mingus himself, because it foregrounds the importance and influence of race on his life and work. His words were originally recorded in 1968, in Thomas Reichman's film *Mingus: Charlie Mingus 1968*, but it was not the only time he addressed being mixed race. He disparagingly referred to his multiracial makeup by pretending to title his autobiography *Memoirs of a Half-Schitt Colored Nigger*.[36] Mingus's explicit rejection of his Blasian mixture ironically became a public acknowledgment of the existence of Blasians.

While he is more than likely not the first Blasian celebrity, I introduce Charles Mingus here to act as a starting point for the emergence of Blasians within the entertainment industry and use the remainder of this chapter to trace out how popular media have created, defined, and represented Blasians, and to explore some of the ways Blasians themselves are destabilizing those media discourses. Others have written about the issues faced by celebrities in disclosing or not disclosing their particular racial makeup.[37] Still, Mingus's statement, which he gave as the Vietnam War raged, came at the height of the Black Power movement and supported the counterhegemonic assertion that "Black is Beautiful." His eschewing of a Blasian identity, memorialized in the documentary and his own writings and music, brings the products of those relationships into the popular imaginary. While famous, Mingus did not become a figure around which multiraciality was discussed significantly, nor is his multiraciality mentioned much, even today. Blasians as a group of people existed before Mingus's identification with and rejection of the label in 1968, but his statement here initiates the moment at which Blasians began to become legible.

1980s Multiculturalism and Blasians' Visibility

While the particular racial formation of multiraciality, and Blasianness in particular, has been taking place for quite some time, it has only been because of a confluence of factors more recently relating to civil rights, for example, the 1967 *Loving v. Virginia* decision, that media have begun to acknowledge the existence and popularity of multiracial celebrities, and Blasians as part of that cadre. Blasians have become what Omi and Winant term "racialized," which means they are the recipients of an "extension of racial meaning to a previously racially unclassified relationship, social practice or group."[38] From that moment in 1968, actors, singers, athletes and models have all availed themselves of Asian/Americanness, Blackness, and multiraciality as necessary in order to negotiate their identity. If I begin the emergence with Mingus's rejection of Blasian identity and embrace of Blackness, then the emergence gathers steam during the multicultural 1980s and 1990s, when Rae Dawn Chong nearly achieves "It Girl" status.

Actor Rae Dawn Chong, daughter of Chinese and Scots-Irish actor Tommy Chong,[39] and Black and Cherokee mother Maxine Sneed, was especially popular in the 1980s, starring in films like *Soul Man* (1986), *Beat Street* (1984), *American Flyers* (1985), *The Color Purple* (1985), and *Commando* (1985). As the daughter of a famous mixed-race Asian/American actor from Canada, who appeared in his films *Cheech and Chong's The Corsican Brothers* (1984) and *Far Out Man* (1990), Chong emphasized her multiraciality, rather than focusing on a monoracial identity. She became the first star to claim a Blasian identity publicly by explicitly rejecting the monoracial identity that media attempted to foist upon her. Chong kicks off a moment that introduces Blasians into mainstream culture, most notably through her role on a popular television show, *St. Elsewhere*. She became accustomed to being neither Black nor Asian/American, but all, because she was always positioned "on the outside looking in"[40] racially. She purposely labeled herself as not a "Blacktor"[41] (Black actor), because she was never considered Black enough to be hired for Black roles, or at all by Black directors. She notes she was accepted by "the establishment" (major Hollywood studios) and rejected by the Black "renaissance" (Black directors[42] making movies in the 1980s and 1990s). That did not keep movie critics and reporters from being torn between referring to her as Black in reviews of her films and roles[43] or letting readers infer that she was Asian/American by mentioning her father.[44] Chong did hold a number of roles not initially meant for a person of color, and she was the primary love interest for many White male stars popular in the 1980s, but in her own comments about her racial identity, she reveals a self-critical awareness of the history of White men and women of color, acknowledging that her being cast in studio films did little to challenge the racial hegemony of Hollywood.[45]

She notes on her personal blog, however, that her branding gamble nearly paid off during her "peak 80s run [when she] almost cracked that glass ceiling by just showing up as 'the girl' instead of THE BLACK girl" [emphasis Chong's].[46] Chong also notes in interviews and on her blog that the biggest consequence of her decision to not be pigeonholed as a Black actor was being ostracized by Black directors, notably Spike Lee, who Chong claims blacklisted her and ensured that she was excluded from being cast in the few large mostly-Black Hollywood studio productions.[47] In making the rounds for the press junket around the rerelease of *The Color Purple* (1985), Chong relayed how Spike Lee declared she was not Black enough, and she talked about the dual struggle of trying to be cast in mainstream productions and proving herself to indeed be enough racially.[48]

While Chong may have distanced herself purposely from being labeled a Black actor, importantly she did not distance herself from Blackness. She recognized people were offended because she "didn't care to take up *our* cause for the struggle ... [and] wasn't applying my afrocentricity into every role."[49] Her strategic use of "our" and "my" is done to mark her membership in the Black community's struggles and to emphasize the fact that she, too, is Black. There are moments, like her inclusion in *Ebony* magazine about the difficulties Black women face in becoming established in Hollywood, that support her membership in Blackness.[50] But she simultaneously stresses the importance of her Asian/American identity and her membership specifically in the Chinese community when she mentions growing up with a grandfather who was ashamed to be Chinese and wanted to be White, and how she was "desperate to know anything about *our* Chinese culture" (emphasis mine).[51] Chong strategically uses her interviews to talk about her racial identity and the impact it had on her career, but it was not until Barack Obama's election as president of the United States that she began to address being multiracial. After Obama's inauguration she remarked that she was "relieved there's a beige face in the White House . . . I'm hoping we can be a little less sensitive about things that make people scared of *us*."[52] Interestingly, her use of "us" works to place them both within multiraciality, but also I would argue she is making a move to position Obama, like she did with herself, within Blasianness. Alternatively, it is possible to read Chong's racial negotiations in the press as ambivalent, but I interpret her maneuvers differently. That these interviews touched on Chong's racial identity, combining both of her self-identification moves against the interviewers' own attempts to label Chong monoracially, is indicative of the difficulty in placing Blasians within the US racial system, not of Chong's uncertainty. This becomes a hallmark of Blasian branding maneuvers: the resistance, maybe even unwillingness, on the part of media to acknowledge that these stars can indeed be both Black and Asian/American.

A watershed moment arrived in this trajectory of emergence when Blasianness was configured as integral to the storyline on an episode of *Law & Order: Special Victims Unit*. This episode is noteworthy because we see the shift from individual Blasians to representations of Blasians, and that shift highlights the struggles media have in making sense of Blasians. The entire *Law & Order* franchise draws attention to its "ripped from the headlines" plots, and while this particular episode seems to not be ripped literally from the headlines, it does work to acknowledge that Blasians exist and are visible if not yet entirely legible. Rae Dawn Chong's brother, Marcus Chong, plays a racially mixed Blasian character, Darryl, in the episode titled "Inheritance." This episode was the eighth in the third season for *Law & Order: SVU*, which marked the year (2001–2002)the series ranked in the top twenty in audience size.[53] The show was averaging 15.2 million viewers an episode, which is a sizable television audience and meant that this episode could have been (and probably was), for many Americans, an introduction to Blasians. The episode follows the unit's investigation of the rapes of several Chinese American women in the Chinatown neighborhood of Manhattan. A break in the case comes when during an interview of a Chinese woman who had filed a police complaint, it is revealed how a man she met through a personal ad in a "Chinese-language newspaper" pulled a knife on her during their date. She also tells the officers, Stabler and Benson, through FBI psychologist and ad hoc Chinese translator George Huang, that "he wasn't Chinese, he was Black." In the next scene is this exchange between Stabler and Huang:

> STABLER: How many African American males speak and write Chinese
>   well enough to fool a native speaker?
> HUANG: Well, he could be a student, or work at the World Bank or the UN,
>   or . . .
> STABLER: Why lie about being Chinese?
> HUANG: Because he knows she'll never go out with him if he's not, and then
>   he expects that once they've met, she'll have been so taken with him that
>   his ethnicity won't matter. Her reaction to his race is what sets him off.

The conversation between the two characters is illuminating, because it speaks to the disbelief that a Black person can also be Asian/American, in this case Chinese, as none of the characters even bring up that possibility. This exchange also shows how identifying as ethnically Chinese, by being able to speak the language and understand the customs, is looked on with suspicion by all of the characters in the show because of Darryl's Blackness. Darryl's Blackness precludes any possibility of, or connection to, authentic Asianness, whatever that is deemed to be.

Marcus Chong's Darryl, the serial rapist in the episode, turns out to be himself the product of rape when the investigation uncovers that his Black father raped his Chinese mother. His mother details the difficulties and isolation Darryl faced growing up, being called "half devil" by her parents, never being accepted by her family, being harassed physically by neighborhood children and verbally by the Chinese neighbors. His mother attends his trial, and as a defense for Darryl is mounted, the show places both Darryl and his mother in the same frame.[54] As the trial progresses, Darryl's difficulties growing up and the circumstances of his existence are used to depict him as mentally defective and unstable. Though this episode aired in 2001, the twin notions of hybrid vigor and multiracial glorification were again coming back into vogue, and this particular narrative is in keeping with popular media's continued deployment of the tragic-mulatto trope. Hybrid vigor initially referred to the crossbreeding of plants and/or animals, and the "empirically observed phenomenon of increased capacity for growth often displayed by hybrid animals or plants."[55] It is now also used in reference to the multiracial children of interracial relationships who are thought to be more attractive, smarter, fertile, and better all around when compared to their monoracial counterparts.[56] Multiracial glorification refers to the notion that mixed-race people, by virtue of their multiraciality, act as a racial salve, their bodies becoming a promise to bridge the racial divides in the United States.[57] Though the tragic-mulatto trope refers to a biracial person's anguish over the abandonment of his or her Black identity in favor of passing as White, which results in some sort of mental, emotional, or psychic instability,[58] it is useful here to describe the depiction of Darryl's mental instability. Though not mulatto,[59] Darryl is depicted as pathologically criminal, because this particular narrative tells us when races mix, the mixed-race person is unable to deal with its attendant tensions and contradictions and subsequently loses his mind and/or succumbs to his baser desires.

Toward the end of the episode, FBI psychologist Huang interviews Darryl to determine if he is competent for trial. After Darryl notes Huang is Chinese and identifies himself as Chinese also, Huang replies, "Actually you're half Chinese." His remark touches on discourses of authenticity and wholeness, where wholeness belongs to monoracially identified people.[60] Racially mixed people, then, are forced to think of themselves in fractions, parts, and pieces.[61] The trial at the end of the episode focuses on essentialist ideas of violence and sexuality tied to Darryl's Blackness. This episode both embraces and eschews essentialist ideas of race. The plot fits within a dominant narrative that violent and criminal behavior is biologically determined: Black man raped, and so his son, who is also Black, rapes; but the plot also refuses to give Darryl entrée into Asianness through his mother. While his treatment by the Chinese community is brought up as the motive for Darryl's rapes, it is never used to talk about Darryl's identity. Darryl's portrayal by both sides is as a Black man, not a Blasian, and definitely not Chinese.

Blasians Represent

The commodification of hip-hop and Black womanhood in the 1990s with the simultaneous emergence of multiracial movement created a move toward broader interest and acceptance of Blasianness vis-à-vis the emergence of Blasian women in music videos. And, it is here, firmly ensconced in the 2000s, that we begin to see not only the beginnings of widespread recognition but the fetishization of Blasianness within hip-hop media culture, a fetishization that resulted in the production of job positions and employment for Blasians. Blasians and Blasianness were now not only plot devices in serial dramas, they were also lyrically and visually appearing in hip-hop and R&B songs. Their employment and subsequent representation ensure their own identities will inform the productions in which they become involved, further shaping the way Blasians become branded.

Rappers and singers mentioned Blasians in song lyrics in such a way that they differentiated from the already popular figure of the light-skinned/biracial Black woman. Despite being marked as different in the songs, these women are met with the same heteronormative objectification as other women in the songs: useful for their looks or as sexual partners and conquests for the rappers. For example, in the D12 song "Chance to Advance" (1997), Black and Asian are used to rhyme with the word *amazing*: "Make moms say 'that's amazing,' all the same like Black and Asian." The lyrics makes little sense in the verse they appear in, but this is possibly the first instance in hip-hop/R&B where they are used together to signify a mixed-race Blasian, rather than Blacks and Asian/Americans as separate entities. The unclear meaning of *Black* and *Asian*, together here, is emblematic of the historical position Blasianness is in prior to broader circulation in media. Nelly, in his song "E.I." (2000), has "a chick rollin' up, half Black and Asian; another one pagin',' tellin' me to come home." In Nelly's song, the Blasian woman is notable enough to warrant a mention of her racial makeup, while the next woman is not. R. Kelly sings in his song "Showdown" (2003) about a "Black and Asian girl" who creates tension between him and his duet partner, Ron Isley. Most revealing is the line "Gotta have you now 'cause me so horny, Black and Asian girl, tattoo on your tummy," which samples the 2 Live Crew song "Me So Horny," which itself used the Kubrick film *Full Metal Jacket* (1987) as a reference. 2 Live Crew took its sample from the scene in which Privates Joker and Rafterman are solicited by a Vietnamese sex worker, who uses the line "Me so horny. Me love you long time." The "me so horny" line, coupled with the focus of the song on a Blasian woman, draws a connection between sex workers, Asian/American women, and this Blasian antagonist.

Other hip-hop and R&B artists have also mentioned Blasians in their songs. Rapper Nas describes his partner at the time, singer Kelis, in the song "Popular Thug" (2003) as his "honey [who is] Black, Puerto Rican and Asian," effectively outing Kelis as a Blasian. Nas again mentions Blasians in the song "Sekou Story" (2003), which is an ode to his "half Haitian, half Asian"[62] titular protagonist, whose life is cut short. Southern rapper Gucci Mane notes in his lyrics for the song "Atlanta Zoo" (2010) that he drinks "with a bad bitch Black 'n Asian." T.I., another southern rapper, mentions Blasians in his collaboration with Nelly on the song "Pretty Toes" (2004). T.I. raps about "light-skinned Asian bitches with pink toes." One of the successful rappers from the South, Big Boi, offers the most specific lyric about Blasians in his song "Flip Flop Rock" (2003), when he asks the listener/critic how they racially identify: "Black, White, Asian, Indonesian, or Borean—that's Black and Korean?" Big Boi's lyrics show a Black Asian mixed person is not only possible but is legible enough to warrant mentioning specific Blasian ethnic combinations. These examples suggest that Blasian began to become a positive attribute, a trendy thing to include, titillating, fashionable, and sexy. There is tension around the emergence of Blasian, and the rappers demonstrate that acceptance is not absolute but conditional, making Blasians what Raymond Williams[63] would term emergent and not yet traditional.

Modeling Blasians

As channels like VH1 and MTV give up the music video in favor of cheaply produced reality television shows, it is niche channels like BET (Black Entertainment Television) and CMT (Country Music Television) that continue to play music videos. The hip-hop video in particular has "collapsed art, commerce, and interactive technology into one mutant animal."[64] As the market for hip-hop music expanded, the need to differentiate among artists called for larger and deeper marketing and promotion budgets, especially during the 1990s, when hip-hop was exploding into mainstream consciousness and becoming a global commodity. As music videos became increasingly more focused on women and their bodies,[65] Tricia Rose notes, women in these videos either became "creatures of male sexual possession or they [were] reified into the status of nonbeing."[66] As a countermeasure to declining record sales, artists regularly appeared on BET music video countdown shows to plug their videos and the guest stars, video models included, who appear in them to drum up fan support for their music. The videos increasingly emphasized the women who appeared in their videos, making sure to feature familiar and more popular models. Black gossip blogs are filled with quotidian posts about women whose fame stems from appearances in hip-hop music videos.[67] Video models are featured on websites focused on everything from celebrity gossip to fashion to music, on their own dedicated blogs, in magazines—especially urban men's magazines and hip-hop magazines (though sometimes those two things are interchangeable), on the *New York Times* bestsellers list, in reality television shows like E!'s *Candy Girls*, and VH1's *Love and Hip Hop* franchise, in movies, and on social media platforms (to varying degrees of success). The presence of models has become so linked to the music that hip-hop magazine *Vibe* created the "*Vibe* Video Vixen" award in the mid-2000s, which was later renamed the "*Vibe* Video Goddess" award. The purpose of the award was to recognize "a woman whose personae [*sic*] and spirit influences urban culture."[68] Sharpley-Whiting[69] points out that hip-hop is now about image just as much as rapping skills and the beats in the songs. Despite the popularity of some women artists in the last decade, it remains a male-dominated genre that is extremely popular and profitable within a male-dominated music industry, which is why the women featured in music videos play such an important role, though they do not reap the same benefits as these men in the industry. Still, despite or maybe because of the male gaze, video models have gone from mere props for mostly male rappers and singers in their videos to major cultural influences in their own right.

It is difficult to determine which came first in hip-hop and R&B music, lyrics about Blasians or the presence of Blasian video models, but they have had a mutually beneficial relationship: artists mention Blasians in their lyrics, and Blasians are highlighted in their music videos in hopes they will draw more (and new) viewers. While Charles Mingus, the Chong siblings, and early-career Tiger Woods began the work of making Blasians legible as a group, it is the popularity of video models that turned Blasians into an identifiable, and therefore consumable, commodity. Shaviro notes that the trend, in his analysis of women in hip-hop music, is "most recently [the] tendency to focus on women who are 'multi-racial,' i.e. black and Asian."[70] Though White women are still the standard by which beauty and femininity are judged, music videos have become the predominant venue for finding images of women of color. Still, the explosion of not-dark-skinned, long- and straight-haired, thin yet acceptably curvy women in music videos has dominated the image of women of color in popular culture.[71] In keeping with racialized ideas of attractiveness, the more popular video models, the ones who "star" in music videos, are racially mixed, or at least ethnically ambiguous, women. While the biracial woman might represent the ultimate and ideal mixture of Black sexuality and White femininity/beauty,[72] Blasian video models do not have the benefit of Whiteness to reflect those beauty standards as neatly. One could argue these women are popular simply because their Black and Asian/American mixture renders them as exotic enough, thanks to conflicting cultural notions that are grounded in anti-Blackness yet simultaneously fascinated by both Blackness and Asianness: meaning that while Blackness is not a hegemonic marker of beauty in the United States, Blackness does operate as a barometer of cool. The cultural trendiness of Blackness coupled with orientalist notions of Asian/American femininity results in the aforementioned conflicting tensions around Blasians. Arguments that dismiss the utility of these Blasian video models because they come close to the ideal White standards of beauty—via multiracial chic—without challenging those standards, dismiss the complexity that accompanies the popularity of ethnic ambiguity. Thornton and Gates note ethnic ambiguity has proven to be beneficial when thinking about the situational nature of racial identification[73] (particularly in hostile environments where blending in is the difference between life and death). The transracial movement of Blasians gives rise to ambiguity, which enables the manipulation and/or performance of race. There are also, of course, the political-economic benefits of ethnic ambiguity; the ability to appeal to a racially broad cross section of people is beneficial for any star, but certainly for mixed-race stars and these Blasian video models specifically. I focus briefly on three Blasian video models because they were prominent enough to allow me the opportunity to delve deeper into how Blasians negotiate their own racial identities alongside the expectations of fans and the music industry.

Tomika Skanes,[74] Denyce Lawton,[75] and La'Shontae Heckard,[76] who all identify as Black and Korean, got their starts in music videos roughly around the same time in the early 2000s and together have been featured in over fifty videos for popular mainstream artists throughout the decade.[77] Interestingly, in an interview with the website HalfKorean.com, Lawton was asked if she had met any other "half/mixed Korean artists," to which she replied that she knew both Skanes and Heckard.[78] The women, during their careers as video models, have also modeled for urban men's magazines and album covers, have been crowned "Video Vixen of the Year" by *Vibe* magazine, and have been featured on a number of websites devoted to tracking the careers and movements of the most popular video models.[79] They have transitioned from being featured in music videos to regular acting roles on Black sitcoms, *The Game* for Heckard and *Tyler Perry's House of Payne* and *Almost Home* for Lawton, and model management for Skanes. This cohort of Blasian video models has strategically leveraged careers in video modeling to negotiate and complicate narratives of non-White multiracial people. Denyce Lawton's 2004 interview with HalfKorean.com fittingly frames the explosion of Blasians, specifically via a tangible presence in the music industry and music videos, by offering a rough timeline. When Lawton's interviewer asks what she thinks of the website and its purpose, she answers: "I do remember thinking, how neat. I never thought this was a hot issue to have a site about or that many people would be interested in half Korean people. You have to understand: to meet half Korean/Black people these days is still weird for me. Up until 3 years ago, the only ones I knew were on the bases with me and my family, now I turn around in this business and everyone is."[80] Though Tiger Woods had been the most visible Blasian since becoming a pro golfer a few years before the rise of these video models, his refusal to discuss his Cablinasian identity after the furor caused by his *Oprah Show* appearance did not help make Blasians a legible category with mainstream visibility until his scandal—which I discuss in a subsequent chapter. In the meantime, the bodies of these women filled the void left by Woods's silence. Though they fit the light-skinned multiracial chic aesthetic popularized in the late 1990s/early 2000s, they also together disrupted the dominant narrative that racial mixing and multiraciality occurred only around Whiteness.

Blasian video models have had to negotiate the attendant sexual representations of women of color in popular culture. The bodies of Black and Asian/American women have been and continue to be a constant site of struggle—over meanings, over power, over control. Moreover, I argue Blasians already exist in a space where they are non-normative, within dominant discourses of race in the United States as mixed-race people, but also within dominant discourses of multiraciality because they are not White mixed-race people; so these Blasian women are launching a "counter-racial-sexualization" that allows them to "redefine sex, race, and representation in an open-ended fashion."[81] Their counter-racial sexualization offers up a transectional space for analysis and a reminder that "race is deployed within pop music videos to not only delimit or sanction sexual behavior, but also sex and gender signify race in ways which tend to reproduce and shore up existing hierarchical power relations."[82]

Research on the role of women in hip-hop/R&B music videos has already parsed the continued hypersexualization of women of color. They are represented through their physicality—never as emotional or intellectual beings[83]—and as sexual commodities.[84] The heteronormative male focus of hip-hop lyrics is depicted in these videos through offering up particular ideals of sexualized and racialized femininity. A great many of the women chosen for these videos have been "either fairer-skinned, ethnically mixed, or of indeterminate ethnic/racial origins, with long, straight or curly hair [which] would suggest that along with the stereotype of hypersexuality and sexual accessibility, a particular type of beauty is offered up as ideal."[85] This type of beauty is one that could approximate Whiteness while still retaining some color. While the aesthetics of many of these women in hip-hop work to reinscribe dominant notions of attractiveness, desirability, and the hypersexuality of raced bodies, their representations of "sexual agency and desire" also work to challenge both the politics of respectability[86] and the heteropatriarchal control of hip-hop. As Miller-Young notes, these videos provide "an arena for . . . self-presentation, mediation, and mobility . . . [and] a space for work, survival, consumption, and identity-formation" for the women highlighted.[87] Importantly, these women "re-identify sexuality as crucial to their social legibility and self-recognition in terms of forging their freedoms from the bonds of racial, gendered, sexual, and classed classifications."[88] In critiquing the binds of representation, Parreñas Shimizu reminds us "to assume that sexuality gives bad impressions of racial subjects [which] keeps us from looking at how these images critique normative subjectivities."[89] She goes on to note that the "perversity unifying their representations, which are palpably different from normal sexuality usually embodied by a white woman, can be interpreted variously: as strength, diversity, or pathology."[90] While she is writing about the sexualized images of Asian/American women in erotic media, her contention is equally applicable to Black women, whose sexuality is also interpreted within those same categories. It is important to analyze and understand Blasian video models, because the representation of women of color, especially as hypersexual beings, happens within a system of social forces that "ground their legibility in culture, as terms for self-recognition and as condition of social marginalization that leads to opportunities for creative self-invention."[91] Furthermore, these representations happen in a system that from its inception has assigned romantic love, marriage, and respectability to middle-class White womanhood, leaving all women of color to express their fulfillment in other arenas. In other words, contextualizing the expressions of women of color in terms of sexual love shows it as "linked inextricably with possibilities of social freedom in the economic and political realms."[92] Davis and Parreñas Shimizu both talk about the sexuality of Black and Asian/American women as a force that both allows them mobility and empowers them. The politics of respectability ignore the ability of sexuality to empower, yet these Blasian video models embody this alternative.

The ways these women were branded hinged not only on how they were racialized by both the music (video) industry and the celebrity industrial complex but also on how they self-identified. The influence from their roles as marquee music-video stars enabled them to strategically utilize the power of the music video and transnational consumption of Black urban music and bodies to effectively promote both themselves, as individuals, and Blasians. Dynastyseries.com, which functions as both an agency for models of color and an aggregator of links mentioning models from other websites, included Heckard in its ranking of the top twenty-five models of the decade. As explanation, the site notes that "in the early to mid 2000 [sic] there was a stint where the Asian/Black model was really sought after; a large part of this was due to Tae Heckard. Her ethnic yet diverse look really changed the game."[93] One interviewer primed his question to Heckard by pointing out that "we all know that your [sic] mixed: African American and Korean," before asking if being Blasian had helped her land more jobs.[94] Heckard replied that "there's too many beautiful & exotic women in the world to be booked solely on your looks. . . . I think most, if not all of the times, it had to do with my character & personality." Her response that Blasianness had very little to do with either her popularity or her success is illuminating, since she has been identified as the most notable Blasian video model by various websites and urban men's magazines and is one of the key players in the progression of Blasian legibility. On the other hand, Lawton points out that actively branding herself as Blasian has both helped and harmed her career: "I get that I'm either too Asian or not Asian enough or too ethnic or not ethnic enough. I have been told I don't look like the All-American girl next door but then not being that has gotten me work so . . . it balances out."[95] Both women are similar in that they both identify alternately as a Blasian, Asian/American, multiracial, or Black. When discussing future opportunities she hoped to gain, Lawton, in a different interview, continues to discuss how branding herself as Blasian is not always successful: "I'm either too light or not light enough, mostly not dark enough.

Not the girl next-door innocent look. I can play a lot of ethnicities but roles aren't being written for those ethnicities!"[96] Critically, she points out that despite the flexibility afforded her by being Blasian, she cannot take advantage of that flexibility because of the lack of opportunities in general for women of color in entertainment. Heckard's willingness to discount the impact and influence of multiraciality on her career is an indication of how branding operates. Though she is identified as a key part of the Blasian brand, Blasians themselves are not completely in control of its meaning, as there are other people who have had active roles in the production of the meaning of the brand. The fact remains these women are commodities that have a particular relationship with both producers and consumers of their Blasianness. The women acknowledge in recognition of their Blasian identity that they are always women of color and refuse to distance themselves, given their flexibility to play different ethnicities/roles, from the systemic problems faced by women of color.

Part of the identity negotiation process for these women is entangled in the rejection they faced from both the Asian/American and Black communities. Heckard's profile on the *XXL* magazine website details in quick fashion her abandonment by her Korean mother when she was five, who had divorced her Black military father, and her subsequent rescue and relocation to the United States at the hands of her Korean grandmother back to her Black father.[97] It would seem part of Heckard's hesitation in explicitly claiming her racial identity/ies as significant to her success is rooted in the rejection she faced from multiple communities during her childhood. While Lawton did not deal with the same abandonment issues as Heckard, she does mention as a result of "growing up Blasian" that "people didn't know how to react to a light skinned Black girl with a lot of crazy hair :) and 'Chinky' eyes. I still get it a little but not by Black people anymore; more so by some Koreans."[98] Kimora Lee Simmons in the following chapter shares similar stories of the slurs and insults hurled at her, usually appended with "chinky." Lawton also shared that speaking in Korean to monoracially identified Koreans would have unpredictable results; sometimes they would be impressed and treat her differently after finding out she was Korean, though most remained indifferent.[99]

I focused briefly on music videos and these Blasian video models because videos, and popular media, have made Blasians visible—literally—and have become contested terrain where these women challenge the meanings and uses of their representations. Fifty years ago or so, Blasians as either a category or an identity did not exist within the popular imaginary, so there were no representations to examine or contest. Now, Blasians are part of a system that is steeped in essentialisms; the branding strategies that make them legible within media rely on dominant notions of what Blackness and Asianness are, cobbling those narratives together in order to understand Blasians. So on one hand, these Blasian video models are part of dominant, stereotypical representations of both Black and Asian/American women. But there are competing claims of Blackness, Asianness, and multiraciality made discursively, empirically, and materially by these women that force us to acknowledge the constitutive aspect of culture and representation. As markers, or logos in brand-speak, of Blasianness, these video models help visualize the emergence of Blasians. The brand itself has progressed from illegibility in the form of nonexistence, to a way of viewing multiracial identity as multiple, intersecting, and perpetually shifting in reaction to societal structures, social conditions, and relations of power.

Blacks and Asian/Americans have been construed as occupying incommensurable positions, whether culturally, economically, or politically, which has not always been the case. There exists a history of Black and Asian/American interactions, which during key moments in history sprang up in opposition to White supremacy. Though not prevented from joining forces by law or policies, political-economic dictates have worked to prevent them from interacting with each other. Yet, during times of war and social protest, they have managed to again forge interconnections "across a variety of cultural, political, and historical contexts."[100] Contemporarily we see the progeny of those interactions through various popular media. The emergence of Blasians operationalizes the utility of using branding and transracial theories to explain how these celebrities are making visible the linkages between essentialist ideas of race and bodies and then disrupting those linkages.

CHAPTER 3

Modeling Race

Refashioning Blasianness

Kimora Lee Simmons, fashion model, fashion designer, and reality television star, has built her career around her Black and Asian/American mixed-race identity. From the onset of her celebrity in the 1990s as the muse for designer Karl Lagerfeld and Chanel, her Blasian identity has been if not the most obvious source of her popularity, than certainly an important dimension of her fame. Simmons has turned her fame into a career, using herself as the template for how women can and should live well. In building her empire that consists of fashion lines for women and children, fragrances, Hello Kitty jewelry collaborations, movie roles, a reality television show, and various philanthropic efforts, she has leveraged her Blasianness to be a unique selling point in bringing together a disparate fan base through maximizing her multiracial visibility. Furthermore, Simmons uses her Blasianness in a way that makes explicit how racialized performances undergird current sociocultural identity categories. Simmons's Blasianness becomes transracial through its campiness as it plays off the racial dissonance wrought by her mixed-race body, which highlights the limitation of our racial categorization system. The

representational moves she makes go back and forth between performing Blackness and performing Asianness by making sure that the moves
are obvious and observable. Her version of Blasianness is especially well
suited stylistically to her branded persona and the over-the-top spirit of
camp. Her winking use of camp is a means of recognizing both the work
put into her image and the work put into subverting dominant ideologies
of race, gender, sexuality, and class. Yet not everyone seems to get what
Simmons represents—as evidenced by the intense criticisms she receives.[1]
The existence of this split within her audience cements Simmons as camp
object, because, as Robertson points out, "for there to be a genuinely
camp spectator, there must be another hypothetical spectator who views
the object 'normally.'"[2] Simmons explains how she built herself into this
campy persona:[3]

> To boost my self-esteem in the early days, I would actively think of and
> write down the words that I felt defined me. Now that I market my clothes
> and products around the world, I see exactly what I was doing then: I was
> creating the "brand of Kimora," and it was a brand that was so fabulous
> and so solid, its import couldn't be denied. To build any successful brand,
> you need a "brand vocabulary." In my beauty-brand vocabulary, I wasn't
> "unconventional-looking": I was "exotic." I wasn't "too tall"; I was "regal."
> I wasn't "too outspoken"; I was "influential." I wasn't too "flashy"; I was
> "show-stopping."

In order to understand Simmons's branding practices, one needs to recognize how camp offers alternatives to dominant notions of race, gender,
class, and even mixed-race identities. This chapter is one such alternate
reading of Simmons, one that emphasizes the resistive potential of her
mixed-race performance.

Race Camp

The last two decades have seen a considerable increase in the amount
of research on camp, which is a testament to the "slipperiness of camp"
and its inability (or perhaps instability) to be defined concretely.[4] While
the majority of the scholarship on camp has focused on its relationship
to queer identity,[5] some has added an emphasis on feminist and racialized discourses.[6] Still, camp has been and continues to be used as a short-
hand for gay culture. Considering the historical context of camp means

acknowledging that a primary emphasis of its use has been to appeal to a male, White, affluent (or at least middle-class) subset of the gay community. This more particularized notion of camp is evident in Babuscio's linking of camp to what he termed "gay sensibilities," or the "creative energy reflecting a consciousness that is different from the mainstream; a heightened awareness of certain human complications of feeling that spring from the fact of social oppression; in short, a perception of the world which is coloured, shaped, directed and defined by the fact of one's gayness."[7] Meyer deepens this connection through his declaration that "rather than a popular style or sensibility, camp is a solely homosexual performance inseparable from the body of the performers."[8] Certainly, in their haste to discuss camp as a knowing nod between gays, these scholars ignore the fact that homosexuals are not a homogeneous community that automatically possesses some preternatural heightened awareness of style and performance. In fact, Padva critiques Babuscio's use of "gay sensibility" as the foundation of camp with the acknowledgment that the gay community is a not a monolith and by questioning whether one needs to be gay in order to have a gay sensibility.[9] He notes:

> Camp, as queer creation and manifestation, objects to the stigmatization that marks the unnatural, extraordinary, perverse, sick, inefficient, dangerous and queer. Camp, as queer counterculture and counterpraxis, undermines and reconsiders the epistemology intended by the bourgeois to produce and reproduce, present and represent its hegemony. Camp not only subverts and revises the dominant ideology, but also creates, produces, and performs counterculture. In its radical interpretation of human existence, camp offers a different point of view, or a broader and vital perspective, of social experience that might be useful not only to members of queer subcultures but also to other groups and subcultures.[10]

Padva's reorientation of camp parallels the utility of transraciality, as they both undermine dominant ideologies while simultaneously transforming those very ideologies. Like the queering of culture and subcultures in the use of camp, transraciality marks the unnatural but alternative transectional perspectives that place it within different moments and spaces and offers a "radical interpretation" of our racial existence.

Writing about the documentary *Paris Is Burning*, hooks and Robertson both note how the inclusion of race somehow confounds critics and culminates in their devaluation of the work of camp. According to

Robertson, "critics tend to treat the African American and Hispanic use of camp to gain access to fantasies of whiteness as a special case, without fully acknowledging [. . .] how inextricably race and sex are intertwined, and without considering whether or how race discourse operates in camp generally."[11] The appearance of race is not the only issue in critiques of camp; the presence of camp for mainstream (read: heterosexual) audiences creates what Rudnick and Andersen have termed "Camp Lite," or straight camp. What Rudnick and Andersen miss in their critique is that differentiating between camp and "straight camp," or ignoring the raced and gendered discourses operating in and around camp, points to the privileging of camp as being for a specific audience, namely, one that is White, male, homosexual, and middle-class. Using Kimora Lee Simmons allows for the explication of camp as more than simply a gay performance, but a performance that is gendered, queered, classed, and racialized as well. Thinking of camp more broadly requires an expansion of it theoretically to include performance and interpretation beyond the aforementioned current iteration, to one that addresses a broader range of identity masquerade and parody practices.

I am not interested in parsing out the differences (if they exist) between "gay camp," "straight camp," "camp lite," "feminist camp," or any other version of camp. More important to this chapter is reinterpreting camp as a process, rather than just a product, which creates an interpretive framework in which to analyze Simmons and her particular brand of Blasian identity. Thus, my use of camp here is not as a thing—a particular performance or identity occurring at a particular moment—but an actively changing performative and identifying process, and interpretations of it, too, can change across time. Thus, camp parallels my use of both branding and transracial as processes of identity formation and negotiation. Robertson notes that using camp as a framework allows for the complication of "how dominant texts and resistant viewers interact to produce camp, and by reconceptualizing resistance and subversion to account for the way in which camp's simultaneous pleasure of alienation and absorption refuse simplistic categories of dominant versus resistant readings."[12] The ability of camp, like transracialness, to upend dominant ideologies by operating in culturally ambiguous and contradictory spaces is crucial to its troubling of a range of hegemonic notions. Additionally, camp as a mechanism, as a purposefully utilized tool, "has the power to force attention onto bodies in a culture that seems increasingly interested in burying, suppressing, or transcending" them.[13] Multiracial bodies have

historically been suppressed through racist state policies like antimiscegenation laws, and cultural practices like passing. Currently, those same
multiracial bodies are used to fortify discourses that imagine a postracial
America and the eventual transcendence of race. Thus, current discourses
on mixed-race people are either celebratory or panicked, and both discourses are an important function of camp. Both Simmons's body and
celebrity become sites where race, mixed race, gender, class, and celebrity intersect with camp's simultaneous embrace and subversion of hegemonic ideologies.

Simmons publicly acknowledges how much of her image is performance, ensuring she is situated queerly amongst other marginalized
groups and deviant people. That she is constructed in myriad contradictory and inconsistent ways is in keeping with Babuscio's determination
that camp "signifies performance rather than existence."[14] Using camp to
understand the way power operates in and around Simmons's Blasian
body allows her audience to view her as possibly deviant, as she does not
fit expectations, while also acknowledging that deviancy might also work
to contest oppressive raced and gendered hierarchies. As a six-foot-tall,
middle-aged woman with children, Simmons's penchant for very high
heels, long hair, full makeup, and body-conscious outfits rejects the disciplining and controlling mechanisms of hegemonic femininity. Her sexuality and the foregrounding of her attractiveness, as opposed to reductive
motherhood-adjacent activities and aesthetics, becomes a critique of the
expectations put on both women and mothers. While Sontag might have
famously declared camp as "apolitical," in her refusal to be normalized
and silenced by dominant ideologies regarding Blackness, femininity,
celebrity, and Asianness, Simmons is unambiguously political.

Visibility and Passing

Babuscio grounds much of the theorization of his "queer sensibility" of
camp within the realm of theatricality, rooting it in the claim that since
gay men violate the moral and social codes of society through their
attraction to other men, they have a "heightened sensitivity to aspects
of a performance which others are likely to regard as routine or uncal-
culated."[15] The social regulation of sexuality is not the only regulatory
system that has led to alternative practices of passing; the regulations
of race, gender, and class have had similar and interlinked effects. For
instance, multiracial people in general, and multiracial celebrities

perhaps especially, have had to pass and take on roles to conform to social, and sometimes legal, expectations.

Passing, for mixed-race celebrities, has become more difficult, as multiracial people are using websites and social media in order to "out" these stars. The increase in the number of websites like www.mixedfolks.com, www.intermix.org.uk, and www.asiansofmixedrace.com has made it easier to affirm and/or confirm the racial mixtures of celebrities. These sites deconstruct and emphasize the racial mixtures of celebrities to rally around these stars as a show of solidarity, because dominant ideas of race have left them out.[16] Role-playing becomes another way to talk about passing, and camp works in similar ways, such that when passers, or campy actors, "are discovered, they expose the fact that despite the failure of the regime of visibility to tell us who is who, such failure is not sufficient to destroy the categories that have been confounded."[17] Drag queens and kings are campy figures because their overt performance of gender during drag shows troubles the authenticity of gender roles. This performative aspect of camp enables the troubling of all sorts of binaries—male/female, black/white, rich/poor, gay/straight, and so on, even though they do not eliminate the binaries altogether.

Similarly, Simmons as a campy figure uses Blasian multiraciality to trouble the Black and White paradigm of race in the United States, as noted by Nishime in her critiques about the race play in Simmons's advertisements for the fashion company Baby Phat. Nishime focuses on two Baby Phat advertisements meant to convey an Asian aesthetic, which feature Simmons and her two daughters, Ming and Aoki. Both advertisements feature stereotypical markers of pan-Asianness—*shoji* screens, fans, and Chinese lanterns, along with a more specific Japanese marker—kanji lettering on the signs. The inference is that the models featured are Japanese, but as Nishime points out, there is a purposeful blurring of the racial and ethnic boundaries between Simmons and the models.[18] All of the models are the same shade of beige as Simmons, dreadlocks and cornrows (hairstyles meant to connote Blackness) appear on two of the male models, and there is eye-obscuring paint or bangs on the women (phenoperceptive markers of Asianness), producing an ambivalent racialized context. The racial identities of the models are ambiguous and conflicting, as is the racial identity of Simmons herself, who is centered in the ad, wearing eye-obscuring sunglasses and straightened hair. Nishime concludes that without "a stable racial reference point," the viewer is unable to concretely racially identify Simmons. She does not ultimately topple racial categories, but she does challenge what it means to be both Black and Asian/American, or, as Nishime states, she "revise[s] the meanings of racial stereotypes and open[s] up a space to question the basis for racial categorization and its hierarchical organization."[19] These advertisements, like Simmons herself, position both the cultural and biological constructions of race into one frame in order to highlight the nonsensical foundations that undergird them.

In *Fabulosity* Simmons introduces a key section, conveniently on image and the body, of her book by asking the reader to "spend a bit of energy considering your image. How are you coming across to the world, and is your image helping your cause? *Does anybody out there know who you are?*"[20] (emphasis in original). She goes on to explain just how much of her image, "the clothes, the home, the office, are deliberate choices, not lucky accidents."[21] Simmons makes clear that her life is not a natural one, and she fulfills what Sontag described as the essence of camp: "love of the unnatural: artifice and exaggeration."[22] Dollimore extends Sontag's description by indicating that the "real, the true, and the authentic are surrendered to, or contaminated by, the fictitious and the contrived. But camp comes to life around that recognition; it is situated at the point of emergence of the artificial from the real, culture from nature—or rather when and where the real collapses into artifice, nature into culture."[23] The image projected by Simmons takes a postmodernist turn by flattening difference and making it impossible to distinguish the "artificial from the real," because she herself does not make that distinction. Collapsing her life into her own personal brand, she makes it impossible for anyone else to draw boundaries and make distinctions either. This is how the Blasian brand functions, by demonstrating the impossibility of drawing boundaries around or parsing out separate racialized identities.

When she explains to her readers how her "personal brand" is created by "taking the icons of old money—diamonds, luxury goods, and decorative arts—and turning them upside down,"[24] Simmons's description of her lifestyle plays on Sontag's claim that extravagance is the hallmark of camp. Simmons's entire brand is predicated on always being "too much," which allows her to manipulate her identity in order to defy social expectations. In writing about appropriating old-money icons to her benefit, she is addressing how she, and other people of color, have not historically had access to these icons of old money. White and White remind us that Black people especially have "rearranged and adapted" objects and created style within "a white world, a world in which black bodies have been

regarded with a mixture of envy and contempt, as something to emu-
late but also as a target for violence."[25] Here, camp becomes immensely
more useful, because it transforms her indirect criticism of the exclusion-
ary property of Whiteness into an obvious critique and subversion of its
dominance. For example, Simmons explains her decision to replace a diamond Rolex watch as the status symbol for wealthy [White] people by
encouraging people to wear Frank Muller watches instead. She notes that
"soon enough one big hip-hop mogul got that same watch, then another
major rapper had one too, and it was on the cover of the luxury magazine,
Robb Report, as the quintessential luxury item!"[26] Similar to the hip-hop
community's appropriation and resignification of specific New England,
preppy, country-club brands like Tommy Hilfiger, Ralph Lauren, and Nau-
tica, Simmons rejects dominant discourses of consumption and appropri-
ateness used to surveil people of color by resignifying the Muller watch
as no longer an exclusive item for Whites. Simmons's campy embrace of
a *ghetto fabulous* ideology and conspicuous consumption does particular racial work. According to Roopali Mukherjeee, ghetto fabulousness
is the "elevation of the black urban experience as [the] ultimate cruci-
ble of cool."[27] Mukherjee goes on to suggest that ghetto fabulousness, a
distant cousin of hip-hop culture, is a product of the post-soul era, the
period immediately following the civil rights era. It is marked by neoliberal demands and policies attacking race, and increased surveillance of
bodies of color.[28] Black consumptive practices have been contradictorily
marked as either pathological[29] or transformative and subversive.[30] What
Simmons does with commodities (including herself) becomes a transformative act, because she exploits them as a subversive play on Black
identity and an indirect critique of Black stereotypes.

Losing the "Baby Phat"

The aesthetic and purpose of Simmons's first fashion line, Baby Phat,[31] is
intimately tied to her attempts to link ghetto fabulousness with fabulosity.
She created Baby Phat because there had "never been a clothing line made
by a young woman like me: a multiethnic woman who has one foot in
Gucci and one foot in the ghetto."[32] In response to the backlash the company received when they used models identifying as either monoracially
White or Black, she became the model for all Baby Phat campaigns. Putting herself in the ads meant highlighting her multiraciality, which would
leave little for people to criticize, because "you can't say I'm too black, or

not black enough. You can't say crap because it's my damn fashion line . . . This is me."[33] Her words both call attention to her identity and reflexively refer to the strategy of making a company based on her image as a creative solution to potential critiques and comments people might make about her mixed racial identity. By creating a company that incorporates her identity, she works to avoid assumptions and arguments around her racial authenticity. Indeed, through the success of her company and her position as spokesmodel, she simultaneously forces questions around what it means to be multiethnic and acceptance of her racial legitimacy.

One of the earliest advertising campaigns to feature Simmons, shot in 2005, shows her coming down the stairs of Air Force One (the Baby Phat logo replacing the president's seal) with her two daughters. In case the viewer misses the president's seal on Air Force One, the background of the image is the Washington monument, effectively locating the scene in Washington, DC. A press corps and Secret Service agents surround Simmons and her daughters. The advertisement is full of bright colors; Simmons and her daughters are in pink, contrasted against the stark black of the Secret Service agents' suits. Simmons is wearing a trench coat with a pattern similar to the plaid used by luxury British brand Burberry. The advertisement is framed so that the viewer is literally looking up to Simmons as she is descending the stairs, and receiving waves from Simmons and her daughters. Simmons explains her vision for the campy ad as such: "Why not? I had married the guy many considered a leader of hip-hop, so I was kind of poking fun at the idea of being a new American leading lady, part preppy, part ghetto fabulous. It was a traditional kind of image with a sneaky, fun twist."[34] The advertisement ran four years before Barack Obama would become president of the United States, and Simmons's preppy chic style becomes a foreshadowing of the preppy chic style Michelle Obama would draw on as First Lady (sans the overt sexiness). Being ghetto fabulous in itself is not necessarily campy, but turning ghetto fabulousness into *fabulosity* definitely is. For Simmons's presentation of ghetto fabulousness to work, economic capital is exchanged in order to gain the cultural and symbolic capital necessary for her campiness to be effective. While it might appear counterproductive to champion the neoliberal tendency toward capitalistic consumerism as a positive, what Simmons does by living excessively and extravagantly aligns precisely with the theatrical performativity inherent in camp.

Camp has been analyzed as a response to oppressive gender hierarchies, and combined here with ghetto fabulousness as a way to critique

dominant notions of race and class. There are many moments in Simmons's career when camp is used to resist racial hegemony through
the deployment of her Blasian identity. Moments when she is depicted
as engaging in what Cleto claims is the "collective, ritual and performative existence, in which it is the object itself to be set on a stage, being,
in the process of campification, subjected."[35] In talking about her childhood, Simmons describes growing up in the Midwest with an absent
Black father and a "very *The Joy Luck Club*" Japanese-Korean mother.[36]
It is interesting that she uses the movie/book *The Joy Luck Club* about
Chinese and Chinese American women as the template for her not-Chi-
nese immigrant mother, given that one of the major criticisms[37] of the
story is that it conflates all Asian/Americans into one muddled orientalist "other" category. The merging of Asian/Americans into one pan-Asian
category eliminates the cultural, political, social, and economic behavior
of what is actually a heterogeneous group of people. She mentions not
being accepted by classmates and being confused by the images on television that did not reflect who she was. She expected public school, with its
diversity of students, to be a place where she would finally be accepted:
"The black kids would high-five me and the Asian kids would trade slap
bracelets with me and I'd get to sit at whatever lunch table I wanted."[38]
Instead as the most visibly different person, she was excluded from every
clique. Simmons described herself as a misfit who was "too-tall, too-
weird, not-black-enough but not-Asian enough, too-ethnic, too kooky-
haired, too-dark, *and* too-light . . . girl most unlikely."[39] She acknowledges
she existed then and continues to exist in a space where she is considered
both not enough and too much. Thus, she uses her celebrity to campily
exploit that liminality to her benefit.

Chinky Giraffes and Barbies

Simmons shares in her book anecdotes about the phrase "chinky giraffe,"
used to taunt her when she was younger because she was tall, skinny, and
Asian/American:

> "Chinky Giraffe," they'd say and laugh hysterically at how funny they
> were and so smart, too, for coming up with a nickname that covered all
> the bases—"giraffe" because I was way too tall and skinny, with long, lop-
> ing legs. And since I definitely had some Asian in me too—horror of hor-
> rors—they added the "Chinky" in a surefire stroke of genius. Pretty soon

the name caught on, and if those kids or their friends were hanging out in the street, they'd yell after me, "Chinky Giraffe!" It really hurt, especially since "chink" was like a slap in the face to my Mom and all the values she believed in.[40]

She explains the slur was hurtful because it would be used to exclude her from lunch tables, activities, and to generally bully her. The website www.disgrasian.com (tagline: "You're a disgrace. To the race") used the epithet when they wrote "chinky giraffe" in a post about Simmons's date with then-partner Djimon Honsou. The site instructs its readers to "enjoy these pictures of our favorite Chinky Giraffe having a leisurely lunch with her boy toy Djimon over the weekend."[41] The site uses "chinky giraffe" again to designate Simmons as their "Disgrasian of the Weak," for "reveling in money-grubbing and excess."[42] Disgrasian.com's use of "chinky giraffe" both embraces and critiques Simmons's Asian/American identity. She is included in a website devoted to Asian/American issues and culture, and is also criticized for failing to embody Asianness in an acceptable manner. Still, the phrase is uttered throughout her book, reality show, and interviews and is used to fulfill camp's purpose, "to dethrone the serious."[43] Simmons says, "I'm the Chinky Giraffe who now collects bejeweled giraffe statues and puts them on display right where everyone can see them. Some of them are in the form of diamond giraffe picture-frames—they're blinged out and totally gorgeous."[44] She even features a giant giraffe topiary at her New Jersey home.

What had been a serious racial slur against Simmons has now been resignified and rendered frivolous. Additionally, Simmons's reclamation of the originally racist "chinky giraffe" epithet becomes a camp critique of social norms, because she has become "simultaneously an embodiment of the target and a parody of it living in the object and turning it upside-down at once."[45] The reappropriation of "chinky giraffe" becomes an empowering act not just because it has been resignified in support of Simmons's Blasianness but also because it returns to her some agency. Her ability to identify using "chink" is like other self-identifying strategies using similarly derogatory labels. Her reappropriation parallels the moves around other stigmatizing terms used to deride identities based on membership in social groups organized by race, class, gender, sexuality, nationality, ability, and the rest. The reappropriation of words like *nigger, queer, bitch, crip, fob, Paki,* and, of course *chink,* provides agency to these group members "because self-labeling with a stigmatizing group label is more than an individual act of defiance, it may influence impressions of group power . . . converting a despised descriptor into an appreciated appellation."[46] The original deployment of the slurs highlights how power operationalizes various ideologies of oppression and marginalization, while reappropriation allows for both individuals and groups to "to position themselves and others in relation to [the slurs] or in relation to each other; to resist oppressive practices, form social relationships, or celebrate a means of identifying."[47]

Kimora Barbie

In the premiere episode of her reality show, *Life in the Fab Lane*,[48] Simmons uses her confessional time to inform the viewer about her collaboration with Mattel for a new Barbie doll, which will be called "Kimora Barbie." On the show, Simmons goes over the mock-up of the Barbie with Tina, her "vice president of branding," when her ex-husband[49] Russell Simmons joins the meeting. As Russell examines the drawing of the doll wearing a full-length faux-fur coat with red miniskirt and halter, and accompanied by a little black dog, Simmons exclaims, "The world is talking to me about this Barbie—I hope she represents a proper ethnic blend. She looks ethnic right? I picked fat face, fat lips, I picked a mixture of colored skin." To which Russell asks, "Why does she have to be so naked, and just so sexy? She's a doll for children. Why she gotta have the tightest little miniskirt, and garter belt?" Kimora Lee Simmons responds by explaining the clothes on the Barbie will actually be sold in department stores, to which Russell Simmons looks visibly relieved, exclaiming, "Oh, this is for adults!" Simmons explains that the doll is still a Barbie, implicitly acknowledging that children will be playing with her very "sexy," nearly "naked" doll. Others have written about Barbie's "overly sexualized body"[50] and not very progressive gender politics. However, the Kimora Barbie, an even more exaggerated version of hypersexualized Barbie, alternatively draws attention to the "exaggerated femininity of Barbie . . . [and] the artificiality of gender."[51] Simmons explains further that Mattel has made professional Barbies before, notably doctor and lawyer Barbies, and that her Barbie would be a "single mother, entrepreneur, mogul Barbie!" In that same meeting Simmons had already stated she was excited about the collaboration, because she could add a little fabulosity to what Barbie already stood for. No doubt single-motherhood is not in keeping with previous iterations of Barbie, and yet the Kimora Barbie offers a counterhegemonic representation of gender and race that is in keeping with Simmons's definition of fabulosity. With this version of Barbie, being a single mother of color[52] is not a source of derision, but rather of celebration. Still, the amount of capital, both cultural and economic, Simmons possesses in order to counter the overwhelming Whiteness of Barbie in general and to call a meeting with Mattel executives in order to ensure that her Blasian Barbie will exist as she has envisioned it, is an important distinction to remember. Her counterhegemonic move is made possible by Simmons's particular brand of Blasianness.

During the same premiere episode of the show, Simmons visits the Mattel office with her daughters, Ming and Aoki, assistant, and Tina, to check the progress of Kimora Barbie. After noting her Barbie needs to be flashier—with more glitter and makeup—drawing attention again to the performative nature of femininity and gender, the Mattel representatives, identified in the episode as Sharon the principal designer for Mattel and Liz in Mattel marketing, tell her that because the doll is tied so closely to Simmons's image they want to drop the name Barbie and name the doll simply Kimora Lee Simmons. Simmons immediately rejects the suggestion, declaring to both the Mattel staffers and audience, "We want it to be a Kimora Barbie. You're trying to take that word away from me, and I will not have it, because I want children to know that there are other colors and textures, and she's still considered Barbie. She doesn't have to be the sidekick." The Mattel people back down and agree with Simmons to keep the Barbie label on the doll.

Then more drama ensues when Sharon and Liz ask Simmons to choose between a full-length fur coat and her dog, Zoe, as accessories for her Barbie, in order to get it within the "right cost structure." Nishime points out the racial undertones that underlie Simmons's reply to Mattel, which questioned why none of the other (read: White) Barbies seemingly have had to choose between having multiple accessories. In the show the representatives do not respond to Simmons, leaving the viewer to fill in the answer: that because the Kimora Barbie is non-White, she cannot have it all. Aoki, Simmons's younger daughter, breaks the silence by announcing that the Barbie should have both the coat and the dog. To which Simmons voices her agreement, refusing to make a choice between the two accessories as the scene ends.

As the meeting ends on the show, the viewer has no idea whether Mattel will really make Simmons choose between accessories, leaving it up in the air until the third episode. While her refusal seems trivial and superficial, especially because it concerns accessories for a doll, it becomes a defining moment for the series. Encapsulated in this one scene is Simmons's resistance to hegemonic ideals of beauty and gender, evidenced in the creation of this multiracial Barbie, and her statement that the Barbie needs to look more "drag queen," because that is a closer representation to how she looks. Referencing drag queens and their explicitly exaggerated version of femininity draws attention to Simmons's own campy performance of identity, and the work she puts in herself to look the way she does, a point underscored in her book when she writes about being an "illusion." Simmons pulls back the curtain on the illusion, exposing the artificiality that passes for normal and explains that it takes "at least an hour and a half (sometimes three hours) of hair styling, makeup, and lighting. Not to mention the waxing, teeth-bleaching, colored contact-lens wearing, hair-straightening, [and] hair-extensions adding" to achieve her look.[53] She has even, via her verified Twitter account (@OfficialKimora), sent out a picture of herself getting her hair touched up, seated in front of cameras and bright lights, as she filmed her reality show. In fact, I focus on her Twitter account in this chapter because it is the only social media account through which she interacts with fans by regularly answering their questions, and in her replies emphasizing how there is no division between her authentic self and the performance she puts on as a celebrity. She reconfigures identity as a theatrical performance, as camp, as "Being-As-Playing-A-Role."[54] Simmons continues to demystify the authenticity of identity by transparently playing with racial narratives.

Autoexoticizing Kimora

Just as Simmons's adaptation of a ghetto fabulous aesthetic does the work of locating her within Blackness, her attempts at autoexoticization[55] (when marginalized people reproduce the same dominant discourses used against them) through the deployment of orientalist tropes place her within stereotypical depictions of Asia. Starting with her aforementioned Baby Phat Asian-themed advertising campaign, Simmons's combination of autoexoticization and racial camp is used to parody stereotypes of Asian/American women, but, as Nishime notes, ends up "disrupt[ing] the discourse of realness surrounding race itself."[56] In the third episode of the first season of *Life in the Fab Lane*, Simmons finally receives the Kimora Barbie, and the viewer sees Mattel ultimately let her keep both the floor-length fur and the dog as accessories. She tells viewers her daughters, Ming and Aoki, then seven and four years old, will decide how authentic the doll is as both a Barbie and a representation of their mother. We see in the next scene Ming and Aoki playing with other dolls while dressed up in matching, differently colored, modified pajama *qípáos*, a traditional Chinese garment. Simmons has referenced her Japanese Korean[57] mother in every medium available to her, so savvy fans and followers of Simmons know that she is not Chinese. One camp reading of this scene would be that Simmons is intentionally parodying the notion that all Asian/ Americans are and/or look the same. This reading becomes more plausible when contextualized with statements from Simmons about growing up in a working-class St. Louis neighborhood, where she was frustrated because there was "no Asian anything."[58] Even the naming of her first three children, Ming (Chinese), Aoki (Japanese), and son Kenzo (where she uses the Japanese kanji letter for "three/third" as part of his name) works to lend Simmons some pan-Asian authenticity. As she writes in her book about being made fun of, partly due to her name, and always being regarded as some sort of inauthentically raced person, her naming practices cannot be chalked up to random baby naming. When coupled with Simmons's emphasis on her role as a mother, the naming of her children becomes an act of resistance against being declared not Asian/American enough. For those fans, viewers, readers, and consumers familiar with her particular racial mixture, the naming of her children is a large part of her camp persona, acting as a "wink" shared between Simmons and those who acknowledge her multiraciality.

The names of Simmons's children are not the only ways she autoexoticizes being Asian/American. Her Twitter avatar for years had been a picture of her sitting next to a giant Buddha head. She sent out the following tweet to alert her fans to the change:

> @*Official Kimora:* 2 all my fabs tht r luvin my new avatar . . . Thku, grazie, merci, danka, gracias!!! This my antique stone Buddha! I'm feeling very ZEN abt things these days! (But dnt push me! Lol!) <3

The Buddha avatar allowed Simmons the flexibility she needed to position herself as Asian/American, as evidenced by this exchange:

> @*Aliya_Rani:* @OfficialKimora the resemblance with you and the statue in your avatar is just so uncanny.

> @*OfficialKimora:* @Aliya_Rani must be a full faced Asian thang! Lol!

While Simmons's Twitter feed is mostly posts wishing her followers to be fabulous, or random bits of advice/encouragement, her tweets about important dates and events like Black History Month and Chinese New Year appear in the timelines of her followers as reminders that she is both Black and Asian/American. Her tweet wishing everyone a happy Chinese New Year resulted in tweets back wishing both her and her mother the same. Without giving her too much undue credit, the fact that she has used her antique stone Buddha as a device to remind her audience just how Asian/American she is, is partly why she is an effective camp subject. At her disposal are oriental objects that can be utilized to prop up (pun intended) her performance as a Blasian media mogul, entrepreneur mother.

In addition to replying to followers who tweet her, Simmons also retweets[59] messages by adding her reply to the original message. Her timeline during the avatar change had numerous messages regarding her appearance, to which she would reply with her thanks. The one message she retweeted, however, is a message that explicitly mentioned her being Asian. She agrees with the follower that she is a "Divine fine sexy sizzlin' Asian," which for most people could be construed as the reification of gendered, racist notions of Asian/American women. This becomes yet another autoexoticizing moment as she both embodies and parodies hegemonic representations of Asian/Americans in order to contest them. In forcing her followers, fans, writers, critics, and detractors to acknowledge that she too is Asian/American, she again challenges, as she did with Blackness, the realness of race.

Refashioning Race

Kimora Lee Simmons, as a former supermodel and president and creative director of two fashion companies, has tangible capital in the fashion realm.[60] Her presence in fashion provided Simmons another platform from which she could resist, and potentially subvert, the hegemonic Whiteness favored by the fashion industry, and her reality show featured some of these key moments. During the second season of her reality show, Simmons met with her staff to get updated on the progress of her New York Fashion Week show when she took a moment to tell her marketing director that the models should be "hot, sexy, multiethnic." When she appeared later in the episode to approve of the model selections for the show, she rejected a few of the choices and then frustratedly exclaimed,

"She's not even Asian!" Her friend and stage manager, J. Alexander[61] asked, "How many Asians do you want in your show?" and she replied, "As many as you can find." The Baby Phat/Phat Farm fall fashion show seen in the episode ultimately featured mainly models of color, which made it an anomaly amongst the other runway shows during Fashion Week.[62] That year the Council of Fashion Designers of America (CFDA) sent letters to designers showing their collections during Fashion Week to encourage them to reflect the multicultural world around them, and still 88 percent of the models used were White,[63] revealing how strong racist ideologies persist within the industry. Contextualized against this particularly discriminatory industry practice, Simmons's featured fashion show becomes one of the few places challenging the Whiteness of Fashion Week and fashion shows. Since camp operates through the materiality of the body, Simmons's directive for multiethnic models, and her subsequent casting of those models, forces attention onto bodies—hers included—the dominant culture has marginalized.

The last season of *Life in the Fab Lane* found Simmons again forcing attention onto bodies of color with the release of her latest product, Shinto Clinical, and a model search to promote the line.[64] Naming the skincare line Shinto Clinical did the same orientalizing, autoexoticizing work as naming her children Ming, Aoki, and Kenzo, or using a Buddha in her avatar on Twitter does. Even if one is unfamiliar with what Shintoism is exactly, the name is Asian enough to work as yet another marker of Asianness for Simmons. While the name of the products is evocative of a spiritual and exotic Asianness, the purpose of the skincare line, according to Simmons, is to appeal to the "multiethnic woman like [herself]."[65] In the quest to appeal to those multiethnic women, Simmons states, "I need to make sure we have enough beautiful multiethnic women to choose from . . . because this is a multicultural skin care line I think the models should show that—a spectrum from light to dark."[66] She goes on to explain that Shinto Clinical is "specifically formulated for women who are of multicultural descent like me. It's all encompassing, it's colorless, universal." During the model search Simmons informed her employees she wanted "real women" instead of models, in order to appeal to her multicultural target audience. When asked what sort of women to scout, she restated her desire for multiracial women: "We need an array of different types of beauties, different skin tone, multiethnic."[67] Though Simmons maintains mixed-race people like her are "colorless," when she described whom she represents specifically she noted, "I represent a woman of color which in my definition is this gold woman."[68] Contradictorily, the multicultural woman is both colorless and a woman of color and, most importantly, if she is like Simmons, golden. Colorless or not, the golden woman's prominence is in keeping with Simmons's view of ghetto fabulousness and fabulosity, as gold connotes luxury whether it is real and valuable or fool's gold, just for show. Importantly, gold here becomes another form of passing, as it is impossible to distinguish without detailed examination whether it is real or not. Her emphasis on gold also aligns with her earlier argument to the Mattel executives that there is no such thing as too much makeup or glitter. The key function of her use of gold, however, is its reference to a beige complexion, which is one of the most familiar phenoperceptive markers for racially mixed people, specifically racially mixed Black people.[69] Thus, Simmons's use of gold fortifies my claim that asserting a Blasian identity for these stars is not a way to avoid Blackness but is in fact necessary for understanding what Blasian means. By the end of the episode, Simmons and her team found the "real"[70] women for the Shinto Clinical campaign, and Simmons closed the episode with the declaration that she feels "really great about this campaign . . . we are showing the world diverse beauty, multi-culti, gold." The women selected do represent diverse versions of beauty, exhibiting a spectrum of complexions, including the sought-after ethnically ambiguous/possibly multiracial gold women.

Simmons's use of ghetto fabulousness and orientalist tropes complemented by her desire for autoexoticization results in a version of camp that suggests a complex racial consciousness. Her camp persona works to very publicly challenge the idea of a colorblind, postracial United States through playing up and exaggerating racial identities. Her transracial movements between being Black and Asian/American, sometimes independently but oftentimes combined, continues to disrupt the biologically and culturally essentialist construction of racial categories. Simmons's beige, or gold as she calls it, body, troubles and transforms the exclusivity and authenticity of dominant understandings of both Blackness and Asianness. Though her wealth gives her access to material and cultural capital not available to most people, her campy use of *ghettofabulosity* allows entrée for other Blasians into this version of Blasianness. Importantly, she uses camp to forge a version of Blasianness that is predicated on the performative nature of identity. This chapter uses her participation, as shown especially in her reality television show and her Twitter stream, to provide a very specific sense of Blasian identity. Her embodied performance of Blasianness is a hopeful position, as she refuses to settle for what is already visible. Simmons is contesting dominant raced, gendered, and classed ideas about what it means to be both Black and Asian/American, subsequently destabilizing hegemonic notions of those aforementioned identity markers, but importantly, of mixed race as well.

CHAPTER 4
"Because I'm Blasian"
Tiger Woods, Scandal, and
Protecting the Blasian Brand

The purpose of this statement is to explain my heritage for the benefit of members of the media who may be seeing me play for the first time. It is the final and only comment I will make regarding the issue. . . . The media has portrayed me as African-American, sometimes, Asian. In fact, I am both. Yes, I am the product of two great cultures, one African-American and the other Asian. On my father's side, I am African-American. On my mother's side, I am Thai. *Truthfully, I feel very fortunate, and equally proud, to be both African-American and Asian* [emphasis mine]. The critical and fundamental point is that ethnic background and/or composition should not make a difference. It does not make a difference to me. The bottom line is that I am an American . . . and proud of it. That is who I am and what I am. Now, with your cooperation, I hope I can just be a golfer and a human being.[1]

Before playing in the 1995 US Open in Southampton, New York, Tiger Woods shared this statement with the sports media. Most ignored is Woods's assertion that he is Blasian—not just Black or Asian/American—but in fact both, equally.[2] In the nearly twenty years since that statement, Tiger Woods's racial identity has come full circle, and he is again reasserting his Blasian identity. Research on Tiger Woods provides a timeline of his racial trajectory throughout his career. This chapter continues that timeline by examining the coverage of Woods post-scandal and charts its impact on Woods's racial trajectory. He offers an interesting analysis because much had been written about him pre-scandal, which makes it possible to follow the shifting logics of race that continue to be mapped onto his body. Woods's image has been crafted to be broadly appealing, racialized throughout his career as Black,[3] then multiracial,[4] and finally as Blasian. Woods has been claimed, oftentimes irregularly, by Blacks, Asian/Americans, and multiracial groups for being a trailblazing athlete. Though he embraced a stance of color-neutrality by refusing to identify himself racially for the majority of his career, his multiraciality has been leveraged to sell everything from golf to Nike products to management consultants. I argue in this chapter that Woods did once enjoy the illusory postracial benefits of multiraciality,[5] but his affairs made it impossible to distance him from both Blackness, via the hypersexuality of Black masculinity, and Asianness through narratives of sexual ineptitude. The multiple ways in which Blackness and Asianness were used to make sense of Woods simultaneously reifies and resists hegemonic racial constructions. Woods's utilization of the term Blasian to describe himself, revealed by news media as the scandal was unfolding, brought Blasians under scrutiny, resulted in moves to recuperate Woods's brand by strategically using the Blasian brand.

Earl Woods once made the claim at a dinner held to honor his son that Tiger was "going to be able to help so many people. He will transcend this game and bring to the world a humanitarianism which has never been known before. The world will be a better place to live in by virtue of his existence and his presence."[6] While the senior Woods's claim was full of puffery, the magnitude of Tiger Woods's presence in golf was corroborated later by the veneration he received from golf fans, media, corporations, and the global public. As such, both Woods and his team (PR persons, managers, agents) have had to use his racial identity to negotiate the devastating blow the scandal around his extramarital affairs dealt to his image and brand, the reluctance of the American public to forgive his affairs, and his poor performance on the golf course.

Cablinasian as Transracial

The year after his first US Open appearance, Tiger Woods became a professional golfer and signed a $40 million endorsement deal with Nike, which used that opportunity to brand him as their Black golfer.[7] Woods's first commercial for Nike, the much-maligned "Hello World" ad,[8] used images of a young Tiger playing golf juxtaposed against text describing his successes. The commercial ended with a rhetorical question asking if the world was ready for Tiger Woods. The commercial revealed itself to be an attempt by Nike to "African Americanize" Woods through the generically vague use of African drumming.[9] The ad also designated Woods as Black when it suggested he was still unwelcome at some golf courses in the United States, because of the color of his skin.[10] In responding to the backlash against the commercial, a Nike spokesperson simultaneously confirmed Nike's purposeful attempt to blacken Woods and informed critics that the ad was not to be taken literally, that Woods was merely a metaphor for other Black golfers who have historically been excluded. Despite the fact that just the year before, Tiger Woods himself had railed against attempts to fix his racial identity as merely Black, Nike used the high-profile advertisement to both racialize Woods as Black and challenge racism in the United States, and to ultimately gain new consumers who similarly saw themselves as challenging racism—by purchasing Nike products.[11] Nike, however, was not the only entity attempting to fix Woods's racial identity as Black.

Much of the media coverage from the earliest moments of Woods's career framed the narrative of his success around the discipline instilled in him by Earl Woods, his retired military father, linking his success to Black militarized masculinity. The "Hello World" commercial ends with the younger Woods hugging his father after his win, connecting him to Blackness through physical proximity to his Black father. Also used to racially "blacken" Woods was the narrative of militarized masculinity through his father's interviews and discussions about his son's success on the golf course, relating it to Earl Woods's determination and training as a Green Beret.[12] Earl Woods would mention employing strategies and tactics he learned as a Green Beret to train his son: breaking him down mentally, distracting him with sounds, intimidating him verbally.[13] The result was the joining of Tiger Woods's accomplishments to the training undertaken by elite soldiers in the US military and the self-discipline of Woods on the golf course. Any Whiteness that Woods could claim as part of his racial makeup is, then, subsumed by his Blackness, and the fact that it is linked so intimately to Black G.I.s and American military intervention.[14]

Habiba Ibrahim details other strategies used in racializing Tiger Woods, like situating him within a lineage of other successful and notable Black athletes. When news media questioned whether Woods would become the next great Black athlete like Jackie Robinson, Arthur Ashe, Lee Elder, or Michael Jordan, they effectively framed him as a challenger of the discriminatory and oppressive treatment meted out to Blacks and a source of Black success. Ibrahim goes on to detail how positioning Woods within a Black genealogy also makes him part of the Black racial family, which is further cemented by the exclusion of Kutilda Woods from the popular narratives about him. Ibrahim goes on to note that Woods's Cablinasian declaration, and subsequent appropriation by the multiracial movement, did not prevent racist declarations like Fuzzy Zoeller's,[15] which effectively established his Blackness. While Ibrahim's essay is an appeal for Black racial solidarity between monoracially and multiracially identified Blacks, I argue here that Woods's use of Cablinasian, and utilization of a multiracial identity, is not rooted in anti-Blackness, nor was it even an attempt to distance himself from Blackness, but rather was an attempt to destabilize Blackness as the anchor for racial hierarchy in the United States.

Of course, both Nike and the media shifted their coverage of Tiger Woods, from framing him via Blackness to situating him as a multiracial flag-bearer for postracial America. Writing about a pre-scandal Woods describe the process of making him America's multiracial son, which involved distancing him from *those* Blacks by commodifying his wholesome image and making him more appealing to Whites through a sanitized racialized narrative.[16] Cole expands on Woods's racial appeal by noting he was beyond established racial classifications and thus allowed to exist in a sort of non-raced space in the public imaginary, making him the perfect figure to market products to diversifying markets. Obviously, he was still racialized within the sorting structures of the US racial hierarchy, but the tensions between how and when he was Black, Asian/American, or neither demonstrate the utility of transraciality.

Henry Yu points out that racial mixing is not a transgressive boundary-crossing experience and that any talk of transgression is really a reaction to the practices of White supremacy.[17] Yu instead uses Tiger Woods to "illustrate the very complex migrations and movements of human bodies around the globe" and to show how he "helps trace the changing politics of racial difference."[18] Yu notes Woods's label of Cablinasian never caught on because the label was too singularly focused; it was a mixture limited to Woods, and racial categories ultimately need to lump large numbers of people together. Yu agrees with Cole's assessment of Woods's marketability based on his multicultural appeal, but what is lost in that process are those complex migrations and movements that have been mapped onto his body. Yu is absolutely correct in his determination that racial mixing is not an automatically transgressive act; it does, after all, need first to establish racialized categories and boundaries before they can be transgressed. This is partly why Blasian is especially effective as a brand; as Blasians effectively move between and transect racial categories, they challenge and transform the fixed nature of those categories through their negotiations.

Hiram Perez, like Yu, takes issue with the trumpeting of Tiger Woods's multiracial identity when it is used to usher in a colorblind era and erase the racialized sexual violence, disenfranchisement, and imperialism that constitute a crucial part of the United States' long and brutal history of racial mixing. Perez notes that Nike's "Hello World" commercial was a huge misstep mostly because the commercial explicitly referenced Blackness and related it to Woods. He finds that the subsequent commercial "I am Tiger Woods" worked much better because it was free from any racial specificity, which made Woods much more serviceable to both colorblind and multicultural ideologies. Perez determines ultimately that Woods "rehabilitate[s] the mulatto" when he is declared America's son, and that results in an "organized forgetting" that elides the history of White sexualized violence against women of color, and the presence of US military occupations in Asian countries.[19] Thus, my focus on a post-scandal Tiger Woods situates him firmly within racialized sexual encounters, forced and consensual. Additionally, Woods uses Blasianness to situate himself within various racial logics. For example, Woods's reception early in his career in Thailand was met with resistance, as its people refused to accept the Thai government's proclamation of Woods as a native son.[20] Even after being granted honorary citizenship through a declaration that he in his heart was Thai, and expressing how he preferred "Asian over American culture,"[21] any recognition of his Thai identity and general Asian/American identity remained fairly contested. There were some who hoped to use his celebrity and brand as an endorsement of Thailand and its culture, and those attempts were visible during his homecoming visit to Thailand.

Yet despite those attempts to burnish his Thai identity by linking him to his mother and a Thai Buddhist upbringing, Thai citizens mostly rejected that narrative. If race is predicated on this biological actuality also known as ancestry, in this instance Woods's Thai mother should be sufficient evidence of his Asianness, yet in Thailand it was not quite enough. Woods's mixed-race Thai status becomes complicated because he is the result of not just US military imperialism but also of Blackness. Eventually, Woods's professional achievements and his later attempts to validate his Asianness via proximity to his mother feature prominently and successfully in his branding efforts.

Nike learned from their initial misstep and the fallout from the "Hello World" commercial, and they responded with the "I am Tiger Woods" advertisement. That commercial featured a rainbow coalition of children all declaring themselves to be Tiger Woods. The year after becoming a professional golfer, Tiger Woods won his first Masters Tournament in 1997. He appeared on the *Oprah Winfrey Show* a few weeks later, where she crowned him "America's son," and he declared himself to be Cablinasian,[22] to explain how he understood his multiracial identity.[23] Fans and critics jumped on his label—using it either to praise him for finally moving America past its racial impasse via his multiracial celebrity,[24] or to excoriate him for trying to distance himself from Blackness.[25] There were also those who understood why Woods self-identified as multiracial but doubted that his Cablinasian moniker was as transgressive or as restrictive as others made it out to be.[26] Whereas Blasian gets traction through its increasing legibility vis-à-vis the bodies of these racially mixed stars, Cablinasian failed because it attempted to assert a distinct racial identity while simultaneously advocating for its ability to conjure up notions of racelessness.[27] When Woods used Cablinasian, the celebrity industrial complex had only just begun to acknowledge the nascent multiracial movement; thus, he was not able to avail himself of the transracial possibilities present in Blasianness. Furthermore, whereas Nishime points out the use of Cablinasian tried to conceal racial norms and in its use instead revealed them, my use of Blasian throughout this book works by replicating essentialist categories of race, as they exist within specific historical and material contexts, while simultaneously highlighting the ways these categories fail. Through its failure, the legitimacy of biological and cultural definitions of race is challenged, and opportunities for transforming how race regulates US culture are created. Though Tiger Woods has never identified himself again as Cablinasian to any media outlet, that label has followed him throughout his career—that is, until news of his extramarital affairs moved from the pages of supermarket tabloids and into the national consciousness in 2009.

Race and Scandal

On November 25, 2009, the *National Enquirer* broke the story about Tiger Woods's extramarital affairs. Not until reports of his car crash on November 27 did the original *Enquirer* story gain any traction. That same day Woods released a statement acknowledging he was in a minor accident. I begin my analysis here of Woods's apologia and the narratives emerging from a variety of media sources to address the discovery and disclosure of his affairs. It is impossible to look only at the multiple discourses deployed against Woods without also looking at the defensive strategies undertaken by his public relations team as a response to the criticism. Since the scandal erupted, there has been some research on the news coverage and the efficacy of Woods's apologia. Sanderson notes that the frames used to understand his actions differed between traditional media, which framed them as a tragic flaw, versus social media, which framed them as "a manifestation of humanness, and evidence of true moral character."[28] Kozman challenges and extends Sanderson's conclusion in her study, which found people were not so much responding to the "humanness" Woods exhibited, but were instead engaged in a "moral decoupling" as a way to support his performance despite his moral failings.[29] Andrews, King, and Leonard claim that Woods escaped mostly unscathed from the usual raced discourses used against athletes of color behaving badly.[30] They note, "Public reaction and media coverage almost universally avoided engaging blackness as it has been so often deployed around the transgressions of black athletes."[31] My analysis shows just the opposite occurred, and that the reaction and media coverage derived from not just his Blackness, but also his Asianness.

Through analysis of a number of texts ranging from newspaper, trade, and magazine articles, entertainment blogs, popular sport websites, television shows, interviews, commercials, press conferences and releases, a divorce agreement,[32] social media, and sundry Internet content,[33] I map both Tiger Woods's apologia and the multiple narratives emerging from the scandal.[34] Three thematic categories—pathological, comical, and recuperative—emerged from the narratives. These narratives were the most common and revealed tensions around race in the United States. The examples highlighted in this chapter were very often the texts referenced by other media in the discussion of Woods and were also representative of Woods's racialization. These narratives delved into sexuality, marriage, success, sport, infidelity, criminality, religion, and class in terms of race and mixed race. In fact, each of the major narrative themes signifies the availability of opportunities to discuss Woods's racial identity in ways that declaring himself Cablinasian had not previously allowed.

The themes, in addition to framing Tiger Woods, also act as a kategoria, or accusations. In evaluating the merits of the accusations, the impossibility of demarcating between Tiger Woods the golfer and Tiger Woods the brand is made clear. The public, golf fans, Woods's fans, and countless media outlets used the scandal to lodge accusations against both Woods's "policy" and his "character."[35] In proffering a defense, Woods's apologia had to account for both his actions and his moral responsibility to the community. As a brand, Woods had to "demonstrate legitimacy [by praising] the values [he was] reputed to have transgressed."[36] That this second part of the apologia is also part of any corporation's image management strategy demonstrates how crucial it was for Tiger Woods, the brand, to situate his apologia within a broader image management campaign. He did not just have to defend, explain, and apologize for his transgressions while mitigating the damage to his moral character; he needed to also use his apologia in such a way that it would repair, or at least attempt to repair, his damaged reputation and restore his social legitimacy. The restoration of his legitimacy and reputation would benefit Woods economically and would come via negotiated branding strategies weaponized through Woods's strategic deployment of his Blasian identity.

Pathology and Race

The most popular and widespread narrative of post-scandal Tiger Woods was one of shame. The shame manifested itself as disappointment and/or disgust at being both duped and betrayed by Woods.[37] Media coverage noted the emergence of the "real" Tiger Woods, by pathologizing his hypersexuality as endemic to Blackness, and then linking Blackness to criminality. Woods went from being "superhuman"[38] to just another athlete bidding "permanent farewell to invincibility."[39] *Vanity Fair* magazine took umbrage at the nonthreatening and noncontroversial image of Woods, when really the abnormal Woods was hidden away, waiting to come out.[40] One *Vanity Fair* article offered accounts from some of Woods's mistresses who relayed their hurt and betrayal at finding out Woods used them for sex.[41] Other coverage offered similar takes on Woods's transition from the "squeaky clean,"[42] "clean-living citizen"[43] golfer who was the "paragon of virtue"[44] to an athlete who had become ruined. Woods's nomination for a Congressional Gold Medal "for promoting good sportsmanship and breaking down barriers in the sport" by Congressman Joe Baca was dropped "in light of the recent developments surrounding Tiger Woods and his family."[45] The scandal and subsequent revelation of Woods's foibles was also too much for the "First Church of Tiger Woods," formed in 1996 to "celebrate the emergence of the true messiah," which was dissolved as the scandal developed.[46] Woods's decline highlights how much postracial hope had been heaped on him, which serves partly as explanation for why this narrative was so intense and abundant as the scandal unfolded.

A dominant mode of representing Blackness is through its conflation with criminality. For example, *Vanity Fair* used an old photo of Woods shirtless, wearing a skullcap, lifting weights, and unsmiling for the cover. Meant to address the blackening of Woods's reputation, the cover did double duty by also blackening Woods vis-à-vis a setting reminiscent of prison. The cover marked a shift in the coverage of Woods as not just a cheater but also potentially criminal, by tapping into a narrative of Blackness as dangerous. The *Vanity Fair* articles, like much of the coverage, also talked about Woods's relationships with retired basketball players Michael Jordan, known for his gambling/womanizing problems, and Charles Barkley, who did not believe athletes should be role models and received a DUI during his quest to receive oral sex.[47] Jordan and Barkley are already framed within the familiar hypersexualized, hyperaggressive Black athlete narrative, and they became signposts for Woods's degeneration.[48] In discussing Woods's loss of multiple endorsements, members of the news media noted the scandal was "different from an NFL or NBA player going bad,"[49] because golf featured mostly White players who rarely dominated news cycles with scandals. The Whiteness of golf has offered cover for its stakeholders—players, professional associations, sponsors, fans—when scandals occur through its ability to keep those scandals from dominating news cycles. The privilege and wealth that surrounds golf often inoculates its key characters, making the Woods scandal even more outrageous and shocking, particularly given the contaminating presence of miscegenation. Since the coverage of Woods pre-scandal framed him as a "nonthreatening" and "non- controversial"[50] athlete and made him a foil for dominant narratives of Black athletes, the swiftness with which he was compared to other Black athletes post-scandal was illustrative. This coverage would often declare that his career was not dead by comparing him to other Black athletes whose personal failings had also been made public.[51] The sympathetic strand in this narrative thread tried to reframe the scandal by asking the public to put his behavior in perspective when compared to other Black athletes. By comparing his affairs to other Black athlete behaviors, this particular narrative utilized positive and negative rhetoric simultaneously to highlight Woods's Blackness.

There were the understandable comparisons between Woods and basketball player Kobe Bryant, who had also cheated on his wife, with some advising Woods to call Bryant for advice "to get the dirt off him with his wife."[52] However, the coverage glossed over that Bryant had been accused of raping the woman, bringing his affair into criminal, rather than simply moral, territory. Woods had not been accused of any abuse against his mistresses, nor were there any allegations of rape or assault. Yet by connecting Woods to Bryant, the coverage criminalized his sexuality by conflating sexual immorality with criminality. When Bissinger explained the ramifications of Woods's accident by comparing it to "one taken by another sports celebrity on the San Diego Freeway, followed by a convoy of Los Angeles police cars, in 1994," he placed Woods even more directly within this familiar and criminal narrative of Black athletes by linking Woods's scandalous behavior to O. J. Simpson's double murder case. Despite Woods's actions not being actual crimes in the way Bryant's and Simpson's actions allegedly were, he was nevertheless linked to them. Together the references to these cases were of a type of narrative constituting a frame that represents men constructed as Black in relation to criminality, regardless of criminality, and thus racializing all three cases in similar ways.

In addition to the *number* of women Woods slept with, much of the press coverage discussed the *types* of women and sex Woods chose for his affairs. These women were waitresses, cocktail servers, nightclub hostesses, porn stars, alleged escorts, and strippers. At one golf tournament in which Woods was to play, dueling airplanes circled the course with banners that read: "We miss you Tiger! Déjà Vu Showgirls," and "We miss you too Tiger! At Dreamgirls."[53] A sports website even cataloged and scored the women involved with Woods, ranking them from "believability" to "hotness."[54] That Woods met some of these women gambling in Las Vegas, and some allegedly via escort services, bolstered the pathology narrative.

By consorting with women deemed, within dominant discourses of race, class, and respectability, as crass and lower class, Woods fulfilled stereotypical notions of Black male sexuality and its appetite for White women. It also linked his Blackness to lower-class tastes and identity. Additionally, articles like the series in *Vanity Fair* noted Woods was "very rough," "tugged [his mistress's] hair and spanked her butt," and had "a voracious appetite for sex."[55] These statements "evoked the age-old specter of the black menace to society by emphasizing how this 'Tiger's' animal desires drove him to brutal, compulsive behavior."[56]

Tiger Woods's media coverage did not include much praise, but the moments in which he garnered praise almost always revolved around his sexual practices. The majority of the public reactions and coverage that praised Woods praised him for having a large penis, and for having sex with a large number of women. Maino, a rapper, created a song he titled "Tiger Woods," which he claimed was more than an homage to the golfer; it was an anthem "to all men who deal with a lot of women."[57] As his mistresses came forward, some similar themes arose from their interviews and focused on how Woods was well endowed.[58] Mindy Lawton, a Perkins waitress, praised Woods's sexual prowess, noting that "he has a very strong sex drive and knows his way around the bedroom. On a scale of 10, I would give him 12."[59] She would later acknowledge in *Vanity Fair* that Woods had the biggest penis she had ever seen.[60] By connecting the hegemonic idea of Black men and large penises to both the amount and type of sex Woods engaged in, this narrative effectively positioned him within a discourse of hypersexualized Blackness.

The socioeconomic status of Woods's mistresses was made even more apparent when contrasted with the coverage Elin Nordegren received. Nordegren became more than the wronged wife—the embodiment of White femininity. By portraying the Swedish Nordegren as a wealthy, supportive, fame-eschewing, college-educated, beautiful blonde mother, the media signaled in so many ways that she was too good for Woods. In her only interview *People* magazine described her state before the divorce by using the example of Nordegren's "long, blonde hair falling out," while also pointing how she good-naturedly laughed at the comedic portrayals of her that appeared during the height of the scandal.[61] By depicting Nordegren as a victim whom Woods had subjected to a "candy shop, open 24/7 and it's certainly not the life for a spouse regardless of sex who takes marriage vows seriously,"[62] continued the pathological depiction of Black male sexuality in general, and Woods's sexuality specifically.

When details of the divorce leaked, the feature most covered was not the $750 million settlement for Nordegren, but the clause that kept Woods from visiting his children if he was in the company of women to whom he was not married or engaged.[63] Nordegren's representation as the ultimate wronged, respectable, White woman victim of Woods's uncontrollable sexual appetite was completed with the contractual demonization of his errant sexuality. In linking Nordegren's behavior to her Whiteness, she could effectively serve as a cautionary tale for the perils of interracial relationships, especially when positioned against Woods's pseudocriminal Blackness.

Race Relations and Humor

The glee with which people could now skewer Woods, who had been above reproach for most of his career, was almost palpable in the many jokes, jabs, parodies, one-liners, and puns delivered at Woods's expense. The Tiger Woods joke cycle revealed the underlying anxieties and tensions wrought by both his Blackness and his Asianness. The jokes employed hegemonic notions of Black male hypersexuality and Asian/American male asexuality/femininity, which were almost all meant to recuperate White masculinity. The equipment and terminology of golf provided a number of puns to address Woods's extramarital affairs, mostly involving a play on wood/clubs and holes as metaphors for male and female genitals.[64] For example: "Tiger's name should be changed to Tiger's wood," and "Is it true that Tiger is playing around? Yeah, he's doing 18 holes."[65] There were countless jokes about Woods's "club," the length of his "iron," the shortening of holes to "hos" to stand in for the women, and sand traps and bogeys to characterize the caliber of the women.

A number of jokes revolved around Woods's mistresses being White, or appearing to be White: "What is Tiger Woods's handicap? White women."[66] SNL had a sketch featuring a character named simply "Mistress 15." During the interview "Weekend Update," host Seth Meyers asked what she thought of the other women who had come forward, to which she replied, "Well, at first I thought they were just me in different outfits and hairs."[67] The joke is, obviously, that these women were so similar aesthetically that they were interchangeable in their Whiteness, which was the characteristic that mattered most to Woods. After Woods checked himself into a sex rehabilitation clinic, a software company released the game *BoneTown: Tiger Woods Affair Tour 10*. The game allows players to be like Woods by "sleeping with pornstars and cocktail waitresses, fighting with other golfers at a nightclub, or just partying and getting drunk."[68] On *GQ* magazine's website, a "Very Tiger Xmas Gift Guide" for Woods displayed gifts ranging from a new Cadillac Escalade "with seating for up to seven Orlando waitresses," to Beyond Seven condoms, because Woods gave "Wilt Chamberlin[69] [*sic*] a run for his money—they don't call you Tiger for nothing! We recommend these Japanese manufactured condoms. . . . They're thin yet strong enough."[70] Woods's hypersexuality was allowable, and even encouraged in this context, because he was not going for the most valuable White women, of which his ex-wife was an example. Woods could be eliminated as a threat to White masculinity, by making it obvious that the mistresses were not a respectable cadre of women.

One of the more popular responses to initial reports about the accident was to reference Woods's Asianness by connecting him to the stereotype of bad Asian/American drivers.[71] The week following the accident, three different comedians, George Lopez, Wanda Sykes, and Jo Koy, told the same joke about Woods: "Tiger Woods is half Black and half Asian. I guess the Black half bought the Cadillac, and the Asian half crashed it."[72] This particular joke provided the audience a chance to laugh at Woods's Blackness as evidenced by his car[73] of choice, and a chance to laugh at his Asianness, as evidenced by crashing his car.[74] Comedian Paul Mooney continued to focus on his Asian/American identity when he joked, "That little White girl beat the Black out of him. That's why the Asian part of him crashed into that tree."[75] Mooney links Woods's Asianness to the absence of an essentialist framing of Black masculinity by noting that "no self-respecting Black man would allow a woman to have her way with him."[76] *Saturday Night Live* drives (no pun intended) this point home in a sketch involving Keenan Thompson as Tiger Woods and Blake Lively as Elin Nordegren. The sketch plays on the idea that Nordegren has beaten Woods over his marital transgressions. This is made obvious when Woods's press conference shows him reading from an apology with "Help" and "She is so strong" written on the back of the papers.[77] Both Mooney's joke and *SNL* allow for reading Woods as emasculated by Nordegren because his Asianness does not provide him with the proper amount of masculinity to avoid such an incident. A derivative telling of this narrative involves interchangeable White golfers hiring Elin Nordegren to teach them how to "beat" Tiger Woods. This particular joke allows for the explicit recovery of White masculinity from both Black domination in sport and Asian/American economic domination. The jokes about Woods's lack of skill with women had the same emasculating effect on the golfer. His use of text message as the preferred mode of communication with his mistresses was deemed to be another feminizing trait. For example, a "Very Tiger Xmas Gift Guide" included the Nokia Twist cellphone as a gift option, because, "OMG! U txt as much as a teenage girl, Tiger :-) Get a Twist so u can txt faster, k? XOXO."[78] Though *GQ* did not mention any racial characteristics in their gift-giving guide, they linked Woods's behavior to teenage girls, part of a familiar feminizing discursive strategy deployed against Asian/American men.[79]

Jokes about Tiger Woods's sexual relationships with White women allowed for the most obvious means of addressing racial tensions. This particular joke thread enabled the discursive equivalent of putting Woods in his place. For example, Mooney, in an interview titled "Tiger Woods's Wake Up Call," states Woods "was running around saying he was cablin-canasian [*sic*], he knows what he is now."[80] Mooney, despite his jokes in the same interview about Woods's Asianness, used the scandal to assert that Woods's use of Cablinasian to distance himself from Blackness was unsuccessful, as evidenced by how quickly media skewered his Blackness after the scandal broke.

In keeping with the idea that Asian/American masculinity is comical, another strand of this narrative made Woods a sympathetic figure by portraying him as a hapless square, incapable of attracting women sans fame and fortune. This theme would begin most often by mentioning how many times Nordegren turned down Woods for a date, then follow up with examples such as the voicemail Woods left asking mistress Jamie Grubbs to change her outgoing message in case Nordegren called. This example was used to show how unskilled, and implicitly how Asian/American, Woods was when it came to women. Despite Woods's status as a professional athlete, he was both a "rookie at having women" and naïve for thinking they would keep the relationships secret.[81] Interestingly, Woods himself played into this narrative of Asian/American masculinity as pathetic as a counter to charges of arrogance. In text messages published by the *New York Post* between Woods and Grubbs, he tells her that "having an asian [*sic*] mother and a military father you cannot and will not ever be full of yourself."[82] This narrative utilized Woods's nonmasculine behavior as evidence he should be pitied.

Recuperating the Image

Tiger Woods's apologia began immediately following the accident. His curt statement acknowledging the accident and his refusal to meet with police regarding the incident[83] were purposeful moves, made in an attempt to quash additional publicity. There was the feeling that Woods's "highly paid image-polishers and truth-benders, the omnipotent sports agency International Management Group, and the assorted lawyers and security gorillas who make up the rest of his coterie" might be able to keep the scandal from spreading.[84] The strategy of silence backfired because his nondisclosure meant information was supplied from other sources. The public's reaction to Woods's silence became the impetus for the kategoria against him. Because Woods's image had been so carefully crafted, the image agents could not prevent his brand from taking a hit, though they predicted his image would be "tarnished only a bit."[85] At the core of the accusations against Woods were assertions that his behavior had violated his responsibility to the public. Underlying the pathological and comical narratives were contentions that he had violated the trust of his sponsors, the sport, his family, and most importantly, his fans. Woods's initial statement on November 29, 2009, was meant to address the violations by alluding to a "situation" that was "obviously embarrassing to my family and me."[86] While he noted, "I'm human and I'm not perfect. I will certainly make sure this doesn't happen again," the statement failed to divert further attention from the "situation," and was thus another misstep in Woods's apologia. Though he had been labeled as "superhuman" and "robotic" before the scandal, humanizing his image did not keep information about his extramarital affairs from being released, and subsequently exploited. While Woods needed to relegitimize his brand, this strategy provided more fodder for attacks against his image.

The chorus of disapproval surrounding Woods's statement about his "situation" was followed with a new statement about his "transgressions" and the abandonment of his "values."[87] This statement addressed the unveiling of yet another mistress, in addition to the criticism regarding his previous statement. His new statement differed from the previous statement in that his self-serving "situation" was replaced with "transgressions" in an effort to acknowledge he was accepting the blame. He also offered an explanation of his actions by stating he had not been "true to [his] values."[88] This statement allowed Woods to dissociate himself from his extramarital affairs and present them as isolated acts that did not represent his true self. His image pre-scandal made him responsible to divergent constituencies, and as such he had a "limited amount of time to explain the events, or risk staining both his own brand and those of his sponsors."[89] Woods's own brand is an entity not entirely separate from the brands he endorsed, and while he lost some endorsements as the scandal deepened,[90] the ineffectiveness of his apologia did major damage to his personal brand. The deployment of his statements as press releases instead of press conferences, Nordegren's refusal to speak on Woods's behalf, and his unavailability to answer questions from entities ranging from the police to reporters to Oprah Winfrey, all seemed to aggravate the public's anger. His statement, however, appeared to be enough for his fellow golfers on tour, who despite the unfolding scandal voted him as their PGA player of the year.[91] Their vote for Woods stands as a testament to the power of his brand, particularly because the Tiger Woods effect causes an increase in television viewership (and subsequently sponsorships) when he is playing in a tournament.[92] Since the golfers seemed to be the only group moving past the scandal, Woods issued yet another statement. This time his statement announced he was taking "an indefinite break from professional golf."[93] Still his critics charged that his behavior, and his responses to having that behavior discovered, continued to violate the public's trust.

As each statement intensified the public scrutiny and pressure, the next tactic in his apologia was entering a sexual rehabilitation clinic. Woods could no longer adopt a strategy of evasiveness; he had already admitted to the transgressions and women continued to come forward. However, by entering rehab, Woods showed he was taking corrective action. Sexual rehabilitation becomes an important part of his apologia and works rhetorically because it demonstrates Woods has established measures of control to ensure it would not happen again. Hearit, in his analysis of organizations and apologia, notes corrective action is only the beginning of reestablishing legitimacy. The next step is demonstrating legitimacy "through a form of epideictic, value-oriented discourse in which they praise the very values they are reputed to have transgressed."[94] Thus, Woods apologized during a nationally televised press conference.[95] He acknowledged he had cheated and also admitted to transgressing the "boundaries" of his marriage, as well as the boundaries of the public's trust. As a measure of sincerity intended to act as a reassurance, Woods spoke about checking himself into "in-patient therapy," where he had been for the last ten weeks. To reassure his many constituencies that he had indeed changed, Woods recognized his Thai mother and their shared Buddhist faith for teaching him "to stop following every impulse and to learn restraint." He ended his apology by asking for help from those "who believed in me" so that they may one day believe in him again. Woods's apology is part of a familiar ritual for celebrities and public figures who transgress social norms. Yet he managed to repair some of the damage done to his reputation by touching on the values—honesty, transparency, not sleeping with (multiple, White) women—he had been accused of violating. He also brought in religion, remorse, repentance, and transformation to continue his brand's restoration process.

There were strategies in Tiger Woods's final apology meant to establish his Blasian brand. His sex addiction situated him squarely within dominant discourses of Black masculinity, effectively depicting his sexuality as something to be feared. His apology addressed rehab and his continued therapy for sex addiction, allowing him to rhetorically allay fears of an out-of-control Black masculinity. Additionally, as he spoke before his carefully vetted audience of family, supporters, and Team Tiger members, the camera maintained a frame that foregrounded Woods's contrite face against the backdrop of Kultida Punsawad Woods's stoic face. The image of Woods set against that of his mother as he spoke about her guidance and his return to Buddhism worked as reminder of Woods's Asianness.[96] Invoking Buddhism conferred to Woods an authentic Asianness, and with it possibly a return to nonthreatening Asian/American masculinity and sexuality. Nishime agrees that Woods relied on "the redemptive power of an Asian cultural identity [to] provide an antidote to the fleshy embodiment of [his] racialization as an African American."[97] Still, there were limits to his invocation of Buddhism. As some pundits explained Buddhism's benefits for both Woods and as a religious practice to their audiences, others like Fox News's Brit Hume had already urged Woods to "turn to the Christian faith, [so] you can make a total recovery and be a great example to the world."[98] Hume's claim that Woods's Buddhist faith did not offer the kind of "redemption and forgiveness offered by the Christian faith," taps into a centuries-old tradition of disciplining non-White bodies through Christianity. When O'Reilly offered Hume a chance to clarify after the public outcry, Hume explicitly linked Buddhism to Woods's Thai mother: "I mentioned the Buddhism only because his mother is a Buddhist, and he has apparently said he was. I'm not sure how seriously he practices that."[99] Deeming Buddhism inferior to Christianity because it was not a "serious" religion allowed Hume to marginalize both the influence of Kutilda Woods and Tiger Woods's claim to an Asian/American identity.

Tiger Woods's apologia did not end with his public apology. As Woods prepared for the Masters Tournament, Nike released a commercial: a black-and-white close shot of Woods on the golf course, while the voice of Earl Woods, his dead father, asked if "he had learned anything."[100] The commercial posed the question the public wanted answered: *Had he learned his lesson?* That question might have made sense if Woods had been racialized only as Black and thus could now recognize his place within US racial hierarchy. However, the scandal had conferred onto Woods some multiracial visibility, as evidenced by the conflicting narratives and tensions analyzed in this article, and thus the commercial was nearly universally panned. By the culmination of the scandal's news cycle Woods had mobilized his Blasianness to demonstrate how identity is ultimately adaptable and contingent and in its flexibility challenges the strictures of racial categorization because the boundaries around race are ultimately meaningless.

Benoit notes apologiae can "reduce, redress, or avoid damage to reputation."[101] Initially Tiger Woods eschewed hiring a crisis management team and relied on his own team of agents, managers, and public relations professionals to contain the fallout from his many affairs.[102] As interest in the scandal continued to mount, Woods's response was a non-response. The missteps in his apologia were blamed on the lack of people specifically trained to manage such a large crisis. Husselbee and Stein note Woods's apologia started off shakily enough to warrant an *antapologia*, which included strengthening the initial attack on Woods and responding in such a way to further weaken his apology.[103] After his first national press conference, Woods hired former White House press secretary Ari Fleischer to help plan his return to golf and respond to the antapologia.[104] While Team Tiger's motivation was the maintenance of Woods's image in order to recoup and retain his endorsement deals, Woods's apologia also worked to protect his own personal Blasian brand identity. Though he had been able to mostly avoid talking about race, especially after the Cablinasian episode of *The Oprah Winfrey Show*,[105] he returned to his Blasian racial identity as the foundation of his apologia and as a response to media misidentification. He strategically deployed his mixed-race identity to counter the popular narratives being used to racialize him. Kruse notes apologiae can include a variety of mediums and methods.[106] Using commercials, statements, a more fan-friendly persona, a televised apology, a column in a national newsmagazine, sex addiction treatment, and sometimes purposeful silence, Woods's apologia has had mixed success based on public reaction and media coverage.

The narratives emerging from the scandal also act as a kategoria, or accusations, against Woods. In evaluating the merits of the accusations, the impossibility of demarcating between Tiger Woods the golfer and Tiger Woods the brand is made clear. Various publics used the scandal to lodge accusations against both Woods's "policy" and "character."[107] Companies whose products Woods endorsed also "suffered greater declines in value, presumably reflecting declines in the asset values or brand equity association with those products."[108] In proffering a defense, Woods's apologia had to account for both his actions and his moral responsibility to the community. Hearit notes the corporate apologia is different from an individual's apologia, mostly because corporations become embroiled in a social legitimation crisis, which compels some sort of corrective action(s). Furthermore, corrective action was only the beginning for Woods's apologia. As a brand Woods also had to "demonstrate legitimacy [by praising] the values [he was] reputed to have transgressed."[109] This second part of the apologia, part of any corporation's image management strategy, demonstrates how crucial it was for Woods to situate his apologia within a broader image management campaign. He did not just have to defend, explain, and apologize for his transgressions while mitigating the damage to his moral character; he needed to also use his apologia in such a way that it would repair, or at least attempt to repair, his damaged reputation and restore his social legitimacy.

Post-scandal but Not Post-race

Woods was praised for acknowledging his transgressions and for attempting to be more fan-friendly, rather than the unemotional "robot" he had long been labeled. For example, the focus upon his return was on how he "smiled and waved and acknowledged most of the applause that came his way. He was even spied signing autographs out on the range Saturday, something he never does."[110] Some fans felt Woods was "gracious,"[111] and they greeted him with cheers and applause at his first tournament post-scandal to "show appreciation for Tiger, an acknowledgement of his significance to golf and his potential significance beyond golf."[112] Those same cheers greeted Woods when he played in his first post-divorce golf tournament in August 2010, and his fans were rewarded with his best golf since the scandal.[113] The cheering and ratings boost for the PGA when Woods played were proof that Woods's apologia had resonated with the public.

When Jamie Grubbs wondered in a text "why I keep falling more and more for u," Tiger Woods replied "because I'm Blasian"[114] While he was locating her romantic attraction to his mixed-race body, I note the universal attraction to the spectacle of Woods was also because of his mixed-race body. Woods began his career asserting his Blasianness, which aided in bolstering his brand throughout his career. Post-scandal he would return to Blasianness to negotiate the fallout and salvage his brand. The production of Woods's Blasian identity worked for the benefit of numerous and concurrent news stories, jokes about his masculinity and sexuality, and the shaming and (scant) praising of his behavior. Although there were very few narratives that addressed race explicitly, all were deployed in very specific ways to reveal the tensions around non-White racially mixed people. In other words, the reaction and coverage engaged not just his Blackness, but his Asianness as well. His restoration came via negotiated branding strategies that positioned his Blasianness in an effort to win back trust. Woods's post-scandal moment reveals some insights about multiracial identity and celebrity that can be applied to other groups. The lack of consistency across media on the coverage of Woods as his scandal played out should be taken as a part of the evolution of the Blasian brand, because it illuminates how quickly some were able to keep up with dynamic transformations in racialization and forces others to begin acknowledging the slipperiness of race and racialization. The lack of consistency also recognizes that Blasians (and by extension other multiracials) are not inscribed with a singular, "right" meaning, despite the presence of hegemonic (or preferred) meanings and the desire to believe in racially pure categories.

A key intervention I make in this chapter is that it is possible to talk about multiracial people in a way that escapes the anti-Black, self-loathing, or celebratory themes of previous research on mixed race, while offering a way of reconceptualizing race through its disruption of the hegemonic order of society. Conventional reading of these news and entertainment sources ignored the variety of ways Woods was racialized. In other words, by reading these sources through a branding theory centered on the untidiness of Blasians, there are possibilities opened up for studying race and mixed race in ways that do not sustain racial hierarchies. Also important is acknowledging there might not be a way to escape the ascription of race by media and society, but the conflict between ascription and personal choice opens up a realm of possibilities. Blasianness challenges extant discursive identity models by recognizing the ways identities and subjectivities evolve, and shift, and potentially change. Furthermore, if prevalent notions of racial authenticity, or realness, can be overcome, then opportunities for building coalitions across the pluralities of subjectivities and identities grow exponentially. Lastly, by not privileging Blasian identity over both monoracial Black or Asian/American identities, examining the branding of Blasians allows for taking a truly antiracist research position.

CHAPTER 5

Sporting the Blasian Body

Shortly after Barack Obama's historic election as president of the United
States, NBC sketch-comedy show *Saturday Night Live* introduced a new
character, "The Rock Obama." The Rock Obama, played by Dwayne "The
Rock" Johnson, was the angry version of perpetually mellow Barack
Obama, played originally by mixed-race Asian/American Fred Armisen,
then later by Jay Pharoah. Armisen's Obama had been met with complaints that he was engaging in a tamer version of blackface in order to
play the president, since he was not Black. In the March 7, 2009, episode,
when "The Rock Obama" made his debut, those complaints immediately
stopped.[1] Interestingly, Armisen, like Obama, is racially mixed, but the
"black-lash" (criticisms about a non-Black person playing a Black person)
against him for playing Obama triggered questions about the politics
of mixed-race representations. Dwayne Johnson's Blasian body was the
answer to those questions, highlighting the utility of multiracial celebrities, which in this case is necessary for ameliorating the tensions around
the representations of race. Furthermore, a Blasian Johnson playing a

potentially Blasian Obama becomes an interesting application of this transracial schema.

This chapter offers an exploration of the utility of Blasian bodies, especially as they relate to nationalism, masculinity, and race by focusing on stars Dwayne Johnson and Hines Ward to discuss the way Blasian identities, masculinity, and nationalism intersect with sport's commodification of athletes.[2] Discourses of sport, race, masculinity, and nation are contradictory and inconsistent, and those multiple narratives mirror the reception of these two celebrities culturally. Furthermore, both of their transracialized bodies are sites of anxiety, as they disrupt racialized hierarchies while also challenging the relationship of those hierarchies to cultural norms. Since representational apparatuses need to be fluid in order to change as discourses for athletes of color change, Blasians mutate along with those changing discourses challenging the essentialist underpinnings of racialized ideologies. The parallels between Ward's and Johnson's experiences with their mothers' home countries, the changing terms of their racialization, and their resistance to the ways they have been racialized provide a compelling push for thinking through new ways of kinship premised on more than race.

Nations and Sport

The role of "celebrity" in sports ensures that athletes are some of the most highly visible figures. The realm of sport is also where narratives of race, gender, class, sexuality, and ability are unambiguously linked to a culture of consumption.[3] As he maps the path sport has taken from ritual to mass consumption, John Alt claims that corporations have made sport a replacement for communities, and the spectacle of sport provides both a diversion from reality and a way to meet the "emotional needs of the masses."[4] We see this happen when athletes win and their victory is shared with people who use the win as a source of cultural identity.[5] Alt and Halberstam both suggest that modern sport, and the spectacle sport has become, emerged as reactions to cultural shifts impacting gender and class, especially the crisis of masculinity men were facing due to new divisions of labor. Furthermore, because class-consciousness was being shaped by corporate rationalizations, and winning and moneymaking were the new ultimate goals, athletes were now subjected to new means of discipline in order to regulate their labor and extract maximum spectacle. The implementation of new rules, spectacle, and theatricality were all designed to bring in audiences, often to the detriment of the players' health and wellbeing.[6]

Masculinity is made all the more salient in sport when it becomes intimately coupled with nationalism, often drawing on the same narratives. There are parallels between the discourses of nationalism and masculinity, where terms like "honour, patriotism, cowardice, bravery and duty are hard to distinguish as either nationalistic or masculinist, since they seem so thoroughly tied both to the nation and to manliness."[7] There are some scholars who think international sport and the globalization of sport have successfully worn down the importance of national identity.[8] However, I argue that globalization operates unevenly and has bypassed a wide range of people and places, such that national identity is still very important in many places. The fact that American/Aussie rules football, indigenous sports, Gaelic games, beauty pageants, and so forth still exist, are popular, and play a central role in the definition and cultural practices of those various national cultures, demonstrates how nationalism has resisted the "encroachment of globalisation's homogenizing tendencies and that sport and globalization have become accomplices in the process whereby the importance of national identity has been ensured."[9] Additionally, the fact that the Olympic Games, World Cup, and other international sporting events seem to be fertile grounds for intensification of nationalisms indicates that the relationship between nationalism and sport is growing rather than shrinking. Jarvie points out that the "symbolism of sport has helped to promote national identity and sentiment at major sporting events [through] the idea that sport and sporting achievements contribute to a nation's greatness, national identity, and at times help to transcend internal strife and social deference".[10] Importantly, sporting celebrities often embody notions of what a nation is, was, should, or can be. Those athletes demonstrate the fluidity of the relationship between nation and sport, helping contextualize the relationship politically, socially, and culturally.

With the flow of goods, technology, information, capital, and people comes the formation of multinational corporations and organizations that benefit from globalization—both economically and culturally. The increase in globalization and the reaches of globalization would ostensibly signal the demise of the nation-state, and yet in sport we find the simultaneous reinforcement of national identities and undermining of nations. In other words, "global expansion is supposed to generate supranational, more cosmopolitan loyalties and identities as part of the emergence of a global culture. But this idea fails to recognize that the entrenchment of national identities and nationalist sentiment places strong limits on the development of global identity and global culture."[11] Thus, sport exists as a contested space where nationalism is simultaneously encouraged and discouraged.

There are numerous forms of identification for people, but national identification is one of the "most intense and demanding."[12] Additionally, linking national identity to sport means recognizing sport(s) as a "potential signifier of oppression and liberation."[13] Sport becomes a signifier for oppression because it re-creates the relations of dominance and subordination found in society. For example, narratives frame women as masculine and violators of heteronormativity if they participate (and excel) in sports, Black athletes are essentialized as physically superior and mentally inferior, Asian/Americans, though rarely discussed, are crafty, gay men are relegated to feminized sports like ice-skating, and Latinx athletes are consigned to baseball and boxing.[14] Thus, sport, as a magnifier of society, is a sexist, racist, classist, homophobic institution. Furthermore, sport behaves as though it is a meritocracy, where those who practice, sharpen their skills, and work hard end up being winners, and those who lose must not have had the ability or work ethic to win. This idealization obscures the way power is structured via ascription and privilege. In this chapter the Blasian sporting figures use masculinity to simultaneously illuminate the discursive maneuvers that attempt to fix them representationally while also offering means for escape from these static representations.

Watching and/or participating in sport becomes an activity fraught with tensions, especially when considering the political economy of sport and its players. The corporatizing of sport and its attendant theatrical, highlight-reel style of play, has resulted in the scouting of athletes from outside traditional borders and has facilitated the emergence of activities that "require cross-border travel and contact on a sustained basis."[15] The economic conditions that require the exploitation of many players of color in order for sport to thrive are the same factors that require the importation of players from overseas—meaning the corporatization of sport has resulted in a two-way flow of talent into and out of the United States, but also in the transformation of sports abroad in becoming more similar to the spectacle of sport seen domestically so as to increase the bottom line of sponsoring corporations. The transnational movements of athletes like Ichiro Suzuki, Pedro Alvarez, Yao Ming, Allen Iverson, and fútbol players makes them "borderless athletes."[16] The flows of globalization explain much of the fanfare greeting both Johnson and Ward on their homecoming visits to Samoa and Korea respectively. However, despite the borderlessness of athletes, the presence of the Olympics—along with the popularity of FIFA's World Cup competition, and other global competitions and title matches—means the globalization of sport continues to be in tension with nationalism. Still, it is the increasing popularity of sports that have long been bound within certain geographical areas (cricket, baseball, basketball, American football) where processes of globalization are becoming more and more apparent—though that process is uneven.

Racializing Athleticism

Bourdieu points out that participation in sports is limited by one's access to various forms of capital—be it economic, cultural, social, symbolic, or political. The historical development of sport in the United States initially allowed men of color entry as long as White men won, in order to maintain the racial order.[17] Even though Jim Crow laws were instituted in the mid-1870s, Black athletes participated in sports alongside Whites. A few years later, however, the more popular sports became segregated; Blacks were pushed out of baseball, and White boxers refused to fight Black boxers.[18] When sport and its athletes began to subvert the racial order in America during the late 1800s, formal segregation was instituted. It was not until 1908, when Tommy Burns agreed to fight Jack Johnson, and 1947, when Jackie Robinson played baseball in the Major Leagues instead of the Negro Leagues, that America's most popular sports became reintegrated. The eventual, inevitable, and uneven integration of sport resulted in the creation of new means of emphasizing racial order in order to maintain White supremacy. As such, key narratives about both Blacks and Asian/Americans have arisen in order to discursively maintain notions of race, nation, and sport.

In response to the segregation and integration of sports, sports and athleticism have played a role in shifting the definitions of manhood and masculinity. For example, narratives of sport had previously framed Black men as excelling in sports due to brute strength and/or natural athleticism, especially when pitted against White men,[19] so it has been only recently that narratives have expanded enough to recognize Black athletes as also skilled. The ability to think, in addition to athletic skill and power, meant Whites had more tools in their arsenal, while Black men had only their strength on which to rely. Tommy Burns's defeat in 1908 at the hands of

Jack Johnson showed just how much the world was not ready for a Black champion athlete, particularly in boxing—then a space for demonstrating White dominance.[20] Jack Johnson was also arguably the first Black celebrity athlete,[21] who spent his time outside of the ring socializing very publicly with White women, which served to intensify the blow his win was to both White masculinity and Whiteness in general. The White public championed Jim Jeffries, then a retired world champion boxer, who they hoped would come out of retirement to beat Johnson. Jeffries was asked to return to the ring in order to beat the "uppity" Johnson and restore the dominance of Whiteness and White supremacy. According to Bederman, Jeffries was labeled a savior "whose intrinsic Anglo-Saxon nature" would naturally lead to Johnson's defeat, and return the title of most powerful man in the world to White men, where it belonged.[22] When Johnson decisively beat Jeffries, the Great White Hope, his victory began to further dismantle hegemonic ideologies of White male power. Though Johnson's win challenged and started shifting the discourse around Black male athleticism and skill, the idea of the thinking White athlete vs. intellectually inferior but physically superior Black athlete persists in contemporary discourses about race and athletes. When contextualized within a meta-narrative of Black inferiority, stemming from the colonialist mind-ver-sus-body dialectic,[23] the persistence of these narratives is understandable.

Inferior intellectual capabilities are just one of the many narratives involving men of color, who have long been commodified in sports and offered up as entertainment for mass consumption.[24] That Cartesian dualism is also evident in discourses of Islander/Indigenous masculinities, whereby colonizers determined that the practices of Pacific Islanders were barbaric, inferior, and abnormal. As with the infantilization of Black men in the United States, Pacific Islanders were thought to be savage, childlike, unsophisticated, physical, and ruled by passion.[25] When Collins writes about how Black men have been reduced to "their bodies [with] their muscles and their penises as their most important sites,"[26] she is merely pointing out a prominent narrative of Black males as one that defines them as hypersexual and physical (read: potentially violent). Holowhitu notes the parallel framing of Pacific Islanders as "emotionally impulsive, aggressive, and violent."[27] The mythogenesis of Pacific Islanders does not include the same sort of overwhelming sexual mythology that steers representations of Black masculinity. In fact, for indigenous Islander masculinities, the emphasis is placed more directly on size as a threat and source of cultural anxieties.[28] Sport has continued to evolve as a way for elites to recognize and discipline bodies of color. Whereas the success of athletes of color in sports is threatening to White male superiority and White social and cultural hegemony, the depictions of these athletes/celebrities reinforce hegemonic ideas of race by centering on the "natural" ability of these athletes to excel at sports—thereby establishing biological racial difference as the reason for their success. Juxtaposing the narratives regarding the innate ability of athletes of color against the accomplishments of White athletes highlights the relationship between race and sport while erasing the labor contributions of these bodies. White athletes are characterized as having "fortitude, intelligence, moral character, strategic preparation, coachability, and good organization";[29] whereas, non-White athletes are reduced to biological characteristics that enable them to succeed, think size, speed, strength, etc. Focusing on natural ability, when taken together with the fact that people of color are rarely in positions of power, as coaches or owners, is in keeping with White supremacist ideology. Punishingly, the narrative of the successful athlete of color is wielded like a double-edged sword, providing, on the one hand, an example of how some men can be successful when using their talents, while simultaneously, on the other, being used to denigrate other men and boys of color who aspire to the same level of success as unrealistic.

Both Ward and Johnson have routinely been identified as natural talents. For example, comments about Ward included such observations as "rushing and receiving came pretty naturally to him,"[30] "blocking is natural [to him],"[31] and "the kid is just a natural athlete."[32] In fact, during Ward's football career there was very little mention of his work ethic or training regimen. Additionally, the use of *natural* as a descriptor of athletic skill and "media-generated images that sustain [the idea of natural talent], probably do more than anything else in our public life to encourage the idea that blacks and whites are biologically different in a meaningful way."[33] Ward is perpetually constructed through traditional media lenses that frame Black athletes as body, not mind. Sport, and essentialist narratives regarding the bodies of athletes, has been and continues to be accepting of embodied racial difference.

Meanwhile, Johnson's familial pedigree adds another layer to a reading of his athletic acumen as natural. As he is a third-generation professional wrestler, the coverage of Johnson's career focused on how wrestling was in his blood.[34] His grandfather, Samoan professional wrestler Peter Maivia, was one of the first Pacific Islanders featured in World Wrestling

Entertainment (known then as the World Wrestling Federation). Maivia subsequently opened up professional wrestling to other Pacific Islander personae, while Dwayne Johnson's father, Rocky Johnson, was one of the first Black WWE champions. Dwayne Johnson began wrestling under the name "Rocky Maivia" as homage to his father and grandfather, eventually shortening it to just "The Rock." As pushback against the natural framing, Johnson utilized media, including his own social media, to talk about the work he puts into his image and his roles. When he revealed his diet and workout regimen to *Muscle & Fitness*, media outlets the world over covered every single calorie of it or attempted to mimic his daily routine themselves.[35] Ultimately, by highlighting how unnatural it was himself, Johnson was able to offer a new media framing focused on how hard he worked rather than the typical essentialist framing.

Perilous Asian/American Athletes

It is not surprising that certain sports have been, and still are, largely associated with particular social classes, races, ethnicities, and nationalities, not to mention gender. Fortunately, the field of Asian/American sport studies is growing quickly as "Asian and Asian American athletes [are] becoming visible" as both participants and fans.[36] Bourdieu's habitus is helpful in explaining and understanding which sports are acceptable for participation in by which athletes. Tiger Woods playing golf successfully becomes a monumental achievement because he represents a break from the notion that golf is a game for wealthy White men, while Michael Jordan playing basketball legitimizes the idea that Black men are good for fast-paced sports that involve little thinking. Within the current racial paradigm that leaves Asian/Americans out of most sporting narratives, Pacific Islanders and Indigenous athletes of color are visible only in physical contact sports like football and rugby.[37] That relative invisibility often results in jokes about Asian/Americans in sports, which, Richard King observes, "not only reinforce dominant ideas about Asian (American) masculinity but also encourage the perpetuation of Black-White understandings of male-centered sporting worlds."[38] Asian/American athletes "have been depicted as anything but normal. They are mysterious competitors, cultural appropriators, cheaters, or simply athletically inept."[39] Narratives that frame the understanding of sport in the United States deemphasize the masculinity of Asian/American men as athletes, while emphasizing (sometimes simultaneously and contradictorily) their model minority status and/or their presence as a threat. Mayeda uses American media portrayal of the two Japanese pitchers Hideo Nomo and Hideki Irabu as an example of how the stories mirrored hegemonic frames of Asian/Americans, thus categorizing the pitchers as "model minorities and economic threats."[40] King demonstrates how dominant ideologies are maintained when the absence of Asian/Americans in sport "embodies the long-standing feminization of all things 'Asian,' which, in turn, reserves desired athletic and leadership qualities for white coaches" and ostensibly Black players.[41]

Even the emergence of professional basketball player Jeremy Lin and the "Linsanity" that ensued served only to reinforce the narratives of Asian/American men as weak and physically ill-equipped for hypermasculine sports through the constant reinforcement of Lin as an anomaly and spectacle.[42] Furthermore, Lin's success was immediately moderated through his Harvard education, with excellence in sport being subsumed by intellectual dominance.[43] The absence of the construction of Lin specifically and Asian/American athletes generally as physically dominant was an instrumental and instructive component of the discursive framing of Lin's success in professional basketball. Lin's presence as an Asian/American athlete did represent "a web of power relations that (re)configures the ways transnational corporations, US cultural imperialism, nation and nationalism, and local cultures negotiate" with each other.[44] Ultimately, however, the coverage of Lin exposed how unmeritocratic US society actually is, since Lin's ascendance showed how often "social inequalities pipeline some players on to and some players off of the NBA's big stage."[45]

Emasculation of Asian/American men has not been the only result of sport. Sport's value to the "colonial project" is evident in moments like the push for physical exercise in American colonies, where there was a "collective (read 'nationalist') concern for upright civic and moral character through proper physical maintenance. Not just the man, but the entire nation, was to be endowed with masculine virility."[46] In response to the emasculation of Asian/American men, particularly as a result of colonization, Pacific Islanders have "use[d] performances of Polynesian warriorhood to make claims to an 'authentic' pre-colonial and premodern masculinity."[47] The images have in turn been commodified by transnational corporations like Adidas and Nike and rearticulated as "hypermasculine spectacles."[48] Pacific Islander and Indigenous men have created a hybridized version of masculinity that includes their own indigenous traditions but have coupled it with the traditions of US militarism and masculinity.

The tradition of US military service for Indigenous and Pacific Islander is especially robust in part because this has been a way to obtain US citizenship.[49] For example, American Samoa has the highest population of military service members among all the territories and states. The overrepresentation of military members from the Pacific coupled with the self-important existence of the US military through imperialism and globalization created an outsized presence of the US in the East. Additionally, this military presence brought Black service members into contact with local Asian and Indigenous women, which provides a context for the relationship that these countries would later have with their native sons Johnson and Ward.

Hines Ward is consistently mentioned in stories and lists that count the number of Asian/American players in the National Football League, so it is not surprising that the depictions of Ward—like fellow athlete Tiger Woods—are framed by narratives of both Black and Asian/American athletes. Ward is rhetorically framed in the usual ways Black male athletes are, as a naturally talented, physical player in a non-thinking position. He had already been a professional football player for years prior to being recognized as the MVP of Super Bowl XL. The ensuing media attention around the MVP, which discovered and highlighted his Blasian identity after the Super Bowl, was enough for the NFL to take notice, as it hoped to profit from his Asianness.[50] Lapchick notes the NFL, since the mid-2000s, had been looking for a way to market itself in Asia, and it hoped that Ward would do for the NFL what Yao Ming and later Linsanity did for the NBA in China (and surrounding countries).[51]

Expansion to or inclusion of Asian countries in sport has been accompanied by US resistance to Asian/American occupation. For example, an earlier instance of this resistance or fear of an Asian economic takeover colored the way sports media discussed the prominence and dominance of East Asian players in baseball during the 1990s. Ono critiques the racist and nationalistic framing of the "un-American" purchase of the Seattle Mariners by Nintendo, linking media criticisms to a fear of what he calls "economic miscegenation"—the mixing of money as a metaphor for racial mixture. During the early 1990s Japan had cemented its position as a legitimate economic threat to the United States, which resulted in Japan's construction as the "newly masculinized Other, attempting to dominate, control, and take over feminized baseball, Seattle, and the U.S."[52] The

Japanese in this instance are both mysterious competitors, with shadowy reasons for wanting to purchase the Mariners, and cultural appropriators trying to taint the pristine nature of "America's" sport. Mayeda's summary of the ways US media frame Asian/Americans is evident in this particular episode. While the NFL's attempts to expand into Asia would not appear to provoke the same intensity in xenophobic feelings as the Mariner purchase, there were complaints about taking "our" game to "those countries."[53] This is due in part to Ward's Blasianness, which provides a partial buffer to the application of yellow peril narratives that play on the fear of Asians taking things from the United States. The forever foreign framing of Asian/Americans is mediated by Blackness, which acts as part of the Blasian brand to complicate the application of anti-Asian rhetoric to these sporting exchanges.

Reinforcing Nationalism in the Face of Globalization

Hines Ward became a barometer for the cultural shifts taking place not only in the United States, but also in Korea. He was located as a transnational figure, a Korean raised as an American, who goes back home after he has "made good" playing an American sport.[54] Similarly, Johnson's homecoming visit, made under similar terms of a native son returning after he has "made good," imparted unto Samoa some mainstream visibility. Obviously, Ward's reimagining of citizenship and Johnson's allegiance were made possible vis-á-vis the movement of global capital and the "relationship between sport and specific national territories [which] cannot be fully understood without recognizing the part played by transnational organizations and international forces of development."[55]

Prior to being named Super Bowl MVP, Ward was a standout football player at both the high school and college levels. In high school he was twice named Offensive Player of the Year in Georgia and earned *USA Today*'s All-American honors his senior year. He played for the University of Georgia and earned All-SEC honors and ended his career as the second all-time receiver (behind only Herschel Walker). After being selected by the Pittsburgh Steelers in the third round of the 1998 NFL draft, Ward went on to become the all-time leader in receptions, receiving yards, and receiving touchdowns for the team. He was selected five times for the Pro Bowl and is a two-time Super Bowl champion. Despite Koreans' unfamiliarity with US football or his career, Hines Ward mania gripped Korea in 2006. There was an extraordinary amount of fanfare surrounding Ward during his Korean visit; as the press reported on his visits with politicians and celebrities, he also gave countless interviews and photo opportunities, took endorsement meetings, and participated in a ceremony granting him honorary Korean citizenship.

Linking sport and nationalism makes it a source for national reconciliation. This narrative of reconciliation comes through in the coverage of Ward's visit to Korea. The Korean news media focused nearly every story on Ward's identity as a multiracial Korean, an inverse of the US coverage, and only in passing did they mention his MVP status and starting position on the Pittsburgh Steelers. Korean news stories reemphasized the nation's inclusion of him: "Ward is Korean, Ward is one of us."[56] The declaration of the press stands in contrast to the experience of Ward and his mother, which he alluded to that during the ceremony conferring on him honorary Korean citizenship. During that ceremony he recalled how he was "angry for the longest time [because Koreans] didn't accept me, they didn't accept my mom."[57] Ward opened the reconciliation process by tearfully proclaiming, after being made an honorary citizen, "I used to be ashamed to say I was Korean, today I just want to thank you guys, because I apologize to you for being ashamed to say I was Korean."[58] Ward was often quoted as saying he was "ashamed to say I was Korean" because he had trouble fitting in as a child.[59] In an ESPN newsmagazine piece, he talks about his birth in Korea, the move from Korea to Atlanta, where his father would abandon both him and his mother, and the difficulties he had growing up in Atlanta largely friendless, poor, and raised by a single mother working multiple jobs. He contrasted his childhood with the difficulties and disadvantages he would have faced had they stayed in Korea. The piece notes biracial Koreans are "poorer and less well–educated," "pariahs," and "outcasts" in Korean society.[60] Ward recalled his mother telling him "people would call her names, spit on her . . . treat [mixed-race] people like dogs."[61] The narrator in the ESPN piece mentions both Ward and his mother had feelings of trepidation upon their return trip to Korea, not knowing what to expect or how they would be treated. As Ward talked about his hero's welcome in Korea, and his surprising acceptance by Koreans, he used his Blasian status as the point of reconciliation, claiming, "If people can accept me for *who I am being Korean*, rather than what I am as a biracial athlete, then I know there is hope for biracial kids here in Korea" [emphasis mine].[62]

Building on the narrative of reconciliation, Ward's exemplary Blasian identity was responsible for constructing an alternative understanding of the role of the US military. Nearly every news account mentioned that the parents of Hines Ward were divorced almost as soon as they got to the United States. However, the Korean reports framed the divorce as Hines Ward Sr. abandoning Kim Young-hee (Ward's mother) and leaving her to fend for herself in the United States with poor English speaking skills and no support system. This particular narrative determination worked, because it accessed prior experiences of "mixed-race children born to US servicemen and Korean women who were often raised by single mothers after the American father returned home."[63] In portraying the relationship as an example of failed Black fatherhood, that relationship became a metaphor for the presence of the American military and its impotency in Korea. Ward's celebrity becomes a powerful tool in the Korean recuperation of masculinity. Ward's father and the military are constructed as a threatening masculine presence in Korea, and the United States as an evil presence in Asia. Against the malevolent presence of the United States, Korea gets to position itself as a moral and benevolent country. The reception in Korea regarding Ward's Super Bowl win allowed Korea to come to the rescue of this poor, abandoned biracial person, bestowing on him the praise he deserved but barely received in America, since familiar narratives of Black athletes rendered his performance as excellent and expected. [64] The celebration of Ward as Korean represented "the symbolic 'rescue' of national policy,"[65] and is in keeping with Jarvie's assertion that sport can act as a substitute for political nationalism. In order for this narrative to be successful, Ward had to be both Black (American) and Korean. Ward's Blackness is recontextualized so that instead of being a source of mistreatment by Koreans, it becomes instead a way for Koreans to position themselves as open and accepting of different iterations of Koreanness. Only Ward's Blasian identity would allow Korea to rhetorically and "systematically erase all but the most innocuous traces of the child's origins."[66] This particular strategy could raise the questions about "whether or not a multiethnic person can have two allegiances or whether she chooses one and, in so doing, betrays the other(s)."[67] However, for this rhetorical strategy to work Ward had to embrace both of his allegiances by asserting his Blasianness, so that politically and symbolically Korea could dominate America through its acceptance of mixed-race Ward.

Johnson's homecoming visit was not nearly as fraught as Ward's. Like Ward, Johnson was greeted with much fanfare and adulation, including front-page newspaper coverage,[68] high-ranking politician visits, and a concert.[69] Unlike Ward, who was not conferred birthright citizenship in

Korea, Johnson's Samoan citizenship was recognized as legitimate though he was born in the United States, because his mother is a Samoan citizen. So instead of citizenship, his honorary award was a title in recognition of his successes in the United States and the visibility and glory he had brought on/to Samoans. Then head of state, Susuga Malietoa Tanumafili II, bestowed on Johnson the title of Seiuli, which at its simplest can be translated to mean "high chief." It was a title also held by his grandfather, who then incorporated it into his wrestling personality. After being awarded the title, Johnson talked about how proud he was to be a Samoan, and he promised "the people of Samoa that he will represent Samoa with dignity and pride."[70]

Shortly after his visit to Samoa, Johnson visited one of the most famous indigenous tattoo artists in Hawai'i to have a traditional Samoan tattoo/*tatau* done. Tradition dictates this is done with a set of tattoo combs (called an *au*), a mallet, and ink, with the pain symbolizing the collective suffering of Pacific Islanders while denoting readiness to face what life demands.[71] Johnson's tattoo took approximately sixty hours, in twenty-hour sessions. He would go on to describe the significance of his tattoo thusly:

> The story of my tattoo is a very elaborate story, that are [*sic*] all the things that are important to me, that I love and are [*sic*] passionate about, that move me and are from the heart. I sat down with my tattoo artists and we talked for hours and we said a prayer, and we went to work. As we're telling the story, it's a story about my life and it's a story about my journey, but bigger than me and my life and my journey, but my ancestors and my culture on my dad's side, on my mom's side—my Black culture, my Samoan culture as well. All the things that are important to me from my family to protecting my family, my ancestors protecting all of us, the spirit of my ancestors. It represents in my tattoos great struggle and overcoming great struggle. Being appreciative of my success as we come up to the sunshine and the sun on my neck . . . it all comes down to three things, my family and protecting my family and having a very aggressive warrior spirit that you can't hold down.[72]

So Johnson's tattoo does the work of making his Samoan identity even more visible, as it can now be literally read on his body, though some Pacific Islanders point out his tattoo is not so authentically Samoan.[73] Still, he acknowledges that his tattoo encompasses the multitudes of his identity, especially racially, by symbolically incorporating both sides of his family. He has not left Blackness out, though he sports a traditional indigenous tattoo—but rather incorporates it into the design purposefully through acknowledgment of his ancestry. Blasianness renders attempts at policing racial boundaries as suspect, because it will always fail racial purity checks. As such, being transracial is not about distancing oneself from a particular identity, but rather about exposing the authenticity tests that accompany race as useless.

Tackling Race

On July 9, 2011, news broke about Blasian football star Hines Ward's arrest for driving under the influence of alcohol in suburban Atlanta. Many of his fans and supporters took to social media, especially Twitter and Facebook, to vocalize their disappointment in him and his actions. His manager and lawyer responded to the fallout with a statement that said Ward was both "not impaired by alcohol" as the arrest alleged and deeply apologetic for the "distraction" caused by his arrest.[74] After Ward pleaded guilty to reckless driving and no contest for failing to maintain his lane, he was sentenced to twelve months of probation, eighty hours of community service, and a $2,000 fine.[75] Incredibly, and in contrast to the fallout from the Tiger Woods scandal, Ward came out of the incident with his reputation intact, endorsements preserved, and a seemingly loyal fan base still behind him. While Ward does not have the same star status Tiger Woods enjoys, Ward did just weeks before his arrest win on ABC's hit show *Dancing with the Stars*, ensuring he had become a recognizable celebrity, not merely a decorated athlete.[76] I argue that part of what differentiated Ward from Woods is that Ward did not have to protect the colorblind multiculturalism that had been affixed to Woods's image, because Ward had already shown himself to be color conscious through his advocacy. In fact, as this excerpt from this *KoreAm* profile of Ward showcases, his version of Blasianness worked by explicitly embracing race:

> It reinforces the central assumption we have about him: that he's a good guy. Even as his fame has grown, there has been little to sully the impression. He seems to be stronger than the modern American celebrity machine. And for a man who has been the defender of biracial children in South Korea, a four-time Pro Bowl selection, a two-time Super Bowl champion, the Super Bowl XL MVP, a likely Hall of Fame inductee, a presidential advisor,

an honorary ambassador, and a *Dancing With the Stars* champion, Hines Ward's greatest accomplishment may be that, somehow, he seems to still just be Hines Ward.[77]

Ostensibly, Ward's very public embrace of his Blasian identity as shown through his homecoming trip and biracial children's foundation, Helping Hands, in Korea allows him to emerge untarnished from the "modern American celebrity machine." Though Ward and Woods enjoy different levels of celebrity, I would argue that the differences between the two lie in the discourses that frame each man, and the purposes of those narratives. Ward's Blasianness, arguably much more so than Woods's, is cemented firmly in discourses that make him much more legible to a multiracial, working-class football fan base, as opposed to the affluent Whiteness Woods must contend with in golf.

Ward did not always recognize the mutability and flexibility of his racial identities as a positive device. In the ESPN *Outside the Lines* documentary, he talked about growing up as a perpetual outsider noting he did not fit in with any group, because he was both Black and Korean, until he started playing and excelling at football:

> WARD: Going to school, Black kids teased me because I was Korean, so it was hard to try to fit in with Black kids because they always made fun of my Korean side. Well, trying to hang out with the Korean kids, they always teased me because I was Black, you know. Trying to hang out with White kids, they teased me because I was Black and Korean.
>
> NARRATOR: For an outcast in two worlds, the playing fields were a natural escape. During Ward's four years at Georgia and his eleven years with the Steelers, performance mattered more than ethnicity.[78]

Separating Ward's performance from his ethnicity is an impossible task, since the myriad ways he is discussed and represented are premised entirely on the recognition and misrecognition of his racially mixed body. It is crucial and necessary to contextualize the representation of Ward within institutionalized sport, because sport is a realm of cultural significance, and it provides a text that has become central to American identity.[79] Televised sport functions as a spectacle where social inequality can be imagined and understood through a competitive framework. The many inequalities of contemporary society are laid bare in the world of entertainment, particularly in the area of sports, since they "are more than just significant events, in and of themselves important, they [also] act as a key signifier for wider questions about identity within racially demarcated societies in which racial narratives about the self and society are read both into and from sporting contests that are imbued with racial meanings."[80] Certainly sport has been crucial in naturalizing gender roles and racial hierarchies in the United States.[81] In this realm of sport, as in so many other areas of popular culture, hegemonic ideas and values are created, maintained, and sometimes subverted, by groups using resources— economic, cultural, and political—to legitimate their ideologies.

Following Ward's homecoming trip to Korea, those questions from his youth about where to place him racially reappear once again but are complicated with the addition of transnational race narratives. Ward's philanthropic efforts in Korea coupled with continued focus on his immigrant Korean mother explicitly address the transnational nature of Blasians, and force a shift in the way US audiences read him. The trip brought out narratives of US military intervention in Asia, and reactions to that presence, and highlighted emergent globalized, national identities. Additionally, Ward has been used to recuperate Asian/American masculinity, both in the face of American military occupation of Asian countries, which itself signifies the emasculation Asians, and as resistance to the continued emasculation of Asian/American men in popular culture. Though he has been framed as both a threat and model minority, he is also used to challenge those perpetual framings. The discussion around Ward centered on nationalism, the work his Super Bowl win did for Blasians in the United States and Korea, and the representation of Blasian male athletes in popular culture. Curiously, narratives about Ward begin as the hypermasculine, athletically superior Black man,[82] progress (regress?) into yellow peril territory as he transforms into the Asian/American who is suspiciously sneaky and a cheater,[83] then finally settle on a discourse of mixed-race exceptionalism. Hines Ward and the negotiation of his Blasian identity provide a symbolic look at how exactly those racial narratives about self and society operate in sport.

Dwayne Johnson similarly negotiates racial representations that threaten to constrain his agency and identification strategies. Johnson openly played with racial identities during his wrestling career and currently does so as an actor in Hollywood. As a third-generation professional wrestler in the WWE, Johnson started out as a "face," meaning he was a good guy. It is worth nothing that he becomes a "heel," or a villain, only after joining the "Nation of Domination," which was a militant, pro-Black, Nation of Islam–parodying cadre of wrestlers.[84] As a heel his popularity soared, and the WWE made him a "face" once again, to capitalize on his immense fan base. In the WWE Johnson was a champion multiple times, semi-retiring as a "superstar" and as one of the most popular wrestlers ever. During his career in the WWE, Johnson was the first wrestler asked to host *Saturday Night Live*. During his first *SNL* episode (March 18, 2000), he told the audience during his opening monologue: "People tell me I look like a sexy Rob Schneider. The ladies have been calling me 'The Deuce Very Bigalow.'" Schneider, one of two mixed-race Asian/Americans[85] cast on *SNL*, had just starred in the movie *Deuce Bigalow: Male Gigolo*. The movie was billed as a "sex comedy," about a hapless male prostitute, and consisted of approximately two hours of dick jokes and twisted sexual banter. So "The Rock," who was at the time a villainous member of the Black Nationalist wrestling crew Nation (of Domination), was simultaneously recognizing his place alongside *SNL*'s first Asian/American cast member and highlighting the size of his penis to place himself within narratives of Black masculinity.

As Johnson started making the transition from the WWE to Hollywood action star, he became a cultural touchstone, particularly around ethnically ambiguous celebrities. *Family Guy*, an animated show on Fox, demonstrates the confusion around Johnson and where to place him racially. In an episode (season 4, episode 19) where the family dog is injured and runs away, the baby Stewie offers this piece of internal dialogue: "If he [Brian the dog] dies, I'm going to have to start hanging out with The Rock again." A fictional movie narrator then chimes in and describes the scene involving Stewie and The Rock: "One's a baby and the other's Black, I think, at least part Black. Or Hispanic. I think you know possibly there's some Filipino in there, yeah possibly some Filipino. I mean if he's Black, it's definitely diluted, I mean one of his parents must be White. What the hell is Jessica Alba, for that matter?" By the mid-2000s Johnson has become legibly Blasian—as evidenced by his being read as both Black and Filipino—but then his Blasian identity is rescinded by shows like *Family Guy* and replaced with a generic biracial identity. Then he is compared to another ethnically ambiguous mixed-race star, Jessica Alba. By this time multiracial chic was in vogue, and ethnically ambiguous people were being celebrated on screen and in print, so the ability to not just recognize multiraciality but to name specific instantiations points toward increasing legibility for Blasians.

When Johnson returned to host *SNL* for the third (March 7, 2009) and fourth (March 28, 2015) times, he played the aforementioned recurring character "The Rock Obama." His first turn as "The Rock Obama" finds Andy Samberg (playing then chief of staff Rahm Emanuel) telling Armisen's Obama to "get angry." Once Barack Obama morphs into The Rock Obama, he speaks in a pidgin English à la Tarzan. He tells the senators assembled for the sketch that he is just like "Barack Obama, just stronger and more impulsive." Which is in keeping with the framing of both Blacks and Pacific Islanders as childlike, impetuous, and passionate. Johnson's second turn as the alter ego for Pharoah's Obama shows him identifying himself to the assembled senators: "The Rock Obama, much like Barack Obama only larger and more violent." This time Johnson repeats the familiar framing of Pacific Islanders as large and couples it with the familiar framing of Blacks as violent. The balancing act between the two representations plays out on Johnson's mixed-race Blasian body, as he parodies the mixed-race Obama.

Equally as interesting as his character The Rock Obama were the choices and risks Johnson took during his opening monologue during his third and fourth visits to *SNL* as host. When he hosted for the third time, Johnson revealed his (quite pleasant) singing voice, with an original song called "Tough Guy." He assured the audience he was "just as tough as ever," while wearing a sequined vest and dancing the same very sexy and feminine, burlesque-like moves as his costars and some professional dancers. The studio audience showed their appreciation for his refusal to stand around as the women danced around him. As he performed every single move in sync with the dancers, his very large and masculine frame served to highlight the absurdity of their moves. When one cast member sings lyrics about a princess, he replies, "Who told you that was my nickname"? He talks about wearing makeup, and working with his "trainer" who is actually his "choreographer-slash-roommate." He ends the number in a bodybuilder pose, biceps flexed. One reading of this number might be that it is a homophobic piece meant to mock stereotypically gay tropes such as having a "roommate" and using feminized nicknames like "Princess." Instead, I read his opening performance as a rebuke of attempts to fix his identity based on some sort of cultural expectation or basis. Though obviously the opening number can be read as both a homophobic piece and a rebuke of those stereotypes, the uncertainty for viewers regarding whether or not he is supposed to be gay mirrors the anxieties around where to place Johnson racially. His Blasian body allows him to more easily adopt and challenge other ambiguities—here, sexuality and gender—as part of the politics of mixed race. The transectional nature of his Blasian identity transforms and is transformed by the ambiguities around both his sexuality and gender as they are implicated in the formation of his racialized identity.

When Johnson hosted *SNL* for the fourth time, he performed another original song for his opening monologue. This time the song was about being "Franchise Viagra." Johnson literally sings about his bankability as a star but pairs it with perceptions of his sexuality and masculinity with lines like, "Been in a lot of sequels and I've added an extra 'ooooomph' to a lot of franchises." This harks back to the utility of mixed-race celebrities and the economic benefit ethnic ambiguity imparts for those who possess it: "Oscar movies this year didn't make no dough, even *Birdman* could have used the People's Elbow." (The People's Elbow is a reference to one of his signature WWE moves.) Notably, however, Johnson sings about playing characters traditionally played by White actors, like "all the characters in Batman" or the next samurai—played confusingly by non-Asian/American actor Tom Cruise. Johnson ends the song by singing about how he could also play "the next president," which, like his character "The Rock Obama," serves to link Johnson to Obama. If the audience is still unclear about the purpose of the song, money rains down at the end of the number, driving home the economic potential of and in his mixed-race body.

Johnson's hypersexualized and commodified Blasian body parallels the commodification of Blasian video models. The success of Johnson's opening monologues hinges on the invocation of sex, the upending of expectations around sexuality and gender in his third appearance, and the perpetuation of hypersexuality in his fourth. Adding to the hypersexualization that already happens around bodies of color, the hypervisibility of racial ambiguity within the celebrity industrial complex becomes a key component of Blasianness. The cultural investment in narratives that script our understanding of racialized bodies, which are then attached explicitly to a language of commerce and consumption, encourages us to think about identities and performances of those identities as being authentically raced. And yet these Blasian entertainers upend those scripts by emphasizing and muddling the performative aspects of these identities and challenging the notions of authenticity that undergird them.

Changing the Game

After Ward's trip to Korea, there were some very public efforts to claim and promote him as Asian/American. Though from the early 2000s he had appeared on lists of Asian/Americans currently in the NFL, there was not as much public acknowledgment of his Korean identity. Upon his return from his first trip to Korea, Ward was asked to comment on topics ranging from the passing of President Roh Moo-hyun[86] to the tsunami and subsequent earthquakes that devastated Japan in 2011.[87] The website Disgrasian.com, which covers Asian/American pop culture and politics, twice named Ward their "Amazian of the Week" for "speaking up for ethnic Koreans . . . [and] kicking arse every time he rocks the Pro Bowl," and for being appointed to President Obama's Advisory Commission on Asian/Americans and Pacific Islanders.[88] He and his Helping Hands Foundation have been profiled in the *New York Times* for helping "half-Korean half something else" children gain acceptance in Korea, where the something-else refers to a self composed of a conflated ethnic, racial, and national identity.[89] His appointment to President Obama's advisory committee[90] was in recognition of the work Ward does on behalf of mixed-race Koreans. As the only celebrity appointed, Ward has emerged as "the public face" for the committee.[91] The coverage of him, and the public reclamation of Ward in the United States as Asian/American, had an impact on his football career, and his reception off the field.

Interestingly and not surprisingly, it was not until the season after Super Bowl XL and Ward's visit to Korea that criticisms about the way he played started. Though Ward's style of play had not changed, he was continually dogged by cries from players, fans, and the sports media that he is the "dirtiest" player in the NFL. The dirtiest-player label is almost always attached to a player of color who is criticized for being too aggressive or aggressive in what has been deemed the wrong ways. Ward's Blackness ensured that he was never described as physically inept, but his newly emphasized Asianness ensured he could be placed within narratives of scheming and untrustworthy Asian/Americans. Indeed, because of his physical prowess, when he "cheats" he does so in a physically overpowering manner, hence how both racial stereotypes converge to construct him effectively as a dirty player. Ward was labeled a dirty player because he blocked unsuspecting defenders, often and "crushingly," which had been a legal move until an NFL rule change.[92] A *Sports Illustrated* poll given to nearly three hundred NFL players labeled Ward *the* dirtiest player in the league at the time.[93] He once hit Keith Rivers of the Cincinnati Bengals so hard that Rivers's jaw was broken. Though that play was deemed a clean play, after that hit the NFL changed its rules on crack-back blocks—blindside blocks using the helmet, forearm, or shoulder to hit a player in the neck or head. Subsequently, sports media dubbed the policy the "Hines Ward Rule."[94] The dirty player label followed him while he was on *Dancing with the Stars*, moving beyond his football persona, suggesting that the cheating dimension of his character became part of his larger image off the field. *DWTS* recaps or comments about his performance on the show were accompanied with statements like, "Ward has developed a reputation around the NFL for being a tough and, at times, dirty player in his thirteen seasons,"[95] and, when Ward dropped his dance partner during a rehearsal for the show, "Around the NFL Hines Ward has a reputation for being a dirty player who dishes out cheap shots when nobody is looking and after he just went WWF pile driver on his Dancing the Start [*sic*] partner, Kym Johnson, I don't think it's gonna help his case."[96]

Still, Ward's turn on *DWTS* show had gone a long way to repair his reputation as a dirty player.[97] He insists he is not a dirty player, pointing out that since the rule change he has seen numerous crack-back hits in other games, but his are the only ones getting called.[98] There are some fans and sports writers who feel he should take the title of the dirtiest player in the NFL as a compliment, especially since the position he plays is rarely known for being tough or physical enough. Interestingly, in defending Ward against criticisms, Jim Rome on his show, *Rome Is Burning*, questions why "the allegedly dirtiest players in the NFL are always some of the best players?" He answers his own question: "It's because they spend their Sundays knocking guys out, making enemies." In the same segment Rome faux-innocently asks, "What has Ward ever done to anybody? I mean besides break their jaw or concuss them." He then differentiates between a dirty player and Ward by listing what dirty players do, "eye-gouging, stepping on [opponents'] hands, taking coin shots in the pile [hitting someone in the crotch]." Rome finishes the segment using words like "nasty," "filthy," and "violent" to explain why Ward should not be labeled a dirty player. He defends Ward's method of playing by noting it is not his fault his opponents are neither ready nor expecting to be hit by a wide receiver like Ward. He also encourages Ward to put his dirtiest player award on the mantel next to his Super Bowl trophies, "because this one is one that you can be proud of." Rome damns Ward with praise by using familiar racialized narratives of violence and aggression to highlight Ward's style of play. Asian/American men, like Black men, have also been framed, via yellow peril discourses, as being destructive, deceptive, and violent, making Ward's Blasianness the perfect vehicle to transport ideas that he is a dirty player.

The converse of the perilous construction of Asian/American athlete is the inferior but model minority. This particular construction of the Asian/ American athlete is a cause for cognitive dissonance within the American psyche, because as model minorities Asian/Americans are focused on assimilating but must then contend with "this Asian stereotype, portraying the Asian athlete as physically inept, that is most pervasive and accepted in American media."[99] Like the naturally skilled Black male athlete, this particular narrative of the Asian/American athlete is rooted in the biological. For example, Asian/Americans are "stereotyped as less athletic but hard working and more intelligent (hence, they are the model minority)."[100] Taking this essentialist approach is especially problematic, because it works together with equally problematic cultural narratives to prescribe acceptable roles and positions. So while Asian/American athletes are portrayed as not being as physically capable as their Black and White counterparts, when they do play they are tracked into positions that require "thinking" (i.e., pitcher) or particular sports where size is not a requirement for success.[101] Sport provides athletes a space where they "can lay claim to a masculine identity as a means of restoring a unified sense of racial identity, freed, if only momentarily, from the emasculating discourses imposed by the ideologies and practices of White racism."[102] Mayeda remarks on how the racialization of Asian athletes is indirectly also a comment on Black athletes: "If this positional racialization goes on without scrutiny, unproven and false images of both Asian and African Americans will be further essentialized in American minds."[103]

While Ferber claims that success in the field of athletics does nothing to undermine the historical propensity to reduce men of color to their bodies, others disagree. The playing field is not level in sports, yet it is possible "to challenge and overturn the dominant hierarchies of nation, race, and class."[104] Berlant points out that the political potential of intimate publics coming together within mass culture produced affective environments,[105] of which sport is obviously a key exemplar. The achievements of athletes of color should be read as a form of both collective and individual resistance. Focusing on multiple and intersecting identities necessarily means taking both identities and representations of those identities into account, while simultaneously also accounting for Blasian identity as specifically informed by the other two, yet different from them as well. It is precisely the hegemonic nature of sport that allows for contestation of the dominant ideologies and hierarchies. After all, as Messner points out, marginalized groups are able to "use sport as a means to resist (at least symbolically) the domination imposed upon them. Sport must thus be viewed as an institution through which domination is not only imposed, but also contested; an institution within which power is constantly at play."[106]

As such, Hines Ward and his position as an "outcast in two worlds" is an illustration of how a Blasian athlete can contest hegemonic norms and expectations of race and nation, both on and off the football field. As an outcast, Ward is able to negotiate the multiplicities of his identities in order to exhibit Asian/American masculinity, or Black congeniality, or a transnational/global identity that is rooted neither in the United States nor Korea, but somewhere in between. This liminality is constitutive of Ward's Blasianness—by which I mean that the contradiction between his subjection to racial stereotypes of both Blacks and Asian/Americans and his inability to be ordered into a familiar racial hierarchy is a critical element of the Blasian brand. As part of the celebrity industrial complex, the NFL attempted to leverage Ward's Blasianness to distinct consumer markets: the aggressive and dirty Ward to fans and corporations domestically, and the genial but appropriately masculine Ward to new markets internationally.

Redefining Nationalism

Muhammad Ali was stripped of his boxing title when he refused to fight in the Vietnam War, kicking off opposition to the war and the US government.[107] Just a year after Ali's conviction for draft evasion, Tommie Smith and John Carlos raised their fists while on the medal stand during the 1968 Olympics, their gesture becoming "one of the most recognized demonstrations of protest and resistance in the history of the United States athletics, and it was the perfect symbol of a generation."[108] Cathy Freeman was derided for carrying the Aboriginal flag after winning during the 1994 Commonwealth Games but praised in the Australian national press when she did it again after winning her race in the 2000 Sydney Olympics. Undoubtedly, sport is integral in building (or undermining) national identity, consciousness, and patriotism. Despite Ward's popularity during his visit to Korea, mixed-race Koreans noted that while they were proud of Ward as biracial Koreans, "[they] see the two faces of Korean society. Since when have they shown so much interest in half-Koreans?"[109] While that article referenced the manic levels of press and adulation Ward received during his trip, the quote can be extended to include the new policies Korea began to enact in recognition of the work done by Ward's Blasian identity. During the months leading up to the visit by Ward and his mother, the focus on the plight of biracial and multi-racial Koreans prompted the government to begin "a long-term project to redefine the meaning of being Korean and the meaning of the nation as well as educating people on cultural relativism."[110] A redefinition of Korean citizenship was necessary, obviously because the previous defi-nitions were created during periods of Chinese and Japanese imperial-ism as a form of resistance to both of those countries. The discrimination faced by mixed-raced Amer/Euro/Afro-Asians stemmed from "lingering memories of past oppression by foreign powers and the continual pres-ence of US troops on [Korean] soil."[111] Ward's Blasian body is instrumental in exposing the contradictions between how Korea had previously vilified its racially mixed subjects, with their intimate connections to US military imperialism, only to glorify those same bodies after they were extended legitimacy via Ward's celebrity status and its cachet within the celebrity industrial complex.

As Korea becomes more globalized, the successes of Blasian celebrities like Ward are emphasized "not [for] merely leading us in becoming more globalized, but also towards becoming more patriotic, as they are proud of their roots."[112] Ward's successes and subsequent lionization in Korea have allowed Korean-born Blasians like Jamie Boyd and Suan Yoo (both included in a profile on Ward for *KoreAm* magazine) to proclaim a Korean identity.[113] When asked how they identify, Boyd replied, "'I'm Korean.' Now it's so natural for me, but before I didn't really want to talk about it. It kind of made me grow seeing how [Ward] handles stuff, and just seeing him, it just changed everything."[114] Through the country's acceptance and recep-tion of Ward, he challenges a Korean nationalism that previously excluded bi/multiracial Koreans. The discourses around him—namely, his skill as a football player, the absence of his father, and the subsequent rescue of a "fatherless" Ward by Korea, together create a specific Korean national identity that centers on Ward as the key player. Ward and this new Korean identity become a symbol for the influences and flows of globalization and sport. With the implementation of new policies regarding mixed-race Koreans and the conferral of honorary citizenship to Hines Ward and actual citizenship to thousands of biracial and multiracial Koreans, the national narrative has been forcibly changed because a Blasian athlete became MVP of a Super Bowl in the United States.

Sport as an institution becomes particularly meaningful in communities of color since it both reinforces inequalities and offers avenues for social change. The utility of these two stars as case studies for Blasianness lies in the ways they both embody hegemonic scripts and disrupt normative racialized masculinist codes, even while concurrently using their Blasian identities to envision empowerment collectively between and amongst people of color. Take, for instance, the way Ward was racialized within a familiar narrative of US military imperialism and the disappearing Black father while simultaneously transforming narratives of nation building and identity. Though I talk about both Ward and Johnson in terms of Asian/American and Black narratives of sporting bodies of color, they draw attention to the precariousness of those narratives. That the hypermasculinity of both men does not constrain Johnson from singing show tunes or Ward from ballroom dancing allows their anomalies to become incorporated into how Blasians are branded.

CONCLUSION

En-Blasianing the Future

In the summer of 2011, the Public Broadcasting Service (PBS) aired a documentary series on Korean cuisine, titled *The Kimchi Chronicles*.[1] The host and focus of the show was Marja Vongerichten, wife of world-famous chef Jean-Georges Vongerichten, and a Blasian. The show was billed as both a look into the rising popularity of Korean food and a journey of self-discovery for Vongerichten, who was born to a Black father and a Korean mother, orphaned, and then adopted by a Black family in the United States.[2] In the concluding segment of the food and identity series, Vongerichten summed up the experience hosting the documentary by summarizing her life:

> Coming back to Korea now as an adult, some thirty years after being put up for adoption, is always in and of itself a special occasion for me. Now when I come back to Korea I'm coming home to family. . . . Most amazing of all, my sweet little grandmother—she's seen it all, Korea's struggles and Korea's triumphs. We may look like two unrelated creatures and live halfway around the world from each other, but I hold her as a role

model. . . . My life has come full circle; it began with a single mom and an orphanage, and now I've come back to chronicle the tastes and traditions of Korea for you."

While she narrates the details of her life, viewers watch her at a beach picnic with members of her extended Korean family—her aunts, her cousins, and her grandmother. They sing traditional Korean folk songs and share stories while they eat. The focus of the scene eventually settles on Vongerichten and her grandmother as they sit next to each other and visibly enjoy each other's company. The producer in an interview noted the plan originally was to use a famous Korean American chef, but ultimately Vongerichten was chosen because her story embodied "the true Korean-American spirit. Somebody born in Korea, but yet gets adopted, and then finds her family. I think a lot of us Korean Americans have that issue, not just necessarily with adoption, but just finding our own identities. . . . Her story made our story even better."[3] That a mixed-race Black and Asian/American person would be chosen to be the global face of Korean cuisine and identity, and for a series intended to be a primer of sorts for those unfamiliar with Korea and its culture, no less, highlights the trajectory this book works to uncover, and symbolizes the successes of Blasian branding within popular culture. Her participation in the series also highlights the utility of her celebrity in the production of this Blasian brand. In addition to being married to one of the world's most visible and successful chefs, Vongerichten goes through the experience with her neighbors, movie stars Hugh Jackman and Heather Graham. Though she is not nearly as recognizable or as popular as her husband or famous neighbors, the status she is afforded via her proximity to those celebrities allows her to benefit from the machinations of the celebrity industrial complex. For example, to garner publicity for the project, she is interviewed by the leading Black women's magazine, *Essence*, where Vongerichten shares important bits of information such as, "I like to refer to Korean food as the soul food of Asia because it really is reminiscent of a lot of the cooking and stewing techniques we use in African-American soul food."[4] She uses "we" to place herself necessarily within Blackness while at the same time promoting her Koreanness. Importantly, as part of the celebrity industrial complex Vongerichten, like the other Blasian celebrities, becomes a barometer for the racial climate both in the United States and globally as we see the shifts and tensions around racialization scripted onto her body.

In the final scene of the documentary Vongerichten and her family offer themselves as a sight/site to behold:

> We have our entire family, which for me is truly a special occasion. My childhood was spent piecing together my family, my loving American parents and a mom back in Korea who I could only try to remember—threads of who I was and where I came from. Now my family is rich in relatives, and when we join our Korean, American, and French forces we are quite the international mixed-race sight to behold.

The value of *transracial* becomes apparent in Vongerichten's story, as the more familiar label to describe international adoptions between parents who do not share the same racial identity as their adopted child, which in turn becomes evidence for how cultural and biological framings of race fall apart. Vongerichten's life highlights the limits of using *transracial* to describe her adoption, particularly since she and her adoptive parents share a racial identity. Though they are linked together phenoperceptively as a Black family, the biological framing of race allows her to also claim a Korean identity. However, since she fails to be phenoperceived as a Korean person and shaped by that perception, the cultural policing of race suggests she should be excluded from Asianness. In other words, if part of the experience of Blackness, Whiteness, or Koreanness, in the case of Vongerichten, is that one be ascribed an identity and then subsequently treated as such, can someone who fails to fit into those discrete categories still have the ability to claim that identity? Obviously, I believe the answer is yes, and I use Blasians to demonstrate the possibilities of that very phenomenon. Like Ward, Johnson, Simmons, Woods, and the other Blasians mentioned herein, Vongerichten becomes a symbol of a radical racial amalgamation. She encapsulates the category-spoiling inherent in Blasianness, the inability to be placed within one or another category. Furthermore, because she does not use her Asian/American identity to distance herself from Blackness, or vice versa, she (and Blasians generally) offers an alternative embodied experience of race and racial performance.

The Future of Mixed-Race Studies

Crucially, a third frame of racialization exists, one that sees mixed race as neither new nor unique nor as a racial salve to move the United States past the problem of the color line. This third paradigm is pluralistic, fluid in its ambiguity, and allows mixed-race people and studies to not only "sustain contradictions," but to "[turn] the ambivalence into something else."[5] This paradigmatic shifting view of race rearticulates what it means to be Black, Asian/American, or Other, and results in the creation of multiracial/other subjectivities that can become a formidable obstacle to the racial order of the United States. Importantly, Blasians trouble the logic of existing US racial classifications without establishing their own. Though Blasians have become increasingly more legible, there will never be a Blasian box on demography forms for people to check. What discourse exists about the racial mixing of Blacks and Asian/Americans with each other reveals there are some different tensions and issues about this particular mixture that do not arise when talking about White + other racially mixed people. It also reveals, unsurprisingly, that media discourses about Blasians follow the path of least resistance: they mostly follow along with hegemonic scripts already created, reproduced, and familiar to their audiences about monoracially identified Blacks and Asian/Americans, and of mixed-race people as "postracial" salves in order to frame them in very particular and recognizable ways.

In the previous chapters I do not offer Blasians as a racial salve, as resistant to or prescription for either race or racism by virtue of their mixed-race bodies. Instead, I have described the emergence of Blasians, not to add to the research that divides monoracials from multiracials, but to muddle the lines between them. The analyses of these celebrities acknowledge that to understand what and who is a Blasian means to first understand hegemonic notions of both Blacks and Asian/Americans. Contextualized against those dominant discourses, Blasians explode the narrow boundaries of authenticity around racialized categories. Blasians do not escape race or erase race, but they do deconstruct normative instantiations of identity. Additionally, the branding of Blasians engages hegemonic Whiteness and its attendant privileges, and helps to reframe the sociopolitical contexts of racial identity formation in the United States. Furthermore, if Blasians can pick and choose which aspects of identity to highlight when it is suitable or beneficial, and media also pick and choose which aspects of identity to highlight, the sheer number of possible identity combinations at any point in time allows Blasians to confront and challenge essentializing discourses by engaging the fluidity of their subjectivities and exposing the nonsensical attempts to fix their race in a particular point or space.

While I have always considered myself Black, Asian/American, and Blasian for a number of reasons, including because I moved transnationally several times as a child and grew up with friends and family members who were also mixed-race Black and Asian/American, this book came about for two reasons: the need to reject the rhetoric of racial math that accompanies racial mixing, and because I noticed an increase in the number and frequency of images and stories in popular culture about Blasians. To the first point, I think about the subject in Kip Fulbeck's *The Hapa Project* who identifies himself as 100 percent Black and 100 percent Japanese. His rejection of an illogical racial formula to explain his identity also acts as a rejection of the idea that individuals are removed from having to do these calculations because they embody racial purity.[6] To the second point and the growing popularity of this Blasian identity, I began to wonder how people came to identify with this label and what sort of maneuvers and discourses enabled Black and Asian/American identity's spread through media and popular culture. Omi and Winant's theory of racial formation suggests that views of race change over time and constitute a new racial milieu and context in which race relations take place. Historical, cultural, and political transformations therefore affect a given racial formation within a particular time period. Thus, there is a new commonsense understanding about race affecting groups and individuals so that the emergence of Blasians is both evidence of a new racial formation and part of the developing racial formation itself. Blasians as a brand, as marketable commodities, challenge current racial hegemony by forcing the contextualization of historical conditions, race and racialized tropes, and resistance to racialization. The emergence of these celebrities has played a not-insignificant role in helping prompt shifts surrounding multiracial identity discourses (like Tiger Woods, as a key celebrity figure, played in the decisive inclusion of racial "options" on the 2000 US Census) and forced popular media to recognize the significant dynamics that have arisen as a result of the boundary-blurring racialization occurring within the ways and means Blasians are represented.

Racecraft

Though this book analyzes the presence, mobility, and utility of these multiracial celebrities within both US and global racial schemas, I use these Blasians to complicate and explore potential alternatives to these racial and racist paradigms. I ask if there is a way to acknowledge that race is an illusion that has inequitable material impact on our lived realities without also strengthening that illusion by reinscribing and maintaining its centrality to the structure of society. Race, as a socially constructed entity, is not measurable in molecular-biological units, yet researchers—from sociologists to geneticists to media and cultural studies scholars—have found ways to racially identify and classify populations. Karen and Barbara Fields coined the term "racecraft" to describe this phenomenon—the application of scientific logic to the fiction, or "folk thought," of race.[7] They note that racecraft is the space that exists between "science and superstition"[8] and involves a "complex system of beliefs, also with combined moral and cognitive content, that presuppose invisible, spiritual qualities underlying, and continually acting upon, the material realm of beings and events."[9] Race becomes a product of the execution of racism, instead of the progenitor of racism.

They go on to invoke witchcraft in their analysis of racism and inequality in order to understand the "processes of reasoning that manage to make both plausible. Witchcraft and racecraft are imagined, acted upon, and re-imagined, the action and imagining inextricably intertwined."[10] Even in my reimagining of the ways Blasian bodies could complicate race, I am still rooting my analysis in extant racial paradigms. In their comparison and examination of the invisible ontologies presupposed by both witchcraft and racecraft, the Fieldses use the falsity of witchcraft to highlight the falsity of racecraft. In the comparison they note that witchcraft and racecraft share intellectual commonalities such as "circular reasoning, prevalence of confirming rituals, barriers to disconfirming factual evidence, self-fulfilling prophecies, multiple and inconsistent causal ideas, and colorfully inventive folk genetics."[11] For example, the visibility, the phenoperceptiveness, of race acts like an index for the invisible traits that have already been ascribed to bodies. In chapter 1 I pointed out the irony of offering mixed-race bodies as a way out of race, since racial mixing centers the existence and importance of races as pure and quantifiable entities capable of being combined into discrete combinations. For that reason I focused on how these stars perform and enact Blasianness (and Asianness, Blackness, Whiteness, et al.), because analyzing race is impossible without examining how beliefs about race and consequently racial differences confer meanings and properties to bodies differently and inequitably. Similarly, the Fieldses emphasize the importance of examining the construction and maintenance of racecraft in order to critique its existence:

> I assign the English suffix -craft to both in the same right for we need the component of socially ratified *making* or *doing* and its companion, the

socially ratified *belief* that travels before and after it, as input and as output. Marking the terms linguistically with–*craft* announces that the workings of those phenomena are not open to objective or experimental demonstration, that is to say by anyone, anywhere, and independent of doing or believing. We all can be more certain that witchcraft exists than that witches do. The same holds for racecraft and races.[12]

Distance allows us to understand witchcraft as nonsensical, but for those who were unable to see the irrationality of witchcraft even as it structured societies then, we are reluctant to engage the irrationality of racecraft even as it structures society currently. The Fieldses illustrate that historically for people grappling with witchcraft (and by extension contemporaneously with racecraft) ,"their understandings about the world took for granted the existence of an active, well-populated invisible realm that manifested itself in the realm of the seen, as real things, events, and persons. Everyday experience reinforced those understandings, which in turn had bearing on everyday behavior and in the recounting of events."[13] In other words, facilitators of racecraft find racial differences so obvious they do not have to be "scientifically demonstrable" to be certain of the existence of race and the consequences of race. It is important to point out here that ignoring the making and doing of racecraft is not an effective strategy for addressing the structuring power of racism and race. In other words this is not an opportunity for those who embrace notions such as reverse racism or take an anti–affirmative action stance to point to this chapter as support for their ideologies. I reiterate that abolishing labels for race[14] or the idea of race itself[15] does not eliminate or change our material realities and the lived experiences.[16] As I have demonstrated with these Blasian celebrities, being mixed race does not automatically challenge the racial schema, as multiracial people are just as capable of upholding hierarchies of gender, sexuality, race, class, and so forth as they are of dismantling the hierarchies. What these mixed-race stars do, however, is draw attention to how risible and absurd the biological and cultural premises for racialization truly are and demonstrate potential alternatives for affiliation that do not rely on genetic material.

Amplifying Ambiguity

Gregory Carter, in his book *The United States of the United Races*, traces the competing narratives of racialization around US President Barack

Obama. In his detailed examination he recounts how stakeholders tried successfully (and not so successfully) to conscript and identify Obama as: Black, biracial, multiracial, African American, White, and postracial. I wondered then, given these various identifications available to Obama, if Obama could also be considered Blasian. Born of a Kenyan father but having been raised by his Indonesian stepfather, in both Hawai'i and Indonesia, he has made references in his biography and in his speeches to being raised in a melting pot that includes an Indonesian mixed-race sister and multiracial Asian/American nieces, and Kenyan siblings and their children:

> In a sense, I have no choice but to believe in this vision of America. As a child of a black man and white woman, someone who was born in the racial melting pot of Hawaii, with a sister who is half-Indonesian but who's usually mistaken for Mexican or Puerto Rican, and a brother-in-law and niece of Chinese descent, with some blood relatives who resemble Margaret Thatcher and others who could pass for Bernie Mac, I've never had the option of restricting my loyalties on the basis of race or measuring my worth on the basis of tribe.[17]

He has championed Asian/American issues, restoring a White House initiative (which counts Hines Ward as a member) whose sole purpose is to address issues concerning the Asian/American and Pacific Islander communities. He has used the extrajudicial shooting of Trayvon Martin to embrace Blackness, including his own. His foregrounding of stories about his mother and her family also places him within some familiar narratives of Whiteness. His concurrent embrace and rejection of racialization strategies mirrors those adopted by Blasian celebrities. Carter, citing the work of John McWhorter, notes the potential of Obama's body politics to "bring us even closer to the goal of the end of race . . . an Obama presidency [suggests] that his presence would change their perception of success, racial authenticity, and racism. Inequality would still exist, but the next generation's understanding of its solutions would move away from the identity politics that the present and past generations had employed to address it."[18] Interestingly, Obama also embodies a critique of race as the sole means for building community and offers an alternative for kinship not predicated on race. Obama exposes the precarity of race by revealing how its place within visual regimes of "truth" does and will result in failure. Though narratives of race are grounded in phenoperception, mixed-race people demonstrate every day why those narratives are flawed and faulty. Fielding quotidian questions about "what are you" or experiencing "racial outings" only serves to underscore the limits of the visual as it pertains to race. So then perhaps it is better to think about race in terms of culture—authentic means of being, acting, speaking, performing race. Yet this idea of culture and race also fails spectacularly, because it is impossible for culture to cover all members of a racialized group. Furthermore, using culture as a stand-in for race is merely a test of authenticity; every time someone tells me, "You don't sound Black," or says backhandedly "I thought all Asians were good at math," only points to failures for the cultural basis of race. Failing to uphold hegemonic tenets of a particular racial group becomes, then, a failure to be that race. Importantly, this cultural framing of race is deployed unevenly, so when Ariana Miyamoto adheres to behaviors and actions that align with Japanese-ness more strictly than monoracially identified Japanese people, she is still denied that particularly identity. This leaves open the possibility of the converse—is it possible to be Black, Asian/American, or a member of any other racialized group, based solely on performance? Certainly, Rachel Dolezal's claim to Blackness was read in some circles as especially strong—she had the performance of Blackness perfected—from head to heart. Yet judging from the reaction to Dolezal, culture as race has its limits. Where Dolezal erred was in her failure to note the unevenness of race as a performance—when she is done performing Blackness, she can always return to the welcoming embrace of Whiteness. For most people of color to perform Whiteness authentically, there must be a complementary chromatic visuality.

Obama exists in the space between being biologically determined and socially constructed. He is part of how I envision the future of multiracials and critical mixed-race studies. It is necessary to peel back the many layers surrounding race and identification in the United States in order to redefine what multiracial means. Just as we have moved away from using blood quantum, matrilineal lineage, and sometimes hypodescent[19] to determine racial identity, the shifting and contestation that occur around multiracials need to be considered within racial formation theories. Specifically, taking into consideration the transracial potential of mixed-race bodies is a call for some new paradigms to accommodate theories about identity, community, and inequality that acknowledge racism (and other oppressions) without centering race. In other words if one thinks, as I have argued in this book, that being Blasian is not the same as combining monoracial Blackness with monoracial Asianness, then labeling Obama our first Asian/American president should bear out my argument.

I spend the greater part of the introductory chapter arguing that theorizing Blasians as a brand allows me to look at the intersections of identity, analyze them as a group of people who are framed by multiple and contradictory discourses, and rearticulate the meaning of race and mixed race. In stressing the transections of identity, and the pluralized view of ourselves these mutually constitutive identity formations command, this book lays the foundation that multiple subjectivities should always be taken into account even if media and societal understandings of race are limiting. These Blasian celebrities self-consciously offer versions of themselves that render the artificial indistinguishable from the real, contributing to a representation that destabilizes what it means to be *both* Black and Asian/American. Their embodied performance of Blasianness indicates a refusal to settle for what is visible and allows for the contestations of hegemonic notions of identity, which in turn opens up a space to question racial categorizations and hierarchies. Blasians are branded by their simultaneous embrace and eschewal of the visual and performative expectations of both Blackness and Asian/Americanness. The lack of consistency in media coverage of these celebrities should be taken as a space of potentiality. They do not offer themselves as a new racial formation; instead they show how different configurations of identification might ultimately aid in formulating new approaches for dismantling systemic oppressions and inequalities.

Blasian celebrities are central to my book because these mixed-race stars have sometimes come to represent "the multiracial neutral in that their images sell the idea of racial pluralism and freedom, and yet their images remain other, available for audiences and consumers of all racial backgrounds to claim or own."[20] The multiraciality of Blasian stars, and other mixed-race celebrities, allows media to use whatever component of those stars they wish, to serve whichever end they choose. Though media stories discussing these Blasian stars are many and varied, my project finds they are mostly incapable of addressing these celebrities as wholes, instead choosing to foreground and commodify particular dimensions of their identity.[21] This has resulted in the idea that mixed-race stars are fragmented, unclear about who they are, and confused, when in reality it is media that have disaggregated and disarticulated Blasian identity in such a way that a complete picture of these Blasians, as with other stars of color, is impossible. I also find that Blasian celebrities differ from other biracial stars in that their marketability is not wrapped up in racial ambiguity they cannot approximate. Unlike stars such as Vin Diesel or Kristin Kreuk, who can access the universalizing potential of Whiteness, Blasian celebrities may not allow most audiences to see themselves reflected in these stars. Blasians, despite potentially offering a multiracial neutrality, are not always able to stand in for *every* body. This book ultimately reveals that, despite the best attempts by media and audiences to fit these stars into familiar frames, it is impossible to squeeze the entirety of their Blasian identity into recognizable categories all of the time. The representations of these celebrities do not always fit our expectations, including of mixed-raceness, and certainly not of singular cultural identities like Blackness or Asianness. In other words, I contextualize some of the material and historical conditions that both enable and constrain Blasian engagement with popular culture. Those conditions have given stars access to sundry representational apparatuses, such as social media and other digital technology, which has allowed for more than one image of these stars to exist simultaneously in the popular imaginary.

Possibly the most important intervention this research on Blasians makes is that *transracial*, despite the handwringing that accompanied Dolezal's usage of it, is a useful and necessary concept. Furthermore these subjectivities escape the anti-Black, self-loathing, blindly celebratory logics of previous research on mixed race and offer a way of reconceptualizing race through its disruption of the racial order of society. Also important is the acknowledgment that the ascription of race by media and society is formidable, but the conflict between ascription and identification opens up a realm of possibilities. This reframing of the centrality of race does not mean that we have entered a postrace era or that colorblindness truly has been the key to solving issues of oppression and discrimination. Blasianness challenges extant discursive identity models by recognizing the ways identities and subjectivities evolve, and shift, and potentially change. Furthermore, if prevalent notions of racial authenticity, or realness, can be overcome, then the opportunities for building coalitions across the pluralities of subjectivities and identities grow exponentially. Lastly, by not privileging Blasian identity over both monoracial Black or Asian/American identities, this book opens up the possibility of studying race and mixed race in ways that do not sustain racial disparities. In other words, *transracial* is not only useful in disrupting race, but it is also an antiracist research position. It complements the aims of Critical Race theorists, ethnic and cultural studies scholars, and others invested in examining and eliminating racial and affiliated oppressions, by allowing critiques of the insidiousness of racism and racial categorization while pushing for alternate strategies for identification and solidarity building.

As I conclude this book, I am looking at a list of Blasians that I began compiling at the inception of this project. The list originally contained names of famous, kind of famous, and slightly famous Blasian people. Then, as friends and family understood the direction of my project, they contributed names to the list. It has now expanded to include the names of people I have met as I was writing who have identified themselves to me as Blasian, and the names of others within their families and communities who also think of themselves as Blasian. I tried not to write this book using the generalizing notion that "all Blasians are like this," since "all" presumes a culture-as-race aspect, which I have noted fails to account for the experiences of every person in a particular group. So I end this book where I started, with a rapidly growing list of people whose existence rejects the ideal of theoretically pure races through their Blasianness, offering less predictable, multifaceted identities ripe for building new avenues of kinship and for subverting current paradigms of racialization.

Notes

Chapter One: Theorizing Blasians

1. Will Ripley, "Biracial Beauty Queen Called Not Japanese Enough," *CNN*, March 25, 2015, http://www.cnn.com/2015/03/25/asia/japans-biracial-beauty-queen/; Peter Holley, "Japan's Half-Black Miss Universe Says Discrimination Gives Her 'Extra Motivation,'" *Washington Post*, May 13, 2015, https://www.washingtonpost.com/news/morning-mix/wp/2015/05/13/japans-half-black-miss-universe-says-discrimination-gives-her-extra-motivation/; Noël Duan, "Biracial Miss Japan Ariana Miyamoto Is Changing Perceptions of Beauty in Japan," *Yahoo.com*, March 24, 2015, https://www.yahoo.com/beauty/biracial-miss-japan-ariana-miyamoto-is-changing-114496707273.html; Martin Fackler, "Biracial Beauty Queen Challenges Japan's Self-Image," *New York Times*, May 29, 2015, http://www.nytimes.com/2015/05/30/world/asia/biracial-beauty-queen-strives-for-change-in-mono-ethnic-japan.html.

2. I capitalize *Black* and *White* throughout this book because its use refers to culture, ethnicity, or a group of people in the same way as Asian, Latinx, Arab, et al. I do not capitalize their use when directly quoting others in transcription, as they might not agree with my reasoning.

3. Fackler, "Biracial Beauty Queen Challenges."

4. Audrey Akcasu, "'Haafu' to Represent Japan at Miss Universe 2015," *Japan Today*, March 17, 2015, http://www.japantoday.com/category/lifestyle/view/haafu-to-represent-japan-at-miss-universe-2015.

5. Ripley, "Biracial Beauty Queen Called."

6. Brian Ashcraft, "The Face of Japan Is Changing but Some Aren't Ready," *Kotaku*, March 13, 2015, http://kotaku.com/the-face-of-japan-is-changing-but-some-arent-ready -1691234262.

7. Ripley, "Biracial Beauty Queen Called."

8. Elaine Lies and Shori Ito, "Multiracial Miss Japan Hopes to Change Homeland's Thinking on Identity," *Reuters*, April 2, 2015, http://www.reuters.com/article/2015/04/02 /us-japan-beauty-multiracial-idUSKBN0MT0TU20150402.

9. Michael Fitzpatrick and Tim Macfarlane, "'I've Been Called N****r and Had Trash Thrown at Me': First Mixed Race Miss Japan Hits Out at the 'Spasmodic Vomit of Racial Abuse' She's Suffered Because Father Is African-American," *Daily Mail*, April 1, 2015, http:// www.dailymail.co.uk/news/article-3021032/First-mixed-race-Miss-Japan-Ariana-Myamoto -hits-spasmodic-vomit-racial-abuse-suffered-father-African-American.html.

10. Duan, "Biracial Miss Japan."

11. Sarah Banet-Weiser, *The Most Beautiful Girl in the World: Beauty Pageants and National Identity* (Berkeley: University of California Press, 1999), 59.

12. Duan, "Biracial Miss Japan."

13. Banet-Weiser, *Most Beautiful Girl*, 3.

14. I use Asian/American to highlight the conflation of Asian American with Asian despite their status in the United States stemming from the refusal to acknowledge the citizenship and/or immigrant status of the group writ large. I opt to use the slash instead of writing Asian and Asian Americans because, as David Palumbo-Liu notes, the slash represents "a choice between two terms, their simultaneous and equal status, and an element of indecidability, that is, as it at once implies both exclusion and inclusion." (*Asian/American: Historical Crossings of a Racial Frontier* [1999], 1).

15. Kevin Lynch, *The Image of the City* (Cambridge: MIT Press, 1960), 2–3.

16. Leslie Bow, "Transracial/Transgender: Analogies of Difference in *Mai's America*," *Signs* 35 (2009): 75–103, 80.

17. Stuart Hall, "Subjects in History: Making Diasporic Identities," in *The House That Race Built*, ed. Wahneema Lubiano (New York: Vintage Books, 1998), 299.

18. "Zak Heaton: Aqua Artistry," *Seattle Times*, February 15, 2001.

19. Wei Ming Dariotis, "Hapa: The Word of Power," *Hyphen Magazine*, December 3, 2007, http://mixedheritagecenter.org/index.php?option=com_content&task=view&id =1259&Itemid=34.

20. Patricia Morton, "From Invisible Man to 'New People': The Recent Discovery of American Mulattoes," *Phylon* 46 (1985): 106–22.

21. Brian Stross, "The Hybrid Metaphor: From Biology to Culture," *Journal of American Folklore* 112 (1999): 254–67.

22. Greg Carter, "Hybrid Vigor: The Transformation of a Scientific Racialist Idea," *American Studies Association National Conference*, November 2004, Atlanta.

23. Daniel McNeil and Leanne Taylor, "Radical Love: A Transatlantic Dialogue about Race and Mixed Race," *Asian American Literary Review* 4 (2013): 15–26.

24. Gayatri Chakravorty Spivak, "Imperialism and Sexual Difference," *Oxford Literary Review* 8 (1986): 225–44.

25. See: Richard Delgado and Jean Stefancic, *Critical Race Theory: An Introduction* (New York: New York University Press, 2001); bell hooks, *Black Looks: Race and Representation*

(Boston: South End Press, 1992); Henry Jenkins, *Textual Poachers: Television Fans and Participatory Culture* (London: Routledge, 1992).

26. Maria P. P. Root, ed., *The Multiracial Experience: Racial Borders as the New Frontier* (Thousand Oaks, CA: Sage, 1996).

27. G. Reginald Daniel, *More than Black: Multiracial Identity and the New Racial Order* (Philadelphia: Temple University Press, 2002).

28. Root, *Multiracial Experience*, 3–14.

29. Lewis Gordon, *Her Majesty's Other Children: Sketches of Racism from a Neocolonial Age* (Lanham, MD: Rowman & Littlefield, 1997).

30. David Parker and Miri Song, eds., *Rethinking "Mixed Race"* (London: Pluto Press, 2001).

31. Laurie M. Mengel, "Triples—the Social Evolution of a Multiracial Panethnicity: An Asian American Perspective," in *Rethinking "Mixed Race,"* ed. David Parker and Miri Song (London: Pluto Press, 2001), 104.

32. Nathan Douglas, "Declaration of Racial Independence," 1997, *Interracial Voice*, 2010, http://www.webcom.com/~intvoice/natdoug2.html.

33. Jared Sexton, *Amalgamation Schemes: Antiblackness and the Critique of Multiracialism* (Minneapolis: University of Minnesota Press, 2008), 17.

34. Ibid.; Rainier Spencer, "Assessing Multiracial Identity Theory and Politics: The Challenge of Hypodescent," *Ethnicities* 4 (2004): 357–79; Paul Spickard, "Does Multiraciality Lighten? Me-Too Ethnicity and the Whiteness Trap," in *Crossing Lines: Race and Mixed Race across the Geohistorical Divide*, ed. Marc Coronado, Rudy P. Guevarra Jr., Jeffrey Moniz, and Laura Furlan Szanto (Santa Barbara: University of California, 2003), 45–62; Naomi Zack, *Race and Mixed Race* (Philadelphia: Temple University Press, 1993); Maria P. P. Root, *Love's Revolution: Interracial Marriage* (Philadelphia: Temple University Press, 2001); Kimberly DaCosta, "Remaking the Color Line: Social Bases and Implications of the Multiracial Movement" (Berkeley: University of California, 2000); Daniel, *More than Black?*

35. Paul Spickard, "Does Multiraciality Lighten?"

36. Susan Koshy, "Morphing Race into Ethnicity: Asian Americans and Critical Transformations of Whiteness," *Boundary* 2 28 (2001): 153–94; Min Zhou, "Are Asian Americans Becoming 'White'?," *Contexts* 3 (2004): 29–37; Mia Tuan, *Forever Foreigners or Honorary Whites? The Asian Ethnic Experience Today* (New Brunswick: Rutgers University Press, 1998).

37. See: George Kitahara Kich, "*Eurasians: Ethnic/Racial Identity Development of Biracial Japanese/White Adults*" (PhD diss., California Institute of Professional Psychology, 1982); Christine Catherine Iijima Hall, "The Ethnic Identity of Racially Mixed People: A Study of Black-Japanese" (PhD diss., University of California, Los Angeles, 1980); Michael C. Thornton, "A Social History of a Multiethnic Identity: The Case of Black Japanese Americans" (PhD diss., University of Michigan, 1983); Michael C. Thornton and Henry Louis Gates, "Black, Japanese and American: An Asian American Identity Yesterday and Today," in *The Sum of Our Parts: Mixed Heritage Asian Americans*, ed. Teresa Williams-Leon and Cynthia L. Nakashima (Philadelphia: Temple University Press, 2001), 93–105; Kent A. Ono, "Communicating Prejudice in the Media: Upending Racial Categories in *Doubles*," in *Communicating Prejudice*, ed. Michael L. Hecht (Thousand Oaks, CA.: Sage, 1998), 206–20; Jungmiwha Suk Bullock, "Multiracial Politics or the Politics of Being Multiracial? Racial Theory, Civic Engagement, and Socio-Political Participation in a Contemporary Society"

(PhD diss., University of Southern California, 2010); Mary Lee, "Mixed Race Peoples in the Korean National Imaginary and Family," *Korean Studies* 32 (2008): 56–85; LeiLani Nishime, *Undercover Asians: Multiracial Asian Americans in Visual Culture* (Urbana: University of Illinois Press, 2013); Jennifer Ho, *Racial Ambiguity in Asian American Culture* (New Brunswick: Rutgers University Press, 2015).

38. Alicia Edison, "The Impact of the Media on Biracial Identity Formation" (master's thesis, University of North Texas, 2007).

39. Kerry A. Rockquemore and David L. Brunsma, *Beyond Black: Biracial Identity in America* (Thousand Oaks, CA: Sage, 2002).

40. Sika Alaine Dagbovie, "Star-Light, Star-Bright, Star Damn near White: Mixed-Race Superstars," *Journal of Popular Culture* 40 (2007): 217–37; Daniel, *More than Black?*; Danzy Senna, "The Mulatto Millennium," in *Half + Half: Writers on Growing Up Biracial + Bicultural*, ed. Claudine C. O'Hearn (New York: Pantheon Books, 1998), 12–27.

41. Stuart Hall, "Subjects in History: Making Diasporic Identities," in *The House That Race Built*, ed. Wahneema Lubiano (New York: Vintage Books, 1998); Cynthia Nakashima, "Servants of Culture: The Symbolic Role of Mixed-Race Asians in American Discourse," in *"Mixed Race" Studies: A Reader*, ed. Jayne O. Ifekwunigwe (London: Routledge, 2004), 271–75; Kimberly DaCosta, "Remaking the Color Line: Social Bases and Implications of the Multiracial Movement" (PhD diss., University of California, Berkeley, 2000); Mary Beltrán, "The New Hollywood Racelessness: Only the Fast, Furious (and Multiracial) Will Survive," *Cinema Journal* 44 (2005): 50–67; Rainier Spencer, *Spurious Issues: Race and Multiracial Identity Politics in the United States* (Boulder, CO: Westview Press, 1999).

42. For a more detailed and in-depth chronology and summary of mixed-race studies, see Reginald G. Daniel, Laura Kina, Wei Ming Dariotis, Camilla Fojas, "Emerging Paradigms in Critical Mixed Race Studies," *Journal of Critical Mixed Race Studies* 1(1): 1–65.

43. Sexton, *Amalgamation Schemes*; Paul Spickard, "The Subject Is Mixed Race: The Boom in Biracial Biography," in *Rethinking "Mixed Race"* (London: Pluto Press, 2001), 76–98; Spickard, "Does Multiraciality Lighten?"; Jon Michael Spencer, *The New Colored People* (New York: New York University Press, 1997).

44. Rudy Guevarra Jr., *Becoming Mexipino: Multiethnic Identities and Communities in San Diego* (New Brunswick: Rutgers University Press, 2002); LeiLani Nishime, *Undercover Asians: Multiracial Asian Americans in Visual Culture* (Urbana: University of Illinois Press, 2014); Ralina Joseph, *Transcending Blackness: From the New Millennium Mulatta to the Exceptional Multiracial* (Durham: Duke University Press, 2012); Minelle Mahtani, *Mixed Race Amnesia: Resisting the Romanticization of Multiraciality* (Vancouver: University of British Columbia Press, 2014); Ho, *Racial Ambiguity in Asian American Culture*.

45. Sexton, *Amalgamation Schemes*, 79.

46. Daniel, Kina, Dariotis, and Fojas, "Emerging Paradigms."

47. Ibid., 8.

48. Minelle Mahtani and April Moreno, "Same Difference: Towards a More Unified Discourse in 'Mixed Race' Theory," in *Rethinking "Mixed Race"*, ed. David Parker and Miri Song (London: Pluto Press, 2001), 72.

49. See: Mahtani, *Mixed Race Amnesia*; Guevarra Jr., *Becoming Mexipino*; Camilla Fojas and Rudy P. Guevarra Jr., eds., *Transnational Crossroads: Remapping the Americas and the Pacific* (Lincoln: University of Nebraska Press, 2012); Ho, *Racial Ambiguity*; Nishime, *Undercover Asian;* Laura Kina and Wei Ming Dariotis, *War Baby/Love Child: Mixed Race*

Asian American Art (Seattle: University of Washington Press, 2013); Mary Beltrán and Camilla Fojas eds., *Mixed Race Hollywood* (New York: New York University Press, 2008).

50. Sexton, *Amalgamation Schemes*; Spencer, *Spurious Issues*; Spencer, "Assessing Multiracial Identity."

51. Anne Fausto-Sterling, "How Many Sexes Are There?" *New York Times*, March 12, 1993, A29.

52. Bow, "Transracial/Transgender," 87.

53. Susan Stryker, "(De)Subjugated Knowledges: An Introduction to Transgender Studies," in *The Transgender Studies Reader*, ed. Susan Stryker and Stephen Whittle (New York: Routledge, 2006), 3.

54. Ibid., 89.

55. Bow, "Transracial/Transgender."

56. Henry Yu, "Tiger Woods Is Not the End of History: Or, Why Sex across the Color Line Won't Save Us All," *American Historical Review* 108 (2003): 1406–1414, 1407.

57. Sumi Cho, Kimberlé Williams Crenshaw, Leslie McCall, "Toward a Field of Intersectionality Studies: Theory, Applications, and Praxis," *Signs* 38 (2013): 795.

58. Kimberlé Crenshaw, "Mapping the Margins: Intersectionality, Identity Politics, and Violence against Women of Color," *Stanford Law Review* 43 (1990–1991): 1244.

59. Parker and Song, *Rethinking "Mixed Race,"* 15.

60. Ibid., 16.

61. Phillip Brian Harper, Anne McClintock, José Esteban Muñoz, and Trish Rosen, "Queer Transexions of Race, Nation, and Gender: An Introduction," *Social Text* 52/53 (1997): 1–4.

62. Parker and Song, *Rethinking "Mixed Race,"* 11.

63. Dolezal, then president of the Spokane NAACP, emerged into national consciousness mid-2015 when her parents "outed" her as White, despite her attempts to identify herself as Black.

64. Rogers Brubaker, "The Dolezal Affair: Race, Gender, and the Micropolitics of Identity," *Ethnic and Racial Studies* 39 (2015): 432.

65. Andrea Kelsey Newlyn, "Undergoing Racial 'Reassignment': The Politics of Transracial Crossing in Sinclair Lewis's *Kingsblood Royal*," *Modern Fiction Studies* 48 (2002.): 1041–1074.

66. Parker and Song, *Rethinking "Mixed Race,"* 17.

67. E.g., Apple users are cool, young, and/or hip, while users of other brands that rely on Windows OS are none of these things.

68. Sarah Banet-Weiser, *Authentic: The Politics of Ambivalence in Brand Culture* (New York: New York University Press, 2012).

69. Ibid.

70. For more research on brands and branding, see: Sarah Banet-Weiser and Charlotte Lapsansky, "Red Is the New Black: Consumer Citizenship and Political Possibility," *International Journal of Communication* 2 (2008): 1248–68; Elizabeth C. Hirschman, "Evolutionary Branding," *Psychology and Marketing* 27 (2010): 568–83; Jonathan E. Schroeder and Miriam Salzer-Morling, eds., *Brand Culture* (New York: Routledge, 2006); Adam Arvidsson, "Brands: A Critical Perspective," *Journal of Consumer Culture* 5 (2006): 235–58; Celia Lury, *Brands: The Logos of the Global Economy* (New York: Routledge, 2004); Douglas Holt, "Why Do Brands Cause Trouble? A Dialectical Theory of Culture and Branding," *Journal*

of Consumer Research 29 (2002): 70–96; Elizabeth Moor, "Branded Spaces: The Scope of 'New Marketing,'" *Journal of Consumer Culture* 3 (2003): 39–60; Wally Olins, "Branding the Nation—the Historical Context," *Journal of Brand Management* 9 (2002): 241–48.

71. Ying Fan, "Branding the Nation: What Is Being Branded?" *Journal of Vacation Marketing* 12 (2005): 5–14.

72. Richard Dyer and Paul McDonald, *Stars* (London: British Film Institute, 1979).

73. Jonathan Gray, "Texts That Sell: The Culture in Promotional Culture," in *Blowing Up the Brand: Critical Perspectives on Promotional Culture*, ed. Melissa Aronczyk and Devon Powers (New York: Peter Lang, 2010), 310.

74. See also Foucault's discussion of self-monitoring in *The History of Sexuality* (1990).

75. Naomi Klein, *No Logo: Taking Aim at the Brand Bullies* (New York: Picador, 1999).

76. E.g.: Cameron Diaz, Raquel Welch, Lynda Carter, Ben Kingsley, Mark-Paul Gosselaar, Rob Schneider, Anthony Quinn, Keanu Reeves, Jennifer and Meg Tilly.

77. E.g.: Barack Obama, Halle Berry, Russell Wong, Alicia Keys, Vin Diesel, Dean Cain, Kelly Hu, Bruce Lee, Slash, Rosario Dawson.

78. Angharad Valdivia extends this claim when she stresses the usefulness of "representational ambiguity" to late capitalism in her essay "Latinas as Radical Hybrid: Transnationally Gendered Traces in Mainstream Media." *Global Media Journal* 3 (2004).

79. Klein, *No Logo*, 117.

80. Maureen Orth, *The Importance of Being Famous: Behind the Scenes of the Celebrity-Industrial Complex* (New York: Henry Holt, 2004); Joshua Gamson, *Claims to Fame: Celebrity in Contemporary America* (Berkeley: University of California Press, 1994).

81. Gamson, *Claims to Fame*, 58.

82. Orth, *Importance of Being Famous*, 19–20.

83. Richard Dyer, *Heavenly Bodies: Film Stars and Society* (London: Routledge, 1986), 2.

84. Jennifer Ho, in her book *Racial Ambiguity*, offers an insightful and helpful alternative frame for understanding race, one that sees *all* racialized identities as "ambiguous" because race is a suspect yet dynamic category. I am not using that reading of ambiguous in this book, in fact I argue that the moments where race is fixed and decidedly unambiguous, is how the racialized hierarchy in the US is created. Importantly, the unambiguity of race does not keep us from denaturalizing the process of racialization.

85. Beltrán, "New Hollywood Racelessness."

86. Ibid., 50.

87. See: Ibid.; Dagbovie, "Star-Light, Star-Bright"; Jan Weisman, "The Tiger and His Stripes: Thai and American Reactions to Tiger Woods's (Multi-) 'Racial Self,'" in *The Sum of Our Parts: Mixed-Heritage Asian Americans*, ed. Teresa Williams-Leon and Cynthia Nakashima (Philadelphia: Temple University Press, 2001), 231–43; Angharad Valdivia, "Mixed-Race on the Disney Channel: From Johnnie Tsunami through Lizzie McGuire and Ending with the Cheetah Girls," in *Mixed Race Hollywood*, ed. Mary Beltrán and Camilla Fojas (New York: New York University Press, 2008), 269–89; Cynthia Nakashima, "Servants of Culture: The Symbolic Role of Mixed-Race Asians in American Discourse," in *"Mixed Race" Studies: A Reader*, ed. Jayne O. Ifekwunigwe (London: Routledge, 2004), 271–75; Spickard, "The Subject Is Mixed Race"; Teresa Kay Williams, "The Theater of Identity: (Multi-)Race and Representation of Eurasians and Afro-Asians," in *American Mixed Race: The Culture of Microdiversity*, ed. Naomi Zack (Lanham, MD: Rowman & Littlefield, 1995).

88. The multiracial movement lobbied for one "multiracial" box to be included with the standing racial categories, and the respondent would then check the two, three, or four of

these racial groups they identified with. They settled for the "check all that apply" option. There were 63 racial mixtures possible with the check-more-than-one option, 126 when the Hispanic/non-Hispanic options were checked. The 2000 census counted 6.8 million multiracial people, but that number was later reduced to 4.2 million after adjusting for those who checked White + Other, with Other = Hispanic (DaCosta, *Making Multiracials*, 2007). The reduction in number of mixed-race people aligned with claims from critics of the 2000 census who felt the population of multiracial people was/is underreported.

89. Discussions on the politics of passing and covering can be found in: Elaine K. Ginsberg, *Passing and the Fictions of Identity* (Durham: Duke University Press, 1996); Lisa Nakamura, "Race in/for Cyberspace: Identity Tourism and Racial Passing on the Internet," in *Reading Digital Culture*, ed. David Trend (Oxford: Blackwell, 2001); Adrian Piper, "Passing for White, Passing for Black," *Transition* 58 (1992): 4–32; Jacquetta Amdahl, "'Perpetual Others': The Role of Culture, Race, and Nation in the Formation of a Mixed-Race Identity" (PhD. diss., University of Minnesota, 2012); Kenji Yoshino, *Covering: The Hidden Assault on Our Civil Rights* (New York: Random House, 2007); Catherine Squires and Daniel Brouwer, "In/Discernible Bodies: The Politics of Passing in Dominant and Marginal Media," *Critical Studies in Media Communication* 19 (2002): 283–310; Erving Goffman, *The Presentation of Self in Everyday Life* (Garden City: Doubleday, 1959); Yiman Wang, "The Art of Screen Passing: Anna May Wong's Yellow Yellowface Performance in the Art Deco Era," *Camera Obscura* 60 (2005):159–91; Dyer, *Heavenly Bodies*.

90. Kent A. Ono and Derek T. Buescher, "Deciphering Pocahontas: Unpackaging the Commodification of a Native American Woman," *Critical Studies in Media Communication* 18 (2001): 23–43.

91. Though Orth does not make the connection, both the military (composed of the military, federal government, defense contractors, corporations that manufacture weapons and technology for war) and prison (made up of state and federal government agencies, politicians and lobbyists, prison labor contractors, corporations who manufacture technology and products for prisons, privately run prisons and companies who benefit from cheap inmate labor) industrial complexes provide a template for how mutually beneficial relationships are motivated by profit, growth or both. To use the phrase *celebrity industrial complex* is not to compare celebrities to prisons or the military and war, but to point out the occurrence of a similar profit-generating strategy.

92. Nakamura, "Race In/For Cyberspace"; danah boyd, "Taken out of Context: American Teen Sociality in Networked Publics" (PhD diss., University of California, Berkeley, 2008); Jenny Sundén, *Material Virtualities* (New York: Peter Lang, 2003).

93. Orth, *Importance of Being Famous*, 21.

94. Dagbovie, "Star-Light, Star-Bright" 232.

95. Eduardo Bonilla-Silva, "New Racism," Color-Blind Racism, and the Future of Whiteness in America," in *White Out: The Continuing Significance of Racism*, ed. Ashley W. Doane and Eduardo Bonilla-Silva (London: Routledge, 2003), 271–84.

96. Catherine Squires, *The Post-Racial Mystique: Media and Race in the Twenty-First Century* (New York: New York University Press, 2014).

97. While the multiracial community is a not a homogeneous group, much of the focus on the significance of mixed race has been on those who identify as Black and White or, oftentimes, White and Asian. In fact, the multiracial movement, since the beginning, has dealt with suspicions that those behind the movement were merely "white parents of mixed-race bambinos bartering for a safety zone for their café-au-lait kids." Lisa Jones,

Bulletproof Diva (New York: Anchor, 2010), 55. Considering that the cofounder and executive director of Project RACE (Reclassify All Children Equally), one of the more effective and influential organizations within the multiracial movement, is a White woman, Susan Graham, who has two biracial children with a Black man, the suspicions do not seem unwarranted. Kimberly DaCosta, "Making Multiracials," points out primarily middle- and upper-class, college-educated people participated in the multiracial movement, especially in the beginning. Motivated possibly by parents wishing to distance their children from the reach of the one-drop rule, the movement fought to have multiracial people recognized as its own group, which some critics argued pushed it closer to Whiteness and away from Blackness: Lisa Tessman, "The Racial Politics of Mixed Race," *Journal of Social Philosophy* 30 (1999): 276–94; Sexton, *Amalgamation Schemes*; Spencer, "Assessing Multiracial Identity"; Spickard, "Subject Is Mixed Race".

98. Fred Ho and Bill V. Mullen, eds., *Afro Asia: Revolutionary Political & Cultural Connections between African Americans & Asian Americans* (Durham: Duke University Press, 2008), 2

99. See: Mary Beltrán, *Latina/o Stars in U.S. Eyes: The Making and Meanings of Film and TV Stardom* (Urbana: University of Illinois Press, 2009); Angharad Valdivia, "Geographies of Latinidad: Deployment of Radical Hybridity in the Mainstream," in *Race, Identity, and Representation in Education*, ed. Cameron McCarthy and Warren Crichlow (New York: Routledge, 2005), 307–20.

100. "Major Differences in Subject-Matter Content between the 1990 and 2000 Census Questionnaires," https://www.census.gov/population/www/cen2000/90vsoo/index.html.

101. J. Kehaulani Kauanui, "Asian American Studies and the 'Pacific Question,'" in *Asian American Studies after Critical Mass*, ed. Kent A. Ono (Malden: Blackwell, 2005), 123–143.

102. Dean Itsuji Saranillio, "Why Asian Settler Colonialisms Matters: A Thought Piece on Critiques, Debates, and Indigenous Difference," *Settler Colonial Studies* 3 (2013): 280–94; Candace Fujikane, "Foregrounding Native Nationalisms: A Critique of Antinationalist Sentiment in Asian American Studies," in *Asian American Studies after Critical Mass*, ed. Kent A. Ono (Malden: Blackwell, 2005), 73–87.

103. These are all different combinations for *Asian/American* and *Pacific Islander*.

Chapter Two: Birth of a Blasian

1. Sarah Buckley, "China's High-Speed Sexual Revolution," *BBC.com*, February 27, 2016, http://www.bbc.com/news/magazine-35525566; Adam Taylor, "China's Sexual Revolution Has Reached the Point of No Return," *Business Insider*, August 31, 2012, http://www.businessinsider.com/the-incredible-story-of-chinas-sexual-revolution-2012–8; Vanessa Brown, "Inside China's Sexual Revolution," *News.com.au*, March 7, 2016, http://www.news.com.au/lifestyle/relationships/sex/inside-chinas-sexual-revolution/news-story/af78160062a11b548530d18908ed164a.

2. Damien Ma, "Chinese Workers in Africa Who Marry Locals Face Puzzled Reception at Home," *Atlantic*, June 20, 2011, http://www.theatlantic.com/international/archive/2011/06/chinese-workers-in-africa-who-marry-locals-face-puzzled-reception-at-home/240662/; Mark Kapchanga, "Bedroom May Be Better Bet than Boardroom for Africans in China," *Global Times*, October 29, 2013, http://www.globaltimes.cn/content/821141.shtml.

3. Yepoka Yeebo, "In China, Mixed Marriages Can Be a Labor of Love," *Christian Science Monitor*, September 21, 2013, http://www.csmonitor.com/World/2013/0921/In-China-mixed-marriages-can-be-a-labor-of-love; Zoe Murphy, "Mixed Marriages

in China a Labour of Love," *BBC.com*, October 24, 2013, http://www.bbc.com/news /world-asia-24371673; "African-Chinese Couples on the Rise in Guangzhou, China," *China Central Television America*, March 1, 2015, http://www.cctv-america.com/2015/03/01 /african-chinese-couples-on-the-rise-in-guangzhou-china.

4. Vijay Prashad, *Everybody Was Kung Fu Fighting: Afro-Asian Connections and the Myth of Cultural Purity* (Boston: Beacon Press, 2001), 4.

5. Ibid., 7.

6. Prashad, *Everybody Was Kung Fu Fighting*; Joseph P. Harris, *Africans and Their History* (New York: New American Library, 1972); Abdul Sheriff, *Slaves, Spices and Ivory in Zanzibar* (Dar es Salaam: Tanzania Publishing House, 1987).

7. Prashad, *Everybody Was Kung Fu Fighting*, 11.

8. Gary Y. Okihiro, *Margins and Mainstreams: Asians in American History and Culture* (Seattle: University of Washington Press, 1994).

9. Vanita Reddy, "Afro-Asian Intimacies and the Politics and Aesthetics of Cross-Racial Struggle in Mira Nair's *Mississippi Masala*," *Journal of Asian American Studies* 18 (2015): 234.

10. Moon-Ho Jung, *Coolies and Cane: Race, Labor, and Sugar in the Age of Emancipation* (Baltimore: Johns Hopkins University Press, 2006).

11. Prashad, *Everybody Was Kung Fu Fighting*, 75.

12. Ibid.

13. Scot Ngozi-Brown, "African-American Soldiers and Filipinos: Racial Imperialism, Jim Crow and Social Relations," *Journal of Negro History* 82 (1997).

14. Daniel Widener, "Seoul City Sue and the Bugout Blues: Black American Narratives of the Forgotten War." In *Afro Asian: Revolutionary Political & Cultural Connections between African Americans and Asian Americans*, ed. Fred Ho and Bill V. Mullen (Durham: Duke University Press, 2008), 67.

15. "This Week in History." *Jet*, May 2, 1994, 23; Prashad, *Everybody Was Kung Fu Fighting*, 146.

16. Chong Chon-Smith, *East Meets Black: Asian and Black Masculinity in the Post–Civil Rights Era* (Jackson: University Press of Mississippi, 2015), 29.

17. The act did not explicitly exclude Black soldiers, but since antimiscegenation laws were intended to keep Whites from marrying into various groups of color, they were the ones to benefit from this act.

18. Pearl S. Buck. *East Wind, West Wind* (New York: John Day, 1930); Christopher M. Lapinig, "The Forgotten Amerasians," *New York Times*, May 27, 2013, http://www.nytimes .com/2013/05/28/opinion/the-forgotten-amerasians.html; *America's Forgotten Children: Amerasian Mixed-Race Children Fathered by US Soldiers Struggle with Discrimination in Asian Societies*, Al Jazeera video, 14:23, posted September 13, 2011, http://stream.aljazeera .com/story/201109132034-0015927.

19. *Gerald Horne, Race War! White Supremacy and the Japanese Attack on the British Empire* (New York: New York University Press, 2004).

20. Fred Ho and Bill V. Mullen, eds., *Afro Asia: Revolutionary Political & Cultural Connections between African Americans & Asian Americans* (Durham: Duke University Press, 2008), 5.

21. Claire Jean Kim, *Bitter Fruit: The Politics of BlackKorean Conflict in New York City* (New Haven: Yale University Press, 2003).

22. Hazel M. McFerson, "Asians and African Americans in Historical Perspective," in *Blacks and Asians: Crossings, Conflict and Community*, ed. Hazel M. McFerson (Durham: Carolina Academic Press, 2006), 19–53.

23. Ibid.

24. Rachel F. Moran, *Interracial Intimacy: The Regulation of Race and Romance* (Chicago: University of Chicago Press, 2001), 18.

25. Ibid.; Roland G. Fryer Jr. "Guess Who's Been Coming to Dinner? Trends in Interracial Marriage over the 20th Century," *Journal of Economic Perspectives* 21 (2007): 71–90; Maria P. P. Root, *Love's Revolution: Interracial Marriage* (Philadelphia: Temple University Press, 2001); Esther Pan, "Why Asian Guys Are on a Roll: Asian-American Were Told for Many Years by Their Own Community to Be Dutiful Sons," *Newsweek*, February 21, 2000; Cynthia Feliciano, Belinda Robnett, and Golnaz Komale, "Gendered Racial Exclusion among White Internet Daters," *Social Science Research* 38 (2009): 39–54; Patricia Hill Collins, *Black Sexual Politics: African Americans, Gender, and the New Racism* (New York: Routledge, 2005); Kyle D. Crowder and Stewart E. Tolnay, "A New Marriage Squeeze for Black Women: The Role of Racial Intermarriage by Black Men," *Journal of Marriage and The Family* 62 (2000): 792–807; Jerry A. Jacobs and Teresa G. Lobov, "Gender Differentials in Intermarriage among Sixteen Race and Ethnic Groups," *Sociological Forum* 17 (2002): 621–46; Zhenchao C. Qian and Daniel T. Lichter, "Social Boundaries and Marital Assimilation: Interpreting Trends in Racial and Ethnic Intermarriage," *American Sociological Review* 72 (2007): 68–94.

26. Wendy Wang, "The Rise of Intermarriage," Pew Research Center, Executive Summary, February 16, 2012, http://www.pewsocialtrends.org/2012/02/16/the-rise-of-intermarriage/?src=prc-headline.

27. Haeyoun Park, "Who Is Marrying Whom," *New York Times*, January 29, 2011, http://www.nytimes.com/interactive/2011/01/29/us/20110130mixedrace.html.

28. Feliciano et al., "Gendered Racial Exclusion"; Qian and Lichter, "Changing Patterns"; George Yancy, "Cross-Racial Differences in the Racial Preferences of Potential Dating Partners: A Test of the Alienation of African Americans and Social Domination Orientation," *Sociological Quarterly* 50 (2009): 121–43.

29. DeNeen L. Brown, "Single Black Women Being Urged to Date Outside Race," *Washington Post*, February 25, 2010, http://www.washingtonpost.com/wp-dyn/content/article/2010/02/24/AR2010022405727.html.

30. Fryer, "Guess Who's Been Coming to Dinner?"

31. Prashad, *Everybody Was Kung Fu Fighting*; Heike Raphael-Hernandez and Shannon Steen, "Introduction," in *AfroAsian Encounters: Culture, History, Politics*, ed. Heike Raphael-Hernandez and Shannon Steen (New York: New York University Press, 2006), 1–14; Nitasha Tamar Sharma, *Hip Hop Desis: South Asian Americans, Blackness, and a Global Race Consciousness* (Durham: Duke University Press, 2010).

32. Squires, *Post-racial Mystique*.

33. Myra Washington, "Interracial Intimacy: Hegemonic Construction of Asian American and Black Relationships on TV Medical Dramas," *Howard Journal of Communication* 23 (2012): 253–71.

34. This was a portmanteau of Tiger Woods's racial mixture: CAucasian BLack INdian ASIAN.

35. Gene Santoro, *Myself When I Am Real: The Life and Music of Charles Mingus* (Oxford: Oxford University Press, 2000).

36. Ibid.

37. LeiLani Nishime, "Guilty Pleasures: Keanu Reeves, Superman, and Racial Outing," in *East Main Street: Asian American Popular Culture*, ed. Shilpa Davé, LeiLani Nishime, and Tasha G. Oren (New York: New York University Press, 2005); Yiman Wang, "Screening

Asia: Passing, Performative Translation, and Reconfiguration," *Positions: East Asia Cultures Critique* 15 (2007): 319–43; Sika Alaine Dagbovie, "Star-Light, Star-Bright, Star Damn near White: Mixed-Race Superstars," *Journal of Popular Culture* 40 (2007): 217–37; Cheryl Black, "Looking White, Acting Black: Cast(E)Ing Fredi Washington," *Theatre Survey* 45 (2004): 19–40; Caroline A. Streeter, "The Hazards of Visibility: 'Biracial' Women, Media Images, and Narratives of Identity," *New Faces in a Changing America: Multiracial Identity in the 21st Century*, ed. Loretta I. Winters and Herman L. DeBose (Thousand Oaks, CA: Sage, 2003).

38. Michael Omi and Howard Winant, *Racial Formation in the United States: From the 1960s to the 1980s* (New York: Routledge, 1986), 64.

39. Who starred in the Cheech & Chong comedy franchise of films popular in the 1960s and 70s, with co-star Cheech Marin.

40. Paul E. Pratt, "Growing up a Chong." *AsianWeek*, November 23, 2005.

41. Bill Muller, "Rae Dawn Chong's Still Here," *Arizona Republic*, February 9, 2007.

42. Directors include Spike Lee, Robert Townsend, John Singleton.

43. Roger Ebert, "Soul Man," *Chicago Sun-Times*, October 24, 1986; Muller, "Rae Dawn Chong."

44. Pratt, "Growing Up a Chong"; Vincent Canby, "Movie: Beat Street," *New York Times*, June 8, 1984.

45. Tim Gordon, "Keeping It Reel 64: Rae Dawn Chong," *FilmGordon Radio*, podcast audio, January 14, 2011, http://www.blogtalkradio.com/filmgordon/2011/01/14/rae-dawn-chong.

46. Rae Dawn Chong, "Oprah," *dawnrae66.blogspot.com*, October 28, 2010, http://dawnarae66.blogspot.com/2010/10/oprah.html.

47. Gordon, *Keeping It Reel*; Muller, "Rae Dawn Chong's"; Eric Deggan, "Let's, Um, Try Talking about Race," *St. Petersburg Times*, November 30, 2008.

48. Gordon, *Keeping It Reel.*

49. Ricardo Hazell, "'Color Purple' Alum Rae Dawn Chong on Film's Legacy," *Electronic Urban Report: eurweb*, January 24, 2011, http://www.eurweb.com/?p=79595.

50. Robin Givens, "Why Are Black Actresses Having Such a Hard Time in Hollywood?" *Ebony*, June 1991, 36–40.

51. Pratt, "Growing Up a Chong."

52. Deegan, "Try Talking about Race."

53. "How Did Your Favorite Show Rate?" *USA Today*, May 28, 2002.

54. Darryl's mother's stoic countenance acts as eerie foreshadowing of the press conference Tiger Woods would hold, with his mother's stern face sharing the same frame as his body.

55. Brian Stross, "The Hybrid Metaphor: From Biology to Culture," *Journal of American Folklore* 112 (1999): 257.

56. See: ibid.; Deborah A. Kapchan and Pauline Turner Strong, "Theorizing the Hybrid," *Journal of American Folklore* 112 (1999): 239–53; Thomas Teo, "The Historical Problematization of "Mixed Race" in Psychological and Human-Scientific Discourses," in *Defining Difference: Race and Racism in the History of Psychology*, ed. Andrew Winston (Washington, DC: American Psychological Association, 2004), 79–108; Emma Jinhua Teng, "Eurasian Hybridity in Chinese Utopian Visions: From 'One World' to 'a Society Based on Beauty' and Beyond," *Positions: Asia Critique* 14 (2006): 131–64; Greg Carter, "Hybrid Vigor: The Transformation of a Scientific Racialist Idea," *American Studies Association National Conference*, November 2004, Atlanta.

57. Mary Beltrán, "The New Hollywood Racelessness: Only the Fast, Furious (and Multiracial) Will Survive," *Cinema Journal* 44 (2005): 50–67; Dagbovie, "Star-Light, Star-Bright'";

Danzy Senna, "The Mulatto Millenium," in *Half + Half: Writers on Growing Up Biracial + Bicultural*, ed. Claudine C. O'Hearn (New York: Pantheon Books, 1998), 12–27; Naomi Zack, *Race and Mixed Race* (Philadelphia: Temple University Press, 1993).

58. Mark P. Orbe and Karen E. Strother, "Signifying the Tragic Mulatto: A Semiotic Analysis of Alex Haley's 'Queen,'" *Howard Journal of Communication* 7 (1996): 113–26; Claudia Tate, "Nella Larsen's *Passing*: A Problem of Interpretation," *Black American Literature Forum* 14 (1980): 142–46; Donald Bogle, *Toms, Coons, Mulattoes, Mammies, and Bucks: An Interpretive History of Blacks in American Films* (New York: Continuum, 2001); Freda Scott Giles, "From Melodrama to the Movies: The Tragic Mulatto as a Type Character," in *American Mixed Race: The Culture of Microdiversity*, ed. Naomi Zack (Lanham, MD: Rowman & Littlefield, 1995), 63–78.

59. *Mulatto* historically denotes a Black and White racially mixed person and continues to culturally connote a biracial person.

60. Stephen Murphy-Shigematsu, *When Half Is Whole: Multiethnic Asian American Identities* (Stanford: Stanford University Press, 2012).

61. David A. Hollinger, "Amalgamation and Hypodescent: The Question of Ethnoracial Mixture in the History of the United States," *American Historical Review* 108 (2003): 1363–1390.

62. Nas is not the only artist to refer to Blasians from the Caribbean. There are a number of artists who allude to the history of Black, Indigenous, and Asian racial mixing that has been occurring on the various islands for generations. See: Fabolous, "Gangsta Don't Play" (2007), Pitbull, "The Anthem" (2007), Black Rob, "Thug Story" (1999), KRS, One "Brown Skin Woman" (1993), Memphis Bleek, "Do My" (2000).

63. Raymond Williams, *Marxism and Literature* (Oxford: Oxford University Press, 1977).

64. Tate, "Nella Larsen's *Passing*," 7.

65. See: S. Craig Watkins, *Hip Hop Matters: Politics, Pop Culture, and the Struggle for the Soul of a Movement* (Boston: Beacon Press, 2005); T. Denean Sharpley-Whiting, *Pimps Up, Ho's Down: Hip Hop's Hold on Young Black Women* (New York: New York University Press, 2007); Tricia Rose, *The Hip Hop Wars: What We Talk about When We Talk about Hip Hop—and Why It Matters"* (New York: Basic Books, 2008); Gwendolyn D. Pough, *Check It While I Wreck It: Black Womanhood, Hip-Hop Culture, and the Public Sphere* (Boston: Northeastern University Press, 2004).

66. Tricia Rose, *Black Noise: Rap Music and Black Culture in Contemporary America* (Middletown, CT: Wesleyan University Press, 1994), 168.

67. http://www.theybf.com/, http://bossip.com/, http://str8nyc.com/, http://dimewars .com/, http://www.rhymeswithsnitch.com/, http://www.crunktastical.net/.

68. Kaila Adia Story, "Performing Venus: From Hottentot to Video Vixen," in *Home Girls Make Some Noise: Hip Hop Feminism Anthology*, ed. Gwendolyn D. Pough, Elaine Richardson, Aisha Durham, and Rachel Raimist (Mira Loma, CA: Parker, 2007), 245.

69. Sharpley-Whiting, *Pimps Up*.

70. Steven Shaviro, "Supa Dupa Fly: Black Women as Cyborgs in Hiphop Videos," *Quarterly Review of Film and Video* 22 (2005): 174.

71. See: Murali Balaji, "Vixen Resistin': Redefining Black Womanhood in Hip-Hop Music Videos," *Journal of Black Studies* 41 (2010): 5–20; Imani Perry, *Prophets of the Hood* (Durham: Duke University Press, 2004); Sharpley-Whiting, *Pimps Up*; Shaviro, "Supa Dupa."

72. Bogle, *Toms, Coons, Mulattoes*; Sharpley-Whiting, *Pimps Up*.

73. Michael C. Thornton and Henry Louis Gates, "Black, Japanese and American: An Asian American Identity Yesterday and Today," in *The Sum of Our Parts: Mixed Heritage Asian Americans*, ed. Teresa Williams-Leon and Cynthia L. Nakashima (Philadelphia: Temple University Press, 2001), 93–105.

74. Mystikal, "Shake It Fast"; Outkast, "Bombs over Baghdad"; Ludacris, "Saturdays Oooh Oooh"; Slimm Calhoun, "It's Okay"; India Arie, "Brown Skin"; Whitney Houston. "One of Those Days," Nelly, "Hott in Herre"; Jagged Edge, "Walked outta Heaven"; Jagged Edge, "Walked outta Heaven Remix"; Ginuwine, "In Those Jeans"; 8-Ball & MJG, "Cadillac Pimpin"; Murphy Lee, "What the Hook Gon Be"; 50 Cent, "Candy Shop"; Metallica, "Unnamed Feeling"; ATL,"Calling All Girls."

75. N.E.R.D., "Rock Star"; 112, "Peaches & Cream"; Nas, "One Mic"; Jaheim "Anything"; Tony Yayo, "Curious"; Plies, "Want It, Need It"; Mobb Deep, "Burn"; Mobb Deep, "Get Away"; Busta Rhymes, "Break Ya Neck"; Prodigy, "Y.B.E."

76. Brandy, "Full Moon"; DTP, "Growing Pains"; Dru Hill, "I Should Be"; Dru Hill, "I Love You"; Busta Rhymes, "I Know What You Want/Give It to Me"; 50 Cent, "Candy Shop"; Ne-Yo, "Do U"; Ne-Yo, "Because of You"; Kanye West, "Gold Digger"; Young Jeezy "And Then What"; Fat Joe, "Get It Poppin,"; Outkast, "Ghettomusik"; Ciara, "Oh"; Gucci Mane, "So Icy"; Romey Rome, "In da Club"; Kelis, "Bossy"; Nelly, "Grillz"; T.I., "What You Know."

77. "Tomika Skanes," *Ethnicelebs*, July 16, 2010, http://ethnicelebs.com/tomika-skanes; Sandra Rose, "Morning Glory: Tomika Skanes by Request," *sandrarose.com*, June 25, 2008, http://sandrarose.com/2008/06/morning-glory-tomika-skanes-by-request/; "So Amazing: This G.I. Jane Is More than Meets the Eye," *xxlmag.com*, August 1, 2005, http://www.xxlmag.com/eye-candy/2005/08/so-amazing/.

78. David Lee Sanders, "HalfKorean.Com: Interviews—Denyce Lawton," HalfKorean.com, February 10, 2004, http://halfkorean.com/interviews/interview_denyce_lawton_2004.php.

79. "Video Vixen La'Shontae Heckard—Blasian Fury," FeedFury.com, April 17, 2009, http://graphics.feedfury.com/content/32003633-video-vixen-la-shontae-heckard-blasian-fury.html; Lesley Téllez, "'Peeps' Making Noise Online," cover story, *Dallas Morning News* April 14, 2006, 2nd ed., sec. Quick.

80. Sanders, "Halfkorean.com: Interviews—Denyce Lawton."

81. Celine Parreñas Shimizu, *The Hypersexuality of Race: Performing Asian/American Women on Screen and Scene* (Durham: Duke University Press, 2007), 17.

82. Diane Railton and Paul Watson, "Naughty Girls and Red Blooded Women: Representations of Female Heterosexuality in Music Video," *Feminist Media Studies* 5 (2005): 52.

83. Cameron Bailey, "Nigger/Lover: The Thin Sheen of Race in *Something Wild*," *Screen* 29 (1988): 28–40.

84. Sharpley-Whiting, *Pimps Up*.

85. Ibid., 27.

86. Aisha Durham, Brittney C. Cooper, and Susana M. Morris, "The Stage Hip-Hop Feminism Built: A New Directions Essay," *Signs: Journal of Women in Culture and Society* 38 (2013): 721–37.

87. Mireille Miller-Young, "Hip-Hop Honeys and da Hustlaz: Black Sexualities in the New Hip-Hop Pornography," *Meridians: Feminism, Race, Transnationalism* 8 (2008): 261–92.

88. Parreñas Shimizu, *Hypersexuality*, 10.

89. Celine Parreñas Shimizu, "The Bind of Representation: Performing and Consuming Hypersexuality in *Miss Saigon*," *Theater Journal* 57 (2005): 248.

90. Parreñas Shimizu, *Hypersexuality*, 4.

91. Ibid., 17.

92. Angela Y. Davis, *Blues Legacies and Black Feminism: Gertrude "Ma" Rainey, Bessie Smith, and Billie Holiday* (New York: Pantheon Books, 1998), 10.

93. Amina, "Top 25 of the Decade—LaShontae Heckard," *dynastyseries.com*, accessed April 28, 2011, http://dynastyseries.com/top25/top-25-of-the-decade-lashontae-heckard/.

94. Mia Milano, "Model Mondays: Featuring La'Shontae Heckard," *nappyboyonline.com*, October 9, 2009, http://nappyboyonline.com/profiles/blogs/model-mondaysgtgt-featuring.

95. Sanders, "Halfkorean.com: Interviews—Denyce Lawton."

96. "Interview with Denyce Lawton," *Cutie Central*, accessed April 28, 2011, http://www .cutiecentral.com/bios/denycelawton/.

97. "So Amazing," *xxlmag.com*.

98. Sanders, "Halfkorean.com: Interviews—Denyce Lawton."

99. Ibid.

100. Raphael-Hernandez and Steen, *AfroAsian Encounters*, 1.

Chapter Three: Modeling Race
Refashioning Blasianness

1. Heben Nigatu points out in her defense of another intensely criticized figure, Kanye West, that "race affects the way people perceive and respond to vanity." Indeed, for both Simmons and West, "self-love is a political act"; https://www.buzzfeed.com/hnigatu/in -defense-of-kanyes-vanity-the-politics-of-black-self-love?utm_term=.uknEa48vG# .eqVXxnkpB.

2. Pamela Robertson, *Guilty Pleasures: Feminist Camp from Mae West to Madonna* (Durham: Duke University Press, 1996), 17.

3. Kimora Lee Simmons, *Fabulosity: What It Is & How to Get It* (New York: HarperCollins, 2006), 38.

4. Fabio Cleto, ed., *Camp: Queer Aesthetics and the Performing Subject: A Reader* (Ann Arbor: University of Michigan Press, 1999), 2.

5. See: Susan Sontag, "Notes on Camp," in *Camp: Queer Aesthetics and the Performing Subject: A Reader*, ed. Fabio Cleto (Ann Arbor: University of Michigan Press, 1999); Philip Core, *Camp: The Lie That Tells the Truth* (London: Plexus, 1984); Mark Booth, *Camp* (New York: Quartet Books, 1983); Richard Dyer, *It's Only Entertainment* (New York: Routledge, 1992); Jack Babuscio, "The Cinema of Camp," in *Camp: Queer Aesthetics and the Performing Subject: A Reader*, ed. Fabio Cleto (Ann Arbor: University of Michigan Press, 1999), 117–35; Jack Babuscio, "Camp and the Gay Sensibility," in *Gays and Film*, ed. Richard Dyer (London: BFI, 1977); Elizabeth Whitney, "Capitalizing on Camp: Greed and the Queer Marketplace," *Text & Performance Quarterly* 26 (2006): 36–46; Hollis Griffin, "Queerness, the Quality Audience, and Comedy Central's Reno 911!" *Television New Media* 9 (2008): 355–70; Gilad Padva, "*Priscilla* Fights Back: The Politicization of Camp Subculture," *Journal of Communication Inquiry* 24 (2000): 216–43.

6. Robertson, *Guilty Pleasures*; Pamela Robertson, "Mae West's Maids: Race, 'Authenticity,' and the Discourse of Camp," in *Camp: Queer Aesthetics and the Performing Subject:*

A *Reader*, ed. Fabio Cleto (Ann Arbor: University of Michigan Press, 1999), 393–408; bell hooks, *Black Looks: Race and Representation* (Boston: South End Press, 1992); Sarina Pearson, "Pacific Camp: Satire, Silliness (and Seriousness) on New Zealand Television," *Media, Culture & Society* 27 (2005): 551–75; Caryl Flinn, "The Deaths of Camp," *Camera Obscura: Feminism, Culture, and Media Studies* 35 (1995): 53–86; Helene A. Shugart and Catherine Egley Waggoner, *Making Camp: Rhetorics of Transgression in U.S. Popular Culture* (Tuscaloosa: University of Alabama Press, 2008).

7. Babuscio, "Cinema of Camp," 117–18.

8. Moe Meyer, "The Signifying Invert: Camp and the Performance of Nineteenth-Century Sexology," *Text & Performance Quarterly* 15 (1995): 277.

9. Padva, "*Priscilla* Fights," 226.

10. Ibid., 237.

11. Robertson, "Mae West's Maids," 393.

12. Robertson, *Guilty Pleasures*, 17.

13. Flinn, "Deaths of Camp," 76.

14. Babuscio, "Cinema of Camp," 122.

15. Ibid., 125.

16. Lisa Nakamura, "Mixedfolks.Com: Ethnic Ambiguity, Celebrity Outing, and the Internet," in *Mixed Race Hollywood*, ed. Mary Beltrán and Camilla Fojas (New York: New York University Press, 2008), 64–87; Leilani Nishime, "Guilty Pleasures: Keanu Reeves, Superman, and Racial Outing," in *East Main Street: Asian American Popular Culture*, ed. Shilpa Davé, Leilani Nishime, and Tasha G. Oren (New York: New York University Press, 2005).

17. Catherine Squires and Daniel Brouwer, "In/Discernible Bodies: The Politics of Passing in Dominant and Marginal Media," *Critical Studies in Media Communication* 19 (2002): 285.

18. Leilani Nishime, "Kimora Barbie: Camp and the Performance of Race," paper presented at Critical Mixed Race Studies Conference, Chicago, November 2010.

19. Ibid., 10.

20. Simmons, *Fabulosity*, 131.

21. Ibid., 135.

22. Sontag, "Notes on Camp," 53.

23. Jonathan Dollimore, "Sexual Dissidence: Augustine to Wilde, Freud to Foucault," *Camp: Queer Aesthetics and the Performing Subject: A Reader*, ed. Fabio Cleto (Ann Arbor: University of Michigan Press, 1999), 221–36.

24. Simmons, *Fabulosity*, 136.

25. Shane White and Graham White, *Stylin: African American Expressive Culture from Its Beginning to the Zoot Suit* (Ithaca: Cornell University Press, 1998), 3, 6.

26. Simmons, *Fabulosity*, 136.

27. Roopali Mukherjee, "The Ghetto Fabulous Aesthetic in Contemporary Black Culture," *Cultural Studies* 20 (2006): 600.

28. See: Eduardo Bonilla-Silva, *White Supremacy and Racism in the Post–Civil Rights Era* (Boulder, CO: Lynne Rienner, 2001); Todd Boyd, *The New H.N.I.C.: The Death of Civil Rights and the Reign of Hip Hop* (New York: New York University Press, 2003); Roopali Mukherjee, *The Racial Order of the Things: Cultural Imaginaries of the Post-Soul Era* (Minneapolis: University of Minnesota Press, 2006); Mark Anthony Neal, *Soul Babies: Black Popular Culture and the Post-Soul Aesthetic* (New York: Routledge, 2002).

29. Bill Cosby, "Pound Cake" speech, NAACP Gala to commemorate the fiftieth anniversary of *Brown v. Board of Education*, May 17, 2004; Regina Austin, "A Nation of Thieves:

Consumption, Commerce, and the Black Public Sphere," in *The Black Public Sphere*, ed. Black Public Sphere Collective (Chicago: University of Chicago Press, 1995), 229–52.

30. Austin, "Nation of Thieves"; Robert E. Weems Jr., *Desegregating the Dollar: African American Consumerism in the Twentieth Century* (New York: New York University Press, 1998); Michael Eric Dyson, Is Bill Cosby Right? Or Has the Black Middle Class Lost Its Mind? (New York: Basic Civitas, 2005).

31. Baby Phat was created for her by then-husband Russell Simmons, who spun it off his already existing Phat Farm fashion company.

32. Simmons, *Fabulosity*, 80.

33. Ibid, 124.

34. Ibid.

35. Cleto, *Camp*, 25.

36. Simmons, *Fabulosity*, 28.

37. Rey Chow notes that the story of *The Joy Luck Club* sacrifices Chinese cultural specificities for an orientalist version of "ethnic diversity" that supports American multiculturalism. Rey Chow, "Ethnicity, Fantasy, and the Film *The Joy Luck Club*," *Feminisms and Pedagogies of Everyday Life*, ed. Carmen Luke (Albany: State University of New York Press, 1996), 204–224. Jing Yin expands on that claim with the argument that the Chinese culture represented in the movie is actually a composite of various Asian values that have been freed from "culture-specific interpretative framework[s]." Jing Yin, "Constructing the Other: A Critical Reading of *The Joy Luck Club*," *Howard Journal of Communication* 16 (2005): 163.

38. Ibid., 29.

39. Ibid., 27.

40. Ibid., 30.

41. Jen Wang, "Life in the Disgrasiab Lane," *disgrasian.com*, June 19, 2007, http://disgrasian .com/2007/06/life-in-the-disgrasiab-lane/.

42. Diana Nguyen, "Disgrasian of the Weak! Kimora Lee Simmons," *disgrasian.com*, November 30, 2007, http://disgrasian.com/2007/11/disgrasian-of-the-weak-kimora-lee -simmons/.

43. Sontag, "Notes on Camp," 62.

44. Simmons, *Fabulosity*, 137–38.

45. Sam Abel, "The Rabbit in Drag: Camp and Gender Construction in the American Animated Cartoon," *Journal of Popular Culture* 29 (1995): 184.

46. Adam D. Galinsky, Cynthia S. Wang, Jennifer A. Whitson, Eric M. Anicich, Kurt Hugenberg, and Galen V. Bodenhausen, "Reappropriation of Stigmatizing Labels: The Reciprocal Relationship between Power and Self-Labeling," *Psychological Science* 24 (2013): 2021.

47. Angela Reyes, "Asian American Stereotypes as Circulating Resource," *Pragmatics* 14 (2004): 189.

48. *Life in the Fab Lane*, "Kimora Cam-Pain," *Style*, August 5, 2007.

49. Though the Simmonses are divorced, Kimora Lee Simmons explains she maintains a great relationship with Russell Simmons because they are co-parenting their children and because they continued to work together.

50. Nishime, "Kimora Barbie."

51. Ibid, 3.

52. It is important to remember that single motherhood has very specific classed dimensions—particularly in the United States—where it is associated with working-class

women. The class status of single mothers might also keep them from seeing themselves reflected in this particular version of Barbie, since they do not have the same access as Simmons to resources.

53. Simmons, *Fabulosity*, 183.

54. Sontag, "Notes on Camp."

55. Soo Ah Kwon, "Autoexoticizing: Asian American Youth and the Import Car Scene," *Journal of Asian American Studies* 7 (2004): 1–26.

56. Nishime, "Kimora Barbie."

57. In a profile on Simmons, the reporter questions whether her mother is actually Japanese rather than an ethnic Korean who fled Kyoto during World War II. Phoebe Eaton, "Kimora Lee Simmons, the New Queen of Conspicuous Consumption," *New York*, May 21, 2005, http://nymag.com/nymetro/shopping/fashion/features/9306/.

58. Ibid.

59. Posting someone else's tweet to her account so that it shows up in her timeline and goes out to her followers.

60. Important enough to be covered by trade magazines and to appear in major fashion magazines.

61. J. Alexander is also a judge on Tyra Banks's *America's Next Top Model*, and a runway coach. He is a familiar face for some reality television viewers and is a campy personality himself—as he often dresses in drag when he shows up on *ANTM*. People on both shows, and he himself, refer to him informally as Ms. Jay, which he started to differentiate himself from *ANTM* cast member Jay Manuel.

62. Trade magazine *Women's Wear Daily* tallied the numbers of Black models for the fashion season before (Fall 2007) this episode was filmed and found that at least a third of the shows featured no models of color. A number of designers had two or fewer, but only a handful of designers featured a substantial number of models of color. The season during which this episode was filmed offered more than 2,278 modeling opportunities, yet women of color were used to fill only 298 spots. Of those 298 models, Asian models were the most popular (124), then Black models (112), then Latinas (62). Though the tally of models of color is a little problematic, in that it assigned the numerous mixed-race models to whichever category they fit into most phenotypically, and Latinas were classified as such if they appeared to be "visibly non-white Hispanic," it does not take away from the incredibly small percentage of models of color working the most elite fashion shows.

63. In 2009 the number of models of color rose to 18 percent overall during the same fashion week.

64. *Life in the Fab Lane*, "A Pretty Face in the Crowd," *Style*, February 20, 2011.

65. *Life in the Fab Lane*, "100 Makeovers for 100 Women," *Style*, February 13, 2011.

66. *Life in the Fab Lane*, "A Pretty Face in the Crowd."

67. Ibid.

68. Ibid.

69. See Ralina Joseph, *Transcending Blackness: From the New Millennium Mulatta to the Exceptional Multiracial* (Durham: Duke University Press, 2012), for a discussion on "beige-ocracy" as a distinction of racial mixing, or Daniel McNeil and Leanne Taylor, "Radical Love: A Transatlantic Dialogue about Race and Mixed Race," *Asian American Literary Review* 4 (2013): 15–26," for examination of "beigeness" as it relates to their identities as racially mixed people navigating a new relationship.

70. Though the show refers to them as real women who are not models, the scene wherein these women are cast for the campaign shows them arriving with professionally photographed headshots. It is possible that they are models, but "real" is meant to refer to women who do not fit within dominant (thin and/or White) representations of models.

Chapter Four: "Because I'm Blasian"
Tiger Woods, Scandal, and Protecting the Blasian Brand

1. Tim Rosaforte, *Tiger Woods: The Makings of a Champion* (New York: St. Martin's Press), 181.

2. Tom Callahan, *His Father's Son: Earl and Tiger Woods* (New York: Gotham, 2010); Mike Kern, "Woods a Product of Two Great Cultures," *Philadelphia Daily News*, June 14, 1995, sec. Sports.

3. For how Woods had been framed as Black via Nike's branding strategy, proximity to his Black father, placement alongside other Black athletes, and the purposeful exclusion of any mentions of his Thai mother, see: Callahan, *His Father's Son*; C. L. Cole and David L. Andrews, "America's New Son: Tiger Woods and America's Multiculturalism," in *Sports Stars: The Cultural Politics of Sporting Celebrity*, ed. David L. Andrews and Steven J. Jackson (New York: Routledge, 2001), 70–86; Larry Dorman, "We'll Be Right Back, after This Hip and Distorted Commercial Break," *New York Times*, September 1, 1996, sec. S13; Habiba Ibrahim, "Toward Black and Multiracial 'Kinship' after 1997, or How a Race Man Became 'Cablinasian,'" *Black Scholar* 39 (2009): 23–31; Hiram Perez, "How to Rehabilitate a Mulatto: The Iconography of Tiger Woods," in *East Main Street: Asian American Popular Culture*, ed. Shilpa Davé, LeiLani Nishime, and Tasha G. Oren (New York: New York University Press, 2005), 222–48; Miki Turner, "Tiger's Stripes: Does It Really Matter What Color They Are?" *Upscale* 9 (1997): 38–41; Jan Weisman, "The Tiger and His Stripes: Thai and American Reactions to Tiger Woods's (Multi-) 'Racial Self,'" in *The Sum of Our Parts: Mixed-Heritage Asian Americans*, ed. Teresa Williams-Leon and Cynthia Nakashima (Philadelphia: Temple University Press, 2001), 231–43; Henry Yu, "How Tiger Woods Lost His Stripes," *Los Angeles Times*, December 2, 1996.

There were also those who saw Woods as trying to distance himself from Blackness: Davis W. Houck, "Crouching Tiger, Hidden Blackness: Tiger Woods and the Disappearance of Race," in *Handbook of Sports and Media*, ed. Arthur A. Raney and Jennings Bryant (London: Lawrence Erlbaum, 2006), 506–23; Jay Nordlinger, "Tiger Time: The Wonder of an American Hero," *National Review*, April 30, 2001; Charles P. Pierce, "The Man. Amen," *GQ*, April 1997; Leonard Pitts Jr., "Is There Room in This Sweet Land of Liberty for Such a Thing as a 'Cablinasian'?" *Baltimore Sun*, April 29, 1997.

4. Andrew C. Billings, "Portraying Tiger Woods: Characterizations of a 'Black' Athlete in a 'White' Sport," *Howard Journal of Communication* 14 (2003): 29–37; Perez, "How to Rehabilitate a Mulatto"; and Henry Yu, "Tiger Woods at the Center of History: Looking Back at the Twentieth Century through the Lenses of Race, Sports, and Mass Consumption," in *Sports Matters: Race, Recreation, and Culture*, ed. John Bloom and Michael Nevin Willard (New York: New York University Press, 2002), 320–53; Henry Yu, "Tiger Woods Is Not the End of History, or Why Sex across the Color Line Will Not Save Us All," *American Historical Review* 108 (2003): 1406–1414.

5. For more on Woods as "America's multiracial son" and the commodification of his "postrace" body for broader audiences, see Cole and Andrews, "America's New Son"; C. L. Cole, "The Place of Golf in U.S. Imperialism," *Journal of Sport & Social Issues* 26 (2002): 331–36, Ronald E. Hall, "The Tiger Woods Phenomenon: A Note on Biracial Identity," *Social Science Journal* 38 (2001): 333–36, Gary Smith, "The Chosen One," *Sports Illustrated*, December 23, 1996; Orin Starn, *The Passion of Tiger Woods: An Anthropologist Reports on Golf, Race, and Celebrity Scandal* (Durham: Duke University Press, 2011); Christopher P. Uchacz, "Black Sports Images in Transition: The Impact of Tiger's Roar," in *African Americans in Sports: Contemporary Themes*, ed. Gary A. Sailes (New Brunswick: Transaction, 1998); and Jack E. White, "I'm Just Who I Am," *Time*, May 5, 1997: 32–36.

6. Smith, "Chosen One."

7. Yu, "How Tiger Woods Lost"; Callahan, *His Father's Son*.

8. Weisman, " Tiger and His Stripes"; Dorman, "'We'll Be Right Back"; Turner, "'Tiger's Stripes"; Cole and Andrews, "America's New Son"; Perez, "How to Rehabilitate a Mulatto."

9. Cole and Andrews, "America's New Son."

10. Ibid., 75–76.

11. Ibid.; Perez, "How to Rehabilitate a Mulatto"; Yu, "How Tiger Woods Lost."

12. Yu, "Center of History": Yu, "End of History"; Callahan, *His Father's Son*; Earl Woods and Pete McDaniel, *Training a Tiger: A Father's Guide to Raising a Winner in Both Golf and Life* (New York: Harper Collins, 1997); Cole, "Place of Golf."

13. Woods and McDaniel, *Training a Tiger*.

14. Weisman, "Tiger and His Stripes," 240.

15. After winning the Masters Tournament in 1997, Zoeller said: "That little boy is driving well and he's putting well. He's doing everything it takes to win. You pat him on the back and say congratulations and enjoy it and tell him not to serve fried chicken next year, got it . . . or collard greens or whatever the hell they serve." Kyle Porter, "A History of Racist Remarks Aimed at Tiger Woods," *CBSSports.com*, May 22, 2013, http://www.cbssports.com /golf/news/a-history-of-racist-remarks-aimed-at-tiger-woods/.

16. Cole and Andrews, "America's New Son."

17. Yu, "End of History."

18. Ibid., 321.

19. Weisman, "Tiger and His Stripes," 223, 226.

20. Ibid.

21. Jennifer Ho, *Racial Ambiguity in Asian American Culture* (New Brunswick: Rutgers University Press, 2015), 85.

22. Cablinasian = CAucasian, BLack, INdian, ASIAN.

23. Cole and Andrews, "America's New Son"; *The Oprah Winfrey Show*, Harpo Productions, April 24, 1997.

24. Perez, "How to Rehabilitate a Mulatto"; Smith, "Chosen One"; Hall, "Tiger Woods Phenomenon"; White, "Who I Am"; Uchacz, "Black Sports Images."

25. Pitts Jr.,"Is There Room"; Nordlinger, "Tiger Time"; Pierce, "The Man. Amen"; Houck, "Crouching Tiger."

26. Yu, "End of History"; Cole, "Place of Golf"; Cole and Andrews, "America's New Son"; Billings, "Portraying Tiger."

27. LeiLani Nishime, "The Case for Cablinasian: Multiracial Naming from *Plessy* to Tiger Woods," *Communication Theory* 22 (2012): 92–111.

28. James Sanderson, "Framing Tiger's Troubles: Comparing Traditional and Social Media," *International Journal of Sport Communication* 3 (2010): 444

29. Claudia Kozman, "The Tiger Woods Scandal in the Media: Measuring Attribute Effects on the Public," *International Journal of Sport Communication* 6 (2013): 228.

30. David L. Andrews, C. Richard King, and David J. Leonard, "America's Son? Tiger Woods as Commodification and Criminalization," in *Commodified and Criminalized: New Racism and African Americans in Contemporary Sports* (Lanham, MD: Rowman & Littlefield, 2011).

31. Ibid., 250.

32. Without the prenuptial and postnuptial stipulations or any settlement details, as those were confidential and not available online.

33. The alert included all results and was delivered to my e-mail inbox every day. From those results, I excluded anything that did not have Tiger Woods in its title, duplicate news items, and blog posts. Videos were excluded if they were not about Tiger Woods explicitly. Included in the videos were commercials featuring Tiger Woods, his public apology, parodies of the commercials or the scandal, and comedy sketches about the cheating, Tiger himself, and/or the accident.

34. I conducted a Lexis-Nexis search for "Tiger Woods" from November 27, 2009, to January 1, 2011, filtering through major world publications, then broadcast transcripts. With these results, I excluded transcripts that did not feature Tiger Woods in the title, were duplicates, or had fewer than two hundred words. I also excluded metacommentary about Tiger Woods, using the original as a source. In total I read over two thousand articles.

35. Halford Ross Ryan, "Kategoria and Apologia: On Their Rhetorical Criticism as a Speech Set," *Quarterly Journal of Speech* 68 (1982): 256.

36. Keith Michael Hearit, "Mistakes Were Made": Organizations, Apologia, and Crises of Social Legitimacy," *Communication Studies* 46 (1995): 11.

37. Buzz Bissinger, "Tiger in the Rough," *Vanity Fair*, February 1, 2010, http://www.vanityfair.com/culture/features/2010/02/tiger-woods-201002; Tim Cowlishaw, "Shame on Us," *Dallas Morning News*, December 3, 2009; retrieved from Lexis-Nexis database; Frank Deford, "Who Can a Young Fan Look Up To? It's Tough," *NPR Morning Edition*, August 25, 2010, http://www.npr.org/templates/story/story.php?storyId=129400452; Simon Houpt, "Will Sponsors Stand by Tiger Woods?" *Globe and Mail*, December 2009, retrieved from Lexis-Nexis database; Emily Kay, "Tavistock Exhibition Key for Tiger Woods says ex-coach Butch Harmon," *Waggle Room*, March 13, 2011, http://www.waggleroom.com/2011/3/13/2047770/tavistock-exhibition-key-for-tiger-woods-says-ex-coach-butch-harmon; Mike Lupica, "Woods Stuck in a Trap of His Own Making but He Can Claw Way Back," *Daily News*, December 9, 2009, retrieved from Lexis-Nexis database; Mark Seal (March 28, 2010); "Tiger Woods's Inconvenient Women," *Vanity Fair*, March 28, 2010, http://www.vanityfair.com/online/daily/2010/03/tiger-woodss-inconvenient-women.html.

38. Charlie Gibson (anchor), "Deep Dismay: Tiger's Story," *World News Tonight*, ABC, December 2, 2009.

39. Bruce Jenkins, "The Tiger Woods Era Is Over," *San Francisco Chronicle*, November 20, 2010, retrieved from Lexis-Nexis database.

40. Bissinger, "Tiger in the Rough."

41. Mark Seal, "Tiger Woods's Inconvenient Women Part Two," *Vanity Fair*, May 1, 2010, http://www.vanityfair.com/online/daily/2010/05/tiger-woods-part-ii.

42. John Feinstein, "Will 'Transgressions' Hurt Tiger Woods's Brand?" *NPR Morning Edition*, December 3, 2009, http://www.npr.org/templates/story/story.php?storyId=121045024.

43. Houpt, "Will Sponsors Stand By?"

44. Cowlishaw, "Shame on Us."

45. "Congressman Drops Effort to Honor Tiger Woods," Associated Press State & Local Wire, December 9, 2009, retrieved from Lexis-Nexis database.

46. "'Church of Tiger' Website Disbands over Golfer's 'Sins,'" *Agence France Presse*, December 3, 2009, retrieved from Lexis-Nexis database.

47. A. J. Daulerio, "Charles Barkley: I Was Gonna Drive around the Corner and Get a Blow Job, "*Deadspin*, December 1, 2008, http://deadspin.com/#!5121873/charles-barkley -i-was-gonna-drive-around-the-corner-and-get-a-blow-job-.

48. Bissinger, "Tiger in the Rough"; Deford, "Young Fans"; Seal, "Inconvenient Women"; Tim Dahlberg, "Woods Shouldn't Stay Quiet for Too Long," *Chicago Daily Herald*, November 29, 2009, retrieved from Lexis-Nexis database; Ronald L. Jackson, *Scripting the Black Masculine Body: Identity, Discourse, and Racial Politics in Popular Media* (Albany: State University of New York Press, 2006); Tim Kawakami. "Tiger Woods's Relaunch Is Coming, and It Will Happen on the Links," *San Jose Mercury News*, December 8, 2009, retrieved from Lexis-Nexis database; John Rohde, "The Masters: Believe Tiger? Bigger Question Is, What Does It Matter?" *Oklahoman*, April 6, 2010, retrieved from Lexis-Nexis database;

49. Iain Marlow, "Key Sponsors Stand by Tiger; Endorsements Have Made Tiger Woods the World's First Billion-Dollar Athlete. So Far, the Swirl of Scandal Has Left His Empire Unscathed," *Toronto Sun*, December 3, 2009, retrieved from Lexis-Nexis database.

50. Bissinger, "Tiger in the Rough."

51. Lupica, "Woods Stuck"; Adam Lazarus, "Tiger Woods: Is the Media Too Quick to Bury Tiger?" *Sport Shots*, March 11, 2011, http://bleacherreport.com/articles/632659 -nfl-labor-talks-2011-nfl-draft-tiger-woods-and-fridays-top-sports-buzz/entry/51749-tiger -woods-is-the- media-too-quick-to-bury-tiger; Mike Lupica, "He'll Roar Again. We Won't Forget What Tiger Did, but We'll Love Him When He Returns," *Daily News*, December 13, 2009, retrieved from Lexis-Nexis database.

52. Mark Lelinwalla, Mitch Abramson, and Samuel Ebenezer, "Here's the Scoop, Tiger," *Daily News*, December 13, 2009, retrieved from Lexis-Nexis database.

53. Ron Kroichick, "Pro Golf Loses Sparkle Minus Brightest Star, Tiger Woods," *San Francisco Chronicle*, February 6, 2010, retrieved from Lexis-Nexis database.

54. Will Brinson, "Tiger Woods Mistresses Cheat Sheet," *aolnews.com*, December 8, 2009, http://www.aolnews.com/2009/12/08/tiger-woods-mistresses-the-still-growing -cheat-sheet/.

55. Seal, "Inconvenient Women."

56. Paul Apostolidis, "Sex Scandals, Racial Domination and the Systemic Correlation of Power-Modalities in Foucault," *Journal of Political Power* 4 (2011): 185.

57. Michael J. Feeney, "A Rap Cheat off Tiger: Brooklyn Artist Maino Creates 'Anthem' to All Men with a Lot of Women," *New York Daily News*, January 11, 2010, retrieved from Lexis-Nexis database.

58. Bissinger, "Tiger in the Rough"; Seal, "Inconvenient Women"; James Fanelli, "Gal #5: Tiger an Animal in Sack; S&M Bombshell, as 2 New 'Mistresses' Are Revealed," *New York Post*, December 6, 2009, retrieved from Lexis-Nexis database.

59. Fanelli, "Gal #5."

60. Seal, "Inconvenient Women,"

61. Nancy Armour, "Woods's Ex-Wife Went 'through Hell,'" *Associated Press Worldstream*, August 26, 2010, retrieved from Lexis-Nexis database; Sandra Sobieraj Westfall, "My Own Story," *People*, August 25, 2010.

62. Monte Poole, "Tiger Woods Is Still in the Rough, and Will Be for a While," *Contra Costa Times*, December 2, 2009, retrieved from Lexis-Nexis database.

63. Vicki Walker and Randy McMullen, "Tiger Woods Pays $750 Million in Divorce Settlement, Report Says," *Contra Costa Times*, June 30, 2010, retrieved from Lexis-Nexis database.

64. John Barry, "With Golf, Puns Go to the Dogs," *St. Petersburg Times*, December 13, 2009, retrieved from Lexis-Nexis database; Cecil Brown "Knocking on Woods," January 13, 2010, retrieved from http://www.counterpunch.org/brown01132010.html; Jimmy Fallon, *Late Night with Jimmy Fallon*, NBC, 2009; Jay Leno, *The Jay Leno Show*, NBC, December 2, 2009; David Letterman, *The Late Show with David Letterman*, CBS, December 7, 2009; Conan O'Brien, *The Tonight Show with Conan O'Brien*, NBC, December 1, 2009, Hollywood.

65. Brown, "Knocking on Woods."

66. Ibid.

67. "Weekend Update: Mistress 15," dir. Danielle Kasen, *Saturday Night Live*, , NBCDecember 12, 2009.

68. Lauren Bans, "Don't Hate the Player, Hate the Game: Tiger Woods Affairs Tour," *GQ*, December 18, 2010, http://www.gq.com/blogs/the-q/2010/04/dont-hate-the-player-hate-the- game-tiger-woods-affair-tour-2010.html.

69. Wilt Chamberlain, a Black professional basketball player, claimed to have slept with over 20,000 women, in his 1991 biography *A View from Above*.

70. Kevin Sintumuang, "Merry Christmas, Tiger Woods!" *GQ.com*, December 18, 2010, http://www.gq.com/entertainment/humor/200912/tiger-wood-sex-scandal-elin -mistresses-golf.

71. Mike Byhoff, "George Lopez and Wanda Sykes Make the Same Exact Racist Joke about Tiger Woods," *Gawker TV*, December 1, 2009, http://tv.gawker.com/#!5416361/george -lopez-and-wanda-sykes-make-the-same-exact-racist-joke-about-tiger-woods; Sven Klemencic, "Tiger Woods Scandal: The Best Jokes We've Heard So Far," *Bleacher Report*, December 3, 2009, http://bleacherreport.com/articles/301919-tiger-woods-scandal-the-best-jokes-weve-heard-so-far; Ann Oldenburg, "Tiger Woods Is Serious Fodder for Jokes," *USA Today*, December 3, 2009, http://content.usatoday.com/communities/entertainment /post/2009/12/tiger-woods-is-serious-fodder-for-jokes/1; Shake, "Interview w/ Paul Mooney pt. 2—Tiger Gets Wake Up Call," *News with Davey D.*, January 5, 2010, https:// www.youtube.com/watch?v=-9kMx_Zd1N8; Ben Wojdyla, "The Worst Car-Related Tiger Woods Jokes on the Internet," *Jalopnik*, December 7, 2009, http://jalopnik.com/#!5420730 /the-worst-car+related-tiger-woods-jokes-on-the-internet/gallery.

72. George Lopez, *Lopez Tonight*, TBS, November 30, 2009; Byhoff, "George Lopez and Wanda Sykes."

73. The Cadillac Escalade has been linked in popular culture overwhelmingly to Black athletes, rappers, and entertainers.

74. This draws on the stereotype that Asian/Americans are bad drivers.

75. Shake, "Interview w/Paul Mooney."

76. Ibid.

77. "Tiger Woods's Accidents," *Saturday Night Live*, dir. Don Roy King, NBC, December 5, 2009.

78. Sintumuang, "Merry Christmas."

79. Jachinson Chan, *Chinese American Masculinities: From Fu Manchu to Bruce Lee.* New York: Taylor & Francis, 2001; Chiung Hwang Chen, "Feminization of Asian (American) Men in the US Mass Media: An Analysis of I." *Journal of Communication Inquiry* 20 (1996): 57–71; Robert G. Lee, *Orientals: Asian Americans in Popular Culture* (Philadelphia: Temple University Press, 1999); David L. Eng, "Out Here and over There: Queerness and Diaspora in Asian American Studies," *Social Text* 52/53 (1997): 31–52.

80. Shake, "Interview w/Paul Mooney."

81. Lelinwalla, Abramson, and Ebenezer, "Here's the Scoop."

82. "Text Messages between Tiger Woods and Jamie Grubbs," *NY Post*, December 9, 2009, http://nypost.com/2009/12/09/text-messages-between-tiger-woods-and-jaimee -grubbs/.

83. Jeffrey Toobin, "Toobin: Why Tiger Woods May Not Be Talking to Police," *CNN com*, November 30, 2009, http://www.cnn.com/2009/OPINION/11/30/tiger.woods.legal/index .html?iref=24hours.

84. Cam Cole, "Tiger's Tale Exposes Private Life of Sports Stars as a Myth," *Vancouver Sun*, December 3, 2009, retrieved from Lexis-Nexis database.

85. Marlow, "Key Sponsors Stand by Tiger."

86. Tiger Woods, "Statement from Tiger Woods," November 29, 2009, www.tigerwoods .com.

87. Tiger Woods, "Transgressions—Statement from Tiger Woods," December 2, 2009, retrieved from www.tigerwoods.com.

88. Ibid.

89. Houpt, "Will Sponsors Stand By?"

90. Accenture, AT&T, Tiger Woods PGA Tour Golf, Gillette, Nike, Gatorade, TLC Laser Eye Centers, *Golf Digest*, and Tag Heuer all dropped Woods once the scandal broke, costing him an estimate $22 million in endorsement monies, and costing the shareholders for these companies an estimated $12 billion (Christopher R. Knittel and Victor Stango, "Celebrity Endorsements, Firm Value, and Reputation Risk: Evidence from the Tiger Woods Scandal," *Management Science* 60 (2013): 21–37.

91. "PGA Tour Player of the Year," Associated Press, December 19, 2009, retrieved from Lexis-Nexis database.

92. Alex Myers, "CBS Owes Tiger a Big Thank-You for These Ridiculous TV Ratings," *Golf Digest*, August 24, 2015, http://www.golfdigest.com/story/cbs-owes-tiger-a-big-thank -you-for-these-ridiculous-tv-ratings; John Strege, "Tiger Woods Effect in Masters Reflected in ESPN's First-Round Ratings," *Golf Digest*, April 8, 2016, http://www.golfdigest.com/story /tiger-woods-effect-in-masters-reflected-in-espns-first-round-ratings; Bob Harig, "Tiger's Impact Felt across Generations," *ESPN*, January 2, 2016, http://espn.go.com/golf/story/_ /id/14360626/tiger-woods-impact-felt-generations; http://www.golf.com/tour-and-news /2008-we-learned-what-happens-tv-ratings-when-tigers-not-around.

93. Tiger Woods, "Indefinite Break—Statement from Tiger Woods," December 11, 2009, www. tigerwoods.com.

94. Hearit, "Mistakes Were Made," 11.

95. Tiger Woods, "Public Apology—Statement from Tiger Woods," February 19, 2010, www. tigerwoods.com.

96. Jennifer Ho, *Racial Ambiguity in Asian American Culture* (New Brunswick: Rutgers University Press, 2015).

97. LeiLani Nishime, *Undercover Asians: Multiracial Asian Americans in Visual Culture* (Urbana: University of Illinois Press, 2013), 60.

98. Britt Hume, *Fox News Sunday*, Fox, January 3, 2010.

99. Bill O'Reilly, *The O'Reilly Factor*, Fox, January 4, 2010.

100. Nike, Earl and Tiger Woods [commercial], 2010.

101. William L. Benoit, *Accounts, Excuses, and Apologies: A Theory of Image Restoration Strategies* (Albany: State University of New York Press, 1995), vii.

102. Cole, "Tiger's Tale Exposes Private Life."

103. L. Paul Husselbee and Kevin A. Stein, "Tiger Woods' Apology and Newspapers' Responses: A Study of Journalistic Antapologia," *Journal of Sports Media* 7 (2012): 59–87.

104. Brian Montopoli, "Tiger Woods Hires Former Bush Aide Ari Fleischer," *In the News*, March 11, 2010, http://www.cbsnews.com/8301-503544_162-20000286-503544.html.

105. Oprah Winfrey, "Tiger Woods," *The Oprah Winfrey Show*, CBS, April 24, 1997, Chicago.

106. Noreen W. Kruse, "The Scope of Apologetic Discourse: Establishing Generic Parameters," *Southern Speech Communication Journal* 46 (1981): 278–91; Noreen W. Kruse, "Apologia in Team Sport," *Quarterly Journal of Speech* 67 (1981): 270–83.

107. Ryan, "Kategoria and Apologia."

108. Christopher R. Knittel and Victor Stango, "Celebrity Endorsements, Firm Value, and Reputation Risk: Evidence from the Tiger Woods Scandal," *Management Science* 1 (2013), 14

109. Hearit, "Mistakes Were Made."

110. Ken Fidlin, "All in All, Not Bad; Tiger's Return to Golf No Disaster—Except by His Standard, Perhaps," *Toronto Sun*, April 13, 2010, retrieved from Lexis-Nexis database.

111. Fred Goodall, "Inside Tiger Woods Mystery," *Mobile Register*, November 29, 2009, retrieved from Lexis-Nexis database.

112. Monte Poole Bay Area News Group, "Tiger Woods Can Use Kobe Bryant's Redemption as Inspiration," *San Jose Mercury News*, August 9, 2010, retrieved from Lexis-Nexis database.

113. Amanda Cochran, "Tiger's Head Back in Right Place?" *CBS News*, August 27, 2010.

114. "Text Messages between Tiger Woods and Jamie Grubbs."

Chapter Five: Sporting the Blasian Body

1. Mary Beltran, "*SNL*'s "Fauxbama" Debate: Facing Off over Millennial (Mixed-)Racial Impersonation," in *Saturday Night Live & American TV*, ed. Nick Marx, Matt Sienkiewicz, and Ron Becker (Bloomington: Indiana University Press, 2013).

2. Even though professional wrestling is scripted, I am including it here as a sport because it involves physical effort, training, practice, skill, and talent.

3. See: John Hoberman, *Darwin's Athletes: How Sport Has Damaged Black America and Preserved the Myth of Race* (New York: Mariner Books, 1997); Richard E. Lapchick, *Five Minutes to Midnight: Race and Sport in the 1990s* (New York: Madison, 1991); Ben Carrington, "Sport, Masculinity, and Black Cultural Resistance," *Journal of Sport and Social Issues* 22 (1998): 275–98; Todd Boyd, "The Day the Niggaz Took Over: Basketball, Commodity Culture, and Black Masculinity," in *Out of Bounds: Sports, Media, and the Politics of Identity*, ed. Aaron Baker and Todd Boyd (Bloomington: Indiana University Press, 1997), 123–42; Mike, "Sport and Stereotype: From Role Model to Muhammad Ali," *Race and Class* 36 (1995): 1–29; Ronald L. Jackson, *Scripting the Black Masculine Body: Identity, Discourse,*

and Racial Politics in Popular Media (Albany: State University of New York Press, 2006); bell hooks, *Black Looks: Race and Representation* (Boston,: South End Press, 1992); Richard Majors, "Cool Pose: Black Masculinity and Sports," in *The Masculinities Reader*, ed. Stephen M. Whitehead and Frank J. Barrett (Malden: Blackwell, 2001), 211–17; Michael Messner, *Power at Play: Sports and the Problem of Masculinity* (Boston: Beacon, 1992); Kent Ono, "America's Apple Pie: Baseball, Japan-Bashing and the Sexual Threat of Economic Miscegenation," in *Out of Bounds: Sports, Media and the Politics of Identity*, ed. Aaron Baker and Todd Boyd (Bloomington: Indiana University Press, 1997), 81–101.

4. John Alt, "Sport and Cultural Reification: From Ritual to Mass Consumption," *Theory, Culture & Society* 1 (1983): 99

5. Boyd, "Day the Niggaz."

6. J .J. Sewart, "The Commodification of Sport," *International Review for the Sociology of Sport* 22 (1987): 171.

7. Joane Nagel, "Masculinity and Nationalism: Gender and Sexuality in the Making of Nations," *Ethnic and Racial Studies* 21 (1998): 251–52.

8. Lincoln Allison, "Sport and Nationalism," in *Handbook of Sports Studies*, ed. Jay Coakley and Eric Dunning (London: Sage, 2000), 344–55; Joseph Maguire, *Global Sport: Identities, Societies and Civilizations* (Cambridge: Polity Press, 1999).

9. Alan Bairner, *Sport, Nationalism and Globalization* (Albany: State University of New York Press, 2001), 176.

10. Grant Jarvie, "Internationalism and Sport in the Making of Nations," in *Identities: Global Studies in Culture and Power* 10 (2003): 539–40.

11. John Hargreaves, "Globalisation Theory, Global Sport, and Nations and Nationalism," in *Power Games: A Critical Sociology of Sport*, ed. John Sugden and Alan Tomlinson (London: Routledge, 2002), 31.

12. Allison, "Sport and Nationalism," 346.

13. Grant Jarvie and Irene Reid, "Race Relations, Sociology of Sport and the New Politics of Race and Racism," *Leisure Studies* 16 (1997): 214.

14. Myra Washington and Megan Economides, "Strong Is the New Sexy: Women, Cross-Fit and the Postfeminist Ideal," *Journal of Sport & Social Issues* 40 (2016): 143–61; Leslie Heywood and Shari Dworkin, *Built to Win: The Female Athlete as Cultural Icon* (Minneapolis: University of Minnesota Press, 2000); Sandra Lee Bartky, "Foucault, Femininity, and the Modernization of Patriarchal Power," in *Feminism and Foucault: Reflections on Resistance*, ed. Irene Diamond and Lee Quinby (Boston: Northeastern University Press, 1988) 61–86; Cheryl Cooky, Ranissa Dycus, and Shari L. Dworkin, "'What Makes a Woman a Woman?' versus 'Our First Lady of Sport': A Comparative Analysis of the United States and the South African Media Coverage of Caster Semenya," *Journal of Sport & Social Issues* 37 (2013): 31–56; Shari L. Dworkin, "Holding Back: Negotiating a Glass Ceiling on Women's Muscular Strength," *Sociological Perspectives* 44 (2001): 333–50; Shari L. Dworkin and Faye L. Wachs, *Body Panic: Gender, Health, and the Selling of Fitness* (New York: New York University Press, 2009); Susan Birrell, "Race Relations Theories and Sport: Suggestions for a More Critical Analysis," in *Sport: Sport and Power Relations*, ed. Eric Dunning and Dominic Malcolm (London: Routledge, 2003), 44–61; Eric Anderson and Mark McCormack, "Comparing the Black and Gay Male Athlete: Patterns in American Oppression," *Journal of Men's Studies* 18 (2010): 145–58.

15. Lloyd L. Wong and Ricardo Trumper, "Global Celebrity Athletes and Nationalism," *Journal of Sport & Social Issues* 26 (2002):169.

16. Naoki Chiba, Osamu Ebihara, and Shinji Morino, "Globalization, Naturalization and Identity: The Case of Borderless Elite Athletes in Japan," *International Review for the Sociology of Sport* 36 (2001): 203.

17. Carrington, "Sport, Masculinity"; Jarvie, "Internationalism and Sport."

18. Gail Bederman, *Manliness and Civilization: A Cultural History of Gender and Race in the United States, 1880–1917* (Chicago: University of Chicago Press, 1995).

19. Andrew C. Billings & Susan Tyler Eastman, "Selective Representation of Gender, Ethnicity, and Nationality in American Television Coverage of the 2000 Summer Olympics," *International Review for the Sociology of Sport* 33 (2002): 351–70; James A. Rada and Tim K. Wulfemeyer, "Color Coded: Racial Descriptors in Television Coverage of Intercollegiate Sports," *Journal of Broadcasting & Electronic Media* 49 (2005): 65–85; Pamela L. Wonsek, "College Basketball on Television: A Study of Racism in the Media," *Media, Culture & Society* 14 (1992): 449–61; Pat Viklund, "Brain versus Brawn: An Analysis of Stereotyping and Racial Bias in National Football League Broadcasts" (master's thesis: Boston College, 2009); Susan Tyler Eastman and Andrew C. Billings, "Biased Voices of Sports: Racial and Gender Stereotyping in College Basketball Announcing," *Howard Journal of Communication* 12 (2001): 183–201; Mikaela J. Dufur, "Race Logic and Being Like Mike: Representations of Athletes in Advertising, 1985–1994," *Sociological Focus* 30 (1997): 345–55; Robert Staples and Terry Jones, "Culture, Ideology and Black Television Images," *Black Scholar* 16 (1985): 10–20.

20. Bederman notes that at the turn of the twentieth century, bodily strength (and size) was equated with public and political power/authority. That the sport of boxing purposely kept men of color out of championship bouts while they were concurrently denied power outside the realm of sport highlights how well sport reflects cultural norms.

21. Theresa Runstedtler's *Jack Johnson, Rebel Sojourner: Boxing in the Shadow of the Global Color Line* (Berkeley: University of California Press, 2012) offers a thorough and incisive analysis of why Jack Johnson's personality, interracial relationships, and boxing skills combined to make him the most famous Black man in the world.

22. Ibid., 2.

23. See: Reginald Leamon Robinson, "Intersection of Dominant White Images, the Violence of Neighborhood Purity, and the Master Narrative of Black Inferiority," *William and Mary Law Review* 37 (1995): 69–155; George Yancy, *Black Bodies, White Gazes: The Continuing Significance of Race* (Lanham, MD: Rowman & Littlefield, 2008); Wonsek, "College Basketball"; Viklund, "Brain versus Brawn"; Hoberman, *Darwin's Athletes*; Sander L. Gilman, *Difference and Pathology: Stereotypes of Sexuality, Race, and Madness* (Ithaca: Cornell University Press, 1985); William B. Helmreich, *The Things They Say behind Your Back: Stereotypes and the Myths behind Them* (Rutgers: Transaction, 1984).

24. Jackson, *Scripting the Black*; Abby L. Ferber, "The Construction of Black Masculinity: White Supremacy Now and Then," *Journal of Sport and Social Issues* 31 (2007): 11–24; Patricia Hill Collins, *Black Sexual Politics: African Americans, Gender, and the New Racism* (New York: Routledge, 2005); David J. Leonard, "The Next M.J. or the Next O.J.? Kobe Bryant, Race, and the Absurdity of Colorblind Rhetoric," *Journal of Sport and Social Issues* 28 (2004): 284–313; Carrington, "Sport, Masculinity"; Richard Majors, "Cool Pose: Black Masculinity and Sports," in *The Masculinities Reader*, ed. Stephen M. Whitehead and Frank J. Barrett (Malden: Blackwell, 2001), 211–17; Hoberman, *Darwin's Athletes*.

25. Brendan Hokowhitu, "Tackling Māori Masculinity: A Colonial Genealogy of Savagery and Sport," *Contemporary Pacific* 16 (2004): 259–84.

26. Hill Collins, *Black Sexual Politics*, 57.

27. Hokowhitu, "Tackling Māori Masculinity," 266.

28. See April K. Henderson, "Fleeting Substantiality: The Samoan Giant in US Popular Discourse," *Contemporary Pacific* 23 (2011): 269–302.

29. Ferber, "Construction of Black Masculinity."

30. Dylan Martin, "The Top 10 Greatest UGA Football Players of All Time," *bleacherreport.com*, February 5, 2010, http://bleacherreport.com/articles/340442-the-top-10-greatest-uga-football-players-of-all-time/page/11.

31. Ken Sugiura, "Ex-Bulldog Ward Surges to Prove Right for Steelers," *Atlanta Journal Constitution*, December 13, 2001, home ed.

32. Scott M. Reid, "Georgia Notebook Hines Has Speed, Toughness of TB," *Atlanta Journal-Constitution*, August 26, 1994, sec. E Sports.

33. Hoberman, *Darwin's Athletes*, xiv.

34. Kirsten Acuna, "How Dwayne 'The Rock' Johnson Went from WWE Wrestler to Hollywood's Box-Office Champ," *Business Insider*, May 29, 2015, http://www.businessinsider.com/dwayne-johnson-biography-2015-5?op=1.

35. Sean Evans, "We Took On the Rock's Diet and Tried to Eat 10 Pounds of Food per Day," *Complex*, May 7, 2015, http://www.complex.com/pop-culture/2015/05/the-rock-diet-plan-attempted-by-a-real-person.

36. Rachael Joo and Sameer Pandya, "On the Cultural Politics of Asian American Sports," *Amerasia Journal* 41 (2015): x.

37. Henderson, "Fleeting Substantiality."

38. Richard C. King, "Defacements/Effacements: Anti-Asian (American) Sentiment in Sport," *Journal of Sport and Social Issues* 30 (2006): 342.

39. David Tokiharu Mayeda, "From Model Minority to Economic Threat: Media Portrayals of Major League Baseball Pitchers Hideo Nomo and Hideki Irabu," *Journal of Sport and Social Issues* 23 (1999): 209.

40. Ibid., 204.

41. King, "Defacements/Effacements," 344.

42. Michael K. Park, "Race, Hegemonic Masculinity, and the 'Linpossible!': An Analysis of Media Representations of Jeremy Lin," *Communication & Sport* 3 (2015): 367–89.

43. Ying Chiang and Tzu-Hsuan Chen, "Adopting the Diasporic Son: Jeremy Lin and Taiwan Sport Nationalism," *International Review for the Sociology of Sport* 50 (2013): 705–21.

44. Daniel Yu-Kuei Sun, "Transpacific Linsanity: Model Minority, Cultural Hegemony, and a Nationalism without Subjectivity," *Amerasia Journal* 41 (2015): 110.

45. Kathleen S. Yep, "Linsanity and Centering Sport in Asian American Studies and Pacific Islander Studies," *Amerasia Journal* 38 (2012): 136.

46. Vicente Diaz, "'Fight Boys 'til the Last': Island Style Football and the Remasculinization of Indigeneity in the Militarized American Pacific Islands," in *Pacific Diaspora: Island Peoples in the United States and across the Pacific*, ed. Paul R. Spickard, Joanne L. Rondilla, and Debbie Hippolite Wright (Honolulu: University of Hawai'i Press, 2002), 180.

47. Ty P. Kāwika Tengan and Jesse Makani Markham, "Performing Polynesian Masculinities in American Football: From 'Rainbows to Warriors,'" *International Journal of the History of Sport* 26 (December 2009): 2413.

48. Ibid.

49. Since these islands are still considered "possessions" and not territories, their citizens are not conferred birthright citizenship.

50. Richard Lapchick, "Promise to Prominence for Asian Athletes," *ESPN*, May 18, 2006, http://sports.espn.go.com/espn/news/story?id=2449595.

51. Gene Wang, "Yao Ming's Influence Was Far-Reaching during Distinguished NBA Career," *Washington Post*, July 20, 2011; Julia Greenberg, "What the NBA Knows about China That Silicon Valley Doesn't," *Wired.com*, June 1, 2016, https://www.wired.com/2016/06/nba-knows-china-silicon-valley-doesnt/; Calvin Watkins, "Yao Ming, the 'Emperor' of Houston and Chinese Basketball," *ESPN.com*, April 4, 2016, http://www.espn.com/nba/story/_/id/15130977/what-yao-ming-means-houston-china-rockets-nba; Cindy Sui, "'Linsanity' Hits Taiwan as Jeremy Lin Conquers NBA," *BBC.com*, February 15, 2012, http://www.bbc.com/news/world-asia-17052383; Michael Wilbon, "Jeremy Lin and the NBA's Horizons," *ESPN.com*, February 23, 2012, http://www.espn.com/espn/commentary/story/_/page/wilbon-120223/international-popularity-jeremy-lin-cements-nba-role-global-sport.

52. Ono, "America's Apple Pie," 100.

53. Michael David Smith, "American Football Is Coming to India," *NBCSports.com*, Profootballtalk: Latest News and Rumors, August 3, 2011, http://profootballtalk.nbcsports.com/2011/08/03/american-football-is-coming-to-india/.

54. Mary Lee, "Mixed Race Peoples in the Korean National Imaginary and Family," *Korean Studies* 32 (2008): 56–85.

55. Jarvie, "Internationalism and Sport," 545.

56. Sang-Hun Choe, "From an Ostracized Class, a Hero for Koreans; Praise for Athlete Seen as Hypocrisy," *International Herald Tribune*, February 23, 2006, p. 2, par. 9.

57. *Sportscenter*, "Hines Ward," dir. Daniel de la Gándara, ESPN, August 21, 2006.

58. Ibid.

59. Charles D. Sherman, "Pure Blood and Political Football," *Korea Times*, April 14, 2006.

60. *Sportscenter*, "Hines Ward."

61. Ibid.

62. Jonathan SanFilippo, "No. 1 Steeler," *Korea Times*, December 20, 2007.

63. Jon Herskovitz, "S. Korea a Lonely Place for Mixed-Race Children," Reuters, March 5, 2006.

64. Lee, "Mixed Race Peoples."

65. Laura Briggs, "Making 'American' Families: Transnational Adoption and U.S. Latin America Policy," in *Haunted by Empire: Geographies of Intimacy in North American History*, ed. Ann Laura Stoler (Durham: Duke University Press, 2006), 343–65.

66. Ibid.

67. Velina Hasu Houston, "To the Colonizer Goes the Spoils: Amerasian Progeny in Vietnam War Films and Owning Up to the Gaze," *Amerasia Journal* 23 (1997): 69–85.

68. Sean Dorney, "The Rock Visits Samoa," *World Today*, August 13, 2004, http://www.abc.net.au/worldtoday/content/2004/s1176011.htm.

69. "Samoa Gives Chiefly Title to Actor Dwayne Johnson," *Radio New Zealand*, August 11, 2004, http://www.radionz.co.nz/international/pacific-news/150109/samoa-gives-chiefly-title-to-actor-dwayne-johnson.

70. Lave Tuiletufuga, "Samoa Homecoming for the 'Rock' Dwayne Johnson," *Event Polynesia*, http://www.eventpolynesia.com/events/samoa/archive/US3_page_rocksamoa04.htm.

71. Rochelle Tuitagava'a Fonoti, "Tau Ave I Le Mita'I, Tau Ave I Le Mamao: Mapping the Tatau-ed Body in Samoan Diaspora" (master's thesis, University of Hawaii).

72. "The Untold Story behind The Rock's Tattoo—AKA Dwayne Johnson," *YouTube*, TheNewStockholm, April 2, 2012, https://www.youtube.com/watch?v=TE9cLdlFRSc.

73. Fonoti, "Tau Ave."

74. Mike Morris, "Steelers Receiver Hines Ward Arrested for DUI in Dekalb County," *Atlanta Journal Constitution*, July 9, 2011, sec. UGA Sports.

75. Marcus K. Garner, "Hines Ward's DUI Charges Dropped; Pleads Guilty to Reckless Driving," *Atlanta Journal Constitution*, March 15, 2012, http://www.ajc.com/news/sports /hines-wards-dui-charges-dropped-pleads-guilty-to-r/nQRXm/.

76. Maria Sciullo, "Hines Ward Discovers a New Fan Base Dancing with Stars," *Pittsburgh Post-Gazette*, May 23, 2011, sec. A&E/Theater & Dance.

77. Eugene Yi, "The Hines Ward Factor," *KoreAm*, July 2011.

78. *Outside the Lines*, ESPN, June 11, 2009.

79. George Sage's *Power and Ideology in American Sport: A Critical Perspective* (Champaign: Human Kinetics Publishers, 1990) offers a useful and necessary explanation on why using critical theory to examine the influence of sports reveals its significance: "In the realm of sport, as in many others, dominant groups use political, economic, and cultural resources to define societal norms and values to sustain their influence. Their interests are legitimized by compatible ideologies disseminated by schools, mass media, and various agencies of social control, and the processes they use to suppress alternative versions" (3).

80. Carrington, "Sport, Masculinity," 280.

81. C. Roger Rees and Andrew W. Miracle, "Education and Sports," in *Handbook of Sports Studies*, ed. Jay Coakley and Eric Dunning (London: Sage, 2000), 277–90; Carrington, "Sport, Masculinity"; Jarvie and Reid, "Race Relations"; Boyd, "Day the Niggaz"; Samantha King, "Homonormativity and the Politics of Race: Reading Sheryl Swoopes," *Journal of Lesbian Studies* 13 (2009): 272–90; Ferber, "Construction of Black Masculinity"; Stephanie Foote, "Making Sport of Tonya," *Journal of Sport & Social Issues* 27 (2003): 3; Nick Trujillo, "Hegemonic Masculinity on the Mound: Media Representations of Nolan Ryan and American Sports Culture," *Critical Studies in Mass Communication* 8 (1991): 290–308; Jackson, *Scripting the Black*.

82. Jackson, *Scripting the Black*.

83. Mayeda, "From Model Minority."

84. Professional wrestling is staged with storylines and character arcs written and agreed upon by the wrestlers as their characters. The producers and wrestlers decide each week on antagonists (heels) and protagonists (faces). Wrestlers also have tag teams (one partner) and stables (a group of wrestlers) when the storylines call for affiliations and group challenges.

85. Fred Armisen was the other mixed-race Asian/American cast member, whose grandfather was Japanese. Schneider had a Filipina grandmother. See Kent A. Ono and Vincent Pham, *Asian Americans and the Media* (Malden: Polity, 2009) for more on these Asian/American cast members.

86. Ed Bouchette, "Ward Gushes over Obama, Mourns S. Korean Ex-President's Death," *Pittsburgh Post-Gazette*, May 27, 2009, sec. Sports/Steelers.

87. Lynn Hoppes, "Hines Ward: Racism toward Asians Isn't New," *ESPN.com*, March 15, 2011, http://espn.go.com/espn/conversations/_/id/6220265/racism-asians-anything-new.

88. Diana Nguyen, "Amazian of the Week! Hines Ward." *Disgrasian.com*, December 3, 2007, http://disgrasian.com/2007/12/amazian-of-the-week-hines-ward/.

89. John Branch, "Ward Helps Biracial Youths on Journey toward Acceptance," *New York Times*, November 9, 2009, New York ed., sec. D1.

90. It is important to note that the initiative that reestablished the AAPI committee is the only race-based committee to come out of the White House during the first Obama administration. "The mission of the committee is to work with 23 agencies and departments across our government to improve the health, education, and economic status of AAPI communities." Barack Obama, AAPI Initiative Executive Order Signing, October 14, 2009.

91. Yi, "Hines Ward Factor."

92. JJ Cooper, "Hines Ward's the NFL's Dirtiest Player?" *Fanhouse*, September 11, 2010.

93. Richard Deitsch, "Dirtiest NFL Player: Steeler's Ward," *SI.com*, November 4, 2009, http://sportsillustrated.cnn.com/2009/football/nfl/11/04/dirty/index.html.

94. Mike Bires, "Ward: 'I Know I'm Hunted. I Hunt, Too,'" *Beaver County Times*, September 24, 2009, sec. Sports.

95. Trey Treutel, "Hines Ward Wins 'Dancing with the Stars,' Continuing Tradition of Athlete Winners," *cardboardconnection.com*, October 12, 2011, http://www.cardboardconnection.com/hines-ward-wins-dancing-with-the-stars-continuing-traditon-of-athlete-winners.

96. Bobby Wooldridge, "Hines Ward Pile Drivers His Dancing with the Stars Partner," *xx1090am.com*—The Woo Wire, May 17, 2011, http://www.xx1090sandiego.com/pages/woo_wire_landing?Hines-Ward-Pile-Drivers-His-Dancing-With=1&blockID=524267&feedID=8750.

97. Matt Carter, "'Dancing with the Stars' Champ Hines Ward Arrested for DUI," *examiner.com Arts & Entertainment*, July 9, 2011: http://www.examiner.com/tv-in-national/dancing-with-the-stars-champ-hines-ward-arrested-for-dui.

98. Bires, "I Know I'm Hunted."

99. Mayeda, "From Model Minority," 208.

100. Ibid.

101. Richard E. Lapchick, "Race and College Sport: A Long Way to Go," *Race & Class: A Journal for Black and Third World Liberation* 36 (1995): 92.

102. Carrington, "Sport, Masculinity," 291.

103. Mayeda, "From Model Minority," 214.

104. Marqusee, "Sport and Stereotype," 5.

105. Lauren Berlant, *The Female Complaint: The Unfinished Business of American Sentimentality* (Durham: Duke University Press, 2008).

106. Michael A. Messner, *Power at Play: Sports and the Problem of Masculinity* (Boston: Beacon Press, 1995), 13.

107. Max Wallace, "Today's Athletes Owe Everything to Ali," *New York Times*, April 30, 2000, late ed., sec. Sports Desk.

108. William C. Rhoden, "For Sale: A Medal Worth More than Gold," *New York Times*, October 15, 2010, sec. Sports.

109. Sang-Hun Choe, "From an Ostracized Class, a Hero for Koreans; Praise for Athlete Seen as Hypocrisy," *International Herald Tribune*, February 23, 2006, p. 2.

110. Chung-A. Park, "Myth of Pure-Blood Nationalism Blocks Multi-Ethnic Society," *Korea Times*, August 14, 2006.

111. Tae Jong Lee, "U.S. Football Star with Korea in His Blood," *Straits Times*, April 11, 2006, sec. Prime News.

112. Lewis Dunn, "Multiculturalism in Modern-Day Korea (Part 2)," *Korea Herald*, August 9, 2006.

113. Yi, "Hines Ward Factor."
114. Ibid.

Conclusion: En-Blasianing the Future

1. *The Kimchi Chronicles*, PBS, 2011.
2. Christy Smith-Sloman, "'Kimchi Chronicles' Host Marja Vongerichten Serves Up Seoul Food," *Essence.com*, August 30, 2011, http://www.essence.com/2011/08/30/kimchi-chronicles-marja-vongerichten-serves-up-seoul-food/.
3. *Making the Kimchi Chronicles*, Korea Society, rec. May 3, 2011, https://vimeo.com/23536789.
4. Smith-Sloman, "Kimchi Chronicles' Host."
5. Gloria Anzaldua, *Borderlands/La Frontera: The New Mestiza* (San Francisco: Aunt Lute Books, 1987), 79.
6. Henry Yu, "Tiger Woods at the Center of History: Looking Back at the Twentieth Century through the Lenses of Race, Sports, and Mass Consumption," *Sports Matters: Race, Recreation, and Culture* (2002), 320–55.
7. Karen Fields and Barbara Fields, *Racecraft: The Soul of Inequality in American Life* (London: Verso Books, 2012).
8. Ibid., 23.
9. Ibid., 202.
10. Ibid., 19.
11. Ibid., 198.
12. Ibid., 203.
13. Ibid., 21.
14. Naomi Zack, *American Mixed Race: The Culture of Microdiversity* (Lanham, MD: Rowman and Littlefield, 1995).
15. Kwame Anthony Appiah, *In My Father's House: Africa in the Philosophy of Culture* (Oxford: Oxford University Press, 1992).
16. Gregory Carter, *The United States of the United Races: A Utopian History of Racial Mixing* (New York: New York University Press, 2013).
17. Barack Obama, *The Audacity of Hope* (New York: Random House, 2006).
18. Carter, *United States*, 215.
19. The undoing of hypodescent and its influence on US racial formations is still in the beginning stages, but as the multiracial movement continues to make gains on both policy and culture levels, it is within the realm of possibility that the one-drop rule will no longer be a viable option for determining blackness.
20. Dagbovie, "Star-Light, Star-Bright."
21. Kirsten Buick's *Child of Fire* (2009) offers a historical examination of mixed-race Black and Native artist Edmonia Lewis, whose identity was similarly fragmented.

Index

CPSIA information can be obtained
at www.ICGtesting.com
Printed in the USA
BVOW09*0727051017
496027BV00011B/5/P